THE BENEVOLENCE OF LAUGHTER

Also by David Farley-Hills
ROCHESTER: THE CRITICAL HERITAGE *(editor)*

THE BENEVOLENCE
OF LAUGHTER:

Comic Poetry of the Commonwealth
and Restoration

DAVID FARLEY-HILLS

Rowman and Littlefield

First published in the United States 1974 by
ROWMAN AND LITTLEFIELD,
Totowa, N.J.
First published in the United Kingdom 1974 by
THE MACMILLAN PRESS LTD
© David Farley-Hills 1974

Library of Congress Cataloging in Publication Data

Farley-Hills, David.
The benevolence of laughter.
  Based on the author's thesis, Oxford.
  Bibliography: p.
  1. English poetry—Early modern
  (to 1700)—History and criticism.
2. Comic, The. I. Title.
PR549.C6F3 821'.07 73–22229

ISBN 0–87471–502–4

Printed in Great Britain

Contents

Preface

The importance of the comic for the Restoration can hardly be exaggerated. In a period of intellectual confusion, in which different ways of looking at the same thing came to replace the more rigid demand for orthodoxy of earlier generations, it was inevitable that a comic spirit should prevail, for comedy is created when the mind has to interpret the same facts or ideas simultaneously in contradictory ways. The bare facts of the triumph of comedy between the years 1650 and 1700 is obvious and does not need labouring: the variety of comic expression is still to be sympathetically examined. This book attempts to cover part of the ground and show how the contradictions and perplexities of the time came to be expressed in comic poetry. It was tempting to try to extend the field by including stage comedy. But this is a large subject worthy of special and separate attention and a subject where the strength of English tradition I believe demands a rather more historical approach. Restoration comic poetry, on the other hand, while owing something to earlier generations is frequently original, especially in its most successful mode, comic satire. Stage comedy of the Restoration, too, has received considerable attention from later generations. Much of Restoration and Commonwealth comic poetry is still unknown and even major writers like Marvell (as comic satirist) and Rochester have had little critical attention. Certainly they have not had the attention they deserve.

That the Restoration period has largely been regarded as a poetic blank until very recently is due to a general misunderstanding about the seriousness of comedy. Modern criticism, like neo-classical criticism, has often fallen into the semantic error of equating the comic with the unserious. I hope to have shown that the Restoration poet frequently took the comic very seriously indeed and that much good poetry results from this. There is a further reason for interesting ourselves in this literature, for in an age of intellectual confusion and doubt like our own it is no coincidence that we are beginning to appreciate again the seriousness of laughter. Restoration literature has much to offer us as a means of understanding the nature of the comic in literature and it can also provide us with a help to understanding ourselves.

This book began, longer ago than I care to remember, as a D.Phil. thesis, which was supervised at Oxford by Mr F. W. Bateson. I must record my thanks to Professor Beck of the Royal University of Malta, for encouraging me to take up the work and for providing me with the opportunity to do it. This is a good place, too, to thank Ian Jack for his interest and support, not for this book in particular, but in general over the years. I have also to thank the Marquis Scicluna and Simonds, Farsons, Cisk Ltd, Malta, for help with financing a trip to the Bodleian library in Oxford that helped to get the work under way. At a later stage of the work I was indebted for much good advice (and for placing the dots correctly) from Karel Capper-Johnson and throughout to my wife for looking after the babies while first the thesis and then the book was written, for helping with the index and for providing life support. I should also like to thank Karen Willey for her care in typing and arranging the typescript.

I have throughout used modern scholarly texts wherever I could, on the grounds that these attempt to get close to the intentions of the authors. This applies even when I have been comparing original work with Restoration translations. Thus I use Robinson's Chaucer not Speght's, with which Dryden was familiar, because I have been keen to discover the difference in the attitude of the two poets to their subjects rather than simply note the words that started the later poet on his way.

D.F.-H.

1 Introduction:
The Benevolence of Laughter

The philosophy of Descartes, Boileau is supposed to have said, had cut the throat of poetry.[1] Subsequently many critics have echoed this comment. The Restoration has become, in popular imagination, the first age of prose, the first age of a dissociated sensibility. And certainly many people of the period itself felt that much of the poetry had gone out of life. John Aubrey described it as an age when 'Printing and Gunpowder . . . frightened away Robin good fellow and the Fayries'.[2] Yet even if this is true, it is only half of a more complicated truth, and it is with part of the other half that this book deals. For the Restoration is also an age of copious poetry, in some ways the last age when poetry was an important means of communication at all levels of society. Charles's court, for instance, was the last in which it was an advantage, as it had been in many an earlier prince's court, to 'dance and eek sing and wel portraye and write'. To write well was still a means of obtaining court preferment, as Etherege's appointment as ambassador to Ratisbon shows, and a poor boy like Matthew Prior could rise to the heights of a senior diplomatic post by showing a deftness at writing verses. Similarly the most exalted in the land, among them the Duke of Buckingham, the Duke of Newcastle, the Earls of Dorset, Mulgrave and Rochester, were not ashamed to versify, though they did not always own up to their parentage or alternatively sometimes owned to offspring where their parentage might reasonably be questioned. Poetry still had an aura of the divine. The Earl of Mulgrave can open his *Essay on Satire* in his own inimitable way with the lines:

> Of all the arts where mankind does excell
> Nature's chief masterpiece is writing well

and if these lines do not convince the reader that Mulgrave is very close to the divine source of inspiration, more talented poets could claim a divine sanction for their calling with some conviction. John Dryden, in his commemoration of the young poetess Anne Killigrew, laments that his age has profaned God's 'Heavenly gift of Posy', but in doing so asserts the primacy of the poet among men. At the coming of the last judgement, he writes, in the grand baroque manner he could handle so well, the poets will be the first to answer God's summons:

> The Sacred Poets first shall hear the sound,
> And formost from the Tomb shall bound;
> For they are cover'd with the lightest Ground;
> And straight, with inborn Vigour, on the Wing,
> Like mounting Larkes, to the New Morning sing.

To Dryden, God was 'the almighty poet'[3] whose act of creation was the type of all poetic activity.

At a humbler level the divine voice could be heard in the great amount of religious verse that came from the presses; apocalyptic works like *The Day of Doom or a description of the Great and Last Judgement*, which appeared in the aftermath of the great plague in 1666, or homiletic poems like a morality poem *Youth's Tragedy* by a certain 'T.S.', a dialogue between Youth and Wisdom and the Devil, published first in 1671, but sufficiently in demand to go on reprinting until 1709. A similar morality poem is the *Dialogue Between a Blind man and Death* of 1686. Such poems as these make us feel that we have accidentally wandered back into the Middle Ages, until we remember that this is the age of John Bunyan as well as of Samuel Pepys. Admonitory poems are common; these warn of the evils of debauchery, like John Mason's *Mentis Humanae Metamorphosis Sive Conversio, the History of a Young Converted Gallant* (1676), which tells of a rake who sees the error of his ways and repents. The dramatic death bed conversion of the wicked Earl of Rochester in 1680 was celebrated in numerous verses[4] whose main aim was to warn the reader of the foolishness of the debaucheries for which the Earl had been notorious. Sometimes these admonitory verses could concern themselves with rather lighter matters; such is a poem called *Directorium Cosmeticum or, A Directory for the female Sex* (1684), where a father advises his daughter to live virtuously and not to use make-up, or the poem called *Know Thyself*, a broadsheet advertised as 'given away by the Author at the Saracen's head within Aldgate'. Occasionally it is difficult to know whether the writer is on the side of God or the Devil, as in the *Letter to a Virtuous Lady to disuade her from . . . being a Nun* (1685). Sectarian poetry, of course, flourished, not only among such humble writers as the author of *Geneva and Rome or the zeal of both boiling over in an earnest dispute for pre-eminance carried on at a private conference between Jack, a Presbyter and Believe-all a Papist* (1679), but at the much more exalted level of Dryden's Anglican *Religio Laici* and Catholic *Hind and the Panther* and John Oldham's ferocious attack on the Jesuits.

Politics was equally favoured as a subject for poetry, though the political writer often had to issue his poems anonymously for fear of prosecution. The most distinguished of these political poets was Andrew Marvell, whose contribution to English verse satire has been grossly under-rated. In the hands of Marvell or Dryden political poetry could achieve the dignity of great art, but there was a mass of political satire and panegyric which never achieved more than topicality. Much of this verse remained in manuscript during the reigns of Charles and James. An extensive collection was published after the revolution of 1688 in a series of volumes with the title *Poems on Affairs of State*. These poems were as likely to be scurrilous attacks on particular personalities as serious attempts at political persuasion, but the lampoons can occasionally produce poetry of distinction in, for instance, Rochester's attacks on Charles II, or Dorset's on Katherine Sedley. Panegyric was a favourite kind, and the importance of verse for the age is amply shown by the effusions of verse congratulation poured out at the birth of royal or noble infants who might equally well be seen to their marriage or their grave by retrospective or prognostic tributes with appropriate tonal alterations. Tributes could take bizarre forms, as, for instance, the volume published by Oxford scholars in 1688 to celebrate the birth of the Prince of Wales under the title *Strenae Natalitiae*, which contains verses written in Latin, Greek, Arabic, Turkish and Hebrew. Their motive may have been like that of those poets described by Samuel Butler:

> Some write in Hebrew, some in Greek,
> And some more wise in Arabique,
> T'avoyd the Critique, and th' expence
> Of Difficulter wit, and Sense,
> And seeme more Learnedish than those
> That at a greater Charge Compose.[5]

It was professional poets who were most expected to show their paces (or feet) on these occasions, and so at Charles's death in 1685 we find John Crowne's *A Poem on the Lamented Death of our Late Gracious Sovereign* jostling with Otway's *Windsor Castle, in a Monument to our Late Sovereign* and Dryden's *Threnodia Augustalis*, and many another from humbler poets.

Verse had many other uses. Verse broadsheets very often served the function of the crime sheets in our popular newspapers. A poem in heroic verse of 1688, for instance, has the fully self-explanatory title (which I abridge) *A Warning Piece to all Married Men and Women, being the full Confession of Mary Hoby, the French Midwife, who murdered her husband on the 27th January 1687/8 . . . For which she receiv'd Sentence to be burnt alive and on Friday 2nd March, between the Hours of Ten and Eleven in the morning, she was drawn upon a Sledge to Leicester Fields where she was burnt to Ashes.* A no less unusual occurrence is recorded in a poem with the intriguing title *Strange and Wonderful News from Newberry Concerning a Youth that was Choak'd by eating Custard.* The freezing of the Thames in 1684, a rare occasion even in a period when winters were rather colder than ours, brought out a rush of verse commemorating, with titles like *Freezland-Fair or the Icy Bear Garden*, which gives an account of the fair that was held on the ice; other titles included *News from the Thames, or the Frozen Thames in Tears, Thamasis's Advice to the Painter, Behold the Wonders of Almighty God* and the pleasantly descriptive poem *A Winter Wonder, or the Thames Frozen Over.* The Thaw was celebrated in *The Thames Uncas'd.*[6]

That verse should be written to celebrate military victories seems perhaps understandable to us, but what does the modern reader make of a poem by Edmund Arwaker in 1686 called *Fons Perennis*, celebrating 'The excellent and useful invention of making sea-water fresh', or of a poem by Nahum Tate, of 1700, called *Panacea* in praise of tea? Songs in praise of beer or wine are found much earlier, but at the turn of the new century there seems to have been a desire to extend the range of lauded beverages to judge from such poems as John Philips's *Cider*, William King's *Frumenty* and a complete broadside devoted to punch in *Bacchinalia Coelestia* (1680). All this verse making was compounded with the traditional ballads, the street ballads, the metrical street-cries of London, the songs that were published both in song books like those of John Playford and verse anthologies. The verse anthologies, the miscellanies or drolleries as they are sometimes known, are a particular feature of the age. There was a spate of them during the Commonwealth and this continued through the whole Restoration period. These anthologies vary widely between extensive collections of fashionable verse like Hobart Kemp's collection of 1672, Robert Veal's *New Court Songs* of the same year, or John Bulteel's *New Collections of Poems* (1674) and grub street productions like the various collections of William Hickes, with such titles as *London Drollery* (1673) and *Grammatical Drollery* (1682).

Many of these collections, like much of the poetry of the day, are collections of comic verse, as the term drollery implies. Some of the titles, like *Mock Songs and Joking Poems* (1675) or *Merry Drollery* (1661) give a clear indication of the tone of their contents. Comedy in this period was more, however, than a sign of light-headedness and irresponsibility; it was often a serious business. It is no coincidence that the finest literary achievements of the age are mostly comic. Dryden might confess himself unfitted by nature to write comedy because, as he said, 'I want that gaiety of humour that is required to it. My conversation is slow and dull, my humour saturnine and reserved' (*Critical Essays*, ed. Watson, i 116). Yet *Mac Flecknoe* and *Absalom and Achitophel*, which he himself described as comic poems, are among his finest works, and the age is littered with examples of writers who find themselves laughing in spite of themselves. It can be no coincidence that while few of the epics that were written are read today, or indeed are readable, the mock epic is one of the great achievements of the whole Augustan period from Dryden to Fielding.

Both Dryden and Pope projected solemn epics that they never managed to write, but produced instead the mock epic masterpieces of *Mac Flecknoe*, *Rape of the Lock*, and *Dunciad*. In drama the picture is the same. In theory both epic and tragedy were held to be superior literary forms, and there was no dearth of either; yet tragedy eluded them as surely as epic. Instead it is in stage comedy that the age excels, producing a series of comic masterpieces from Etherege to Farquhar that still hold the stage today, unlike the comedy of the Elizabethan and Jacobean playwrights (with the perennial exception of Shakespeare) whose plays tend to have been treated more respectfully by academic critics, but which rarely get professional productions.

The reasons for the Augustan preference for and excellence in comic writing are so complex that they can only be fully explained in terms of the whole range of attitudes and experiences of the age – which means that they are ultimately inexplicable. Certainly an explanation would connect the preference for the comic with the break-up of traditional values and the consequent juxtaposition of divergent attitudes; it would connect it with the Cavalier reaction against the restrictive piety of the Puritans and with the growing cult of individualism and the consequent diminution of respect for convention and orderliness. One important consequence of this breakdown of traditional modes of thought for poetry was that it freed the poet from the Renaissance preoccupation with abstract, derived forms, both of word and idea, and allowed him to talk more directly of actual things. Few poets prescribed to the austere doctrine that the Royal Society adopted to guide its prose: 'to return back to the primitive purity and shortness, when men deliver'd so many *things* almost in an equal number of *words*';[7] yet the poetry of the Restoration reflects the same spirit. The change we shall see between the Marvell of the lyrics and the Marvell of the later satire, for instance, is the change between a poet manipulating conventional forms and ideas, and a poet who had things to say of vital and immediate importance to the society for which he wrote. From the puerilities of number symbolism and the strangeness of the unseen world of ideas the poet now turned to look at the world about him. He rarely liked what he saw, but to come to terms with it was part of a process of growing up.

But the only way of telling what these comic attitudes imply is by looking at particular examples of the way the mood is expressed and to do that we shall have both to understand the wide variety of possible comic attitudes and the relationship between them, as well as to give detailed attention to individual comic poems. Because of the predominance of comedy in the period modern critics have found it difficult to take the poetry seriously, forgetting that the comic has its seriousness equally with the tragic or epic. So much of the best poetry of the period is comic and so little serious attention has been given to it, that an assessment of Restoration comic poetry seemed to be called for.

The seventeenth century itself often spoke disparagingly of the comic. In the hierarchical division of literature into kinds, the comic genres were almost invariably given a lowly ranking. John Dennis in *The Grounds of Criticism in Poetry* (1704) divides poetry into two major categories, 'the greater' and 'the less': comic literature is included under the second heading. In this Dennis was expressing neo-classical orthodoxy. The general agreement about the inferiority of the comic kinds probably stems in particular from Aristotle's *Poetics*, though in general it reflects an age-old association of the comic with deformity and inadequacy. Aristotle says very little about the comic in the *Poetics*, but it is quite clear that he regards it as an inferior mode:

> Poetry soon branched into two channels, according to the temperaments of individual poets. The more serious minded among them represented noble actions and the doings of noble persons, while the more trivial wrote about the meaner sort of people; thus while the one type wrote hymns and panegyrics these others began by writing invectives.[8]

The charge against laughter could often be more damaging still. Many of his contemporaries would agree with Hobbes that laughter was essentially malicious and destructive:

> ... it is incident most to them that are conscious of the lowest abilities in themselves; who are forced to keep themselves in their own favour by observing the imperfections of other men. And therefore much laughter is a sign of pusillanimity. For of great minds one of the proper works is to help and free others from scorn, and compare themselves only with the most able. (*Leviathan*, ch. VI)

This view of laughter as mean and destructive was especially common during the Restoration period when moralists were concerned to point to the ribaldry and immorality of Charles II's court. Laughter was associated with atheism, immorality and disorderliness in works like Joseph Glanvill's *A Whip for the Droll, Fidler to the Atheist . . . with reflections on Drollery and Atheism* (fourth edition 1668), *Seasonable Reflections and Discourses to the Conviction and cure of Scoffing and Infidelity* (1676), Clement Ellis's *Vanity of Scoffing* (1674) and *The Gentile Sinner* (seventh edition 1690). By one of those multiple ironies that abound in the period, Hobbes was frequently singled out in these attacks as the principal droll, and not without some justice, for as Aubrey tells us in his *Brief Life*, Hobbes was extremely popular as a wit with Charles II and his witty courtiers. It was so difficult to avoid the pervading spirit of comedy and irony at this time that the witty scorner of wit became almost a stock type: Samuel Butler, having in *Hudibras* provided the Restoration wits (and Charles) with their favourite comic poem, turned on the Court wits: 'What fops would the sober men of the past appear nowadays', he writes in the *Satire on the Licentiousness of the Age of Charles II*:

> Where the best reason 's made ridiculous;
> And all the plain and sober things we say
> By raillery are put beside their play.[9]

Butler himself associated laughter with malice, writing sardonically in the notebooks: 'Men cannot laugh heartily without showing their teeth.'[10] Butler sees malice as the origin of satire, abandoning the stock explanation of the motivation of satire in the charitable desire to correct one's neighbour:

> There is nothing that provokes and Sharpens wit like Malice, and Anger . . . And hence perhaps came the first occasion of calling those Raptures Poeticall Fury. For Malice is a kind of Madnes (For if Men run mad for Love, why should they not as well do so for Hate?) . . . So much Power has Malice above all other Passions, to heighten wit and Fancy, for Malice is Restles, and never findes ease untill it has vented it self. And therefore Satyrs that are only provok'd with the

Madnes and Folly of the world, are found to contein more wit, and Ingenuity than all other writings whatsoever, and meet with a better Reception from the world . . . [11]

Butler seems always to assume that satire and comedy are closely related, if not identical.[12] His view of the malicious inspiration of satire did not, however, prevent him from regarding the satiric genres as the highest forms of poetry. Rochester, who seems to have been greatly influenced by Butler, explains the motivation of satire in a similar way in his conversations with Gilbert Burnet. Burnet argues that detached satire can be legitimate as 'no improfitable way of Reproof', but that indulgence in personal spleen is unjustifiable. Rochester replies:

A man could not write with life, unless he were heated by Revenge: For to make a Satyre without Resentments, upon the Cold Notions of *Phylosophy*, was as if a man would in cold blood, cut men's throats who had never offended him.

Only a natural poet could go on to add, as he does:

the lies in these Libels came often in as Ornaments that could not be spared without spoiling the beauty of the Poem.[13]

Dryden, protesting his unsuitability for writing in a comic vein and pointing out respectfully in *The Parallel between Painting and Poetry* that Christ never laughed, produced in *Mac Flecknoe* and *Absalom and Achitophel* two of the comic masterpieces of the day. In the next generation Addison is in one breath aiming to 'enliven morality with wit' (*Spectator*, 10) and in another scornfully contrasting the noble arts of the ancients with the modern achievement in 'Doggerel, Humour, Burlesque and all the trivial Arts of Ridicule', and quoting without comment a Frenchman's view that 'laughter was the Effect of the original sin, and that Adam could not laugh before the Fall' (*Spectator*, 249). Addison admittedly made this excuse in *The Freeholder* (no. 45, 1716):

Our nation are such lovers of mirth and humour that it is impossible for detached papers, which come out on stated

days, either to have a general run or long continuance,
if they are not diversified and enlivened from time to time
with subjects and thoughts accommodated to this taste,
which so prevails among our countrymen.

'Malheur à vous qui riez' was the Jansenist motto in the age
that produced both the solemn Puritans and Molière and
Restoration comedy.

The destructive power of the comic was not always held
against it, for it was argued that laughter could be used to
destroy evil. This, indeed, was the recognised apology for the
satirist. Burnet makes this assumption in his argument with
Rochester. It is also the line of self-defence Milton takes in this
answer to Joseph Hall in the *Apology for Smectymnuus* where he
rakes around for scriptural and classical precedent to justify
himself against Hall's accusations that he is a ribald and a
jester:

So that the question ere while mov'd, who he is that spends
the benevolence of laughter and reproofe so liberally upon
such men as the Prelats, may return with a more just demand, who he is, of place and knowledge never so mean,
under whose contempt and jerk these men are not deserv-
edly falne.

The phrase 'the benevolence of laughter and reproofe' as a
description of comic satire contains a nice ambiguity; for whom
is it benevolent, the biter or the bit? The Bible itself is ambiguous on the subject of laughter and for every quotation in
favour of the phenomenon at least two could be quoted
against.[14] The satirists made full use of the ambiguity, though
they never managed to explain it. Milton here is not himself
aware of any incongruity in this passage, I think, for he is
simply referring to what a later seventeenth-century divine
calls the Christian 'Duty of Rebuking'.[15] This moral interpretation of the function of laughter is the chief theoretical
excuse for comic satire throughout the period, a theory that
reaches its most subtle expression in the philosophical essays of
Anthony Ashley Cooper, third Earl of Shaftesbury. In two
essays in particular, *Sensus Communis: An Essay on the Freedom*

of Wit and Humour (1709) and *Soliloquy, or Advice to an Author*
(1710), he presents the argument that laughter, by deflating
enthusiasms, makes men less passionate and intolerant and,
therefore, more civilised:

> The only manner left in which criticism can have its just
> force amongst us is the ancient comic . . . In effect we may
> observe that in our own nation the most successful criticism
> or method of refutation is that which borders most on the
> manner of the ancient Greek comedy. The highly rated
> burlesque poem [*Hudibras*], written on the subject of our
> religious controversies in the last age, is a sufficient token of
> this kind. And that justly admired piece of comic wit given
> us some time after by an author of the highest quality
> [Buckingham's *Rehearsal*], has furnished our best wits in all
> their controversies, even in religion and politics, as well as in
> the affairs of wit and learning, with the most effectual and
> entertaining method of expressing folly, pedantry, false
> reason and ill writing.

Like Milton, though much more circumspectly, Shaftesbury
views the comic as a destructive force which has constructive
results; it destroys illusions and crooked ways of thinking. At
the same time, however, as the comic destroys illusions it
destroys itself, for the mood it leaves behind is presumably a
mood of sober reasonableness, not of facetiousness. It is not
surprising, therefore, that Milton (though in his early verse
sometimes facetious enough) in *Paradise Lost* tends to ally
comedy with evil, giving Satan witty language, 'scoffing in
ambiguous words' (VI 568); for it is a sign of disruption in the
rational order of things. But would Milton have agreed with
Addison's French Curate that Adam did not laugh before the
Fall?
    Some writers in the seventeenth and eighteenth century
acknowledge a completely different kind of laughter; a benevolent laughter that is sometimes contrasted with this satirical,
destructive laughter. Isaac Barrow for instance, in a sermon
published in 1678, *Against Foolish Talking and Jesting*, distinguishes nine legitimate from seven illegitimate kinds of
mirth, while a rather less precise sermon by John Straight, *The*

Rule of Rejoycing or a Direction of Mirth (1671) makes a simpler distinction between Christian joy and the false mirth of secular revelry. Pepys records a sermon on the same subject by George Morley, Bishop of Winchester, at Christmas 1662:

> By and by down to the Chapell again, where Bishop Morley preached upon the song of the Angels, 'Glory to God on high, on earth peace, and good will towards men'. Methought he made but a poor sermon, but long, and reprehending the mistaken jollity of the Court for the true joy that shall and ought to be on those days, he particularized concerning their excess in plays and gaming, saying that he whose office it is to keep the gamesters in order and within bounds, serves but for a second rather in a duell, meaning the groomporter. Upon which it was worth observing how far they are come from taking the reprehensions of a Bishop seriously, that they all laugh in the Chapell when he reflected on their ill actions and courses. He did much press us to joy in those public days of joy, and to hospitality. But one that stood by whispered in my ear that the Bishop himself do not spend one groat to the poor himself.

It would be difficult to find in so short a space a better illustration of the range of possible comic attitudes than this: no wonder that the literature of the age presents us with such complexities of comic treatment.

The distinction between Christian joy and ribald mirth, between 'cheerfulness and mirth' as he puts it, is a subject of one of Addison's *Spectator* essays (no. 381). Here mirth is thought of in Hobbesian terms as 'a certain triumph and insolence of Heart' and reminds us again of the observation that Christ never laughed. Cheerfulness, on the other hand, is a severe attitude of mind that 'naturally flows out into Friendship and Benevolence.' Steele also shows a preference for 'cheerfulness' over 'mirth' in the Epilogue to the *Lying Lover*. Clearly referring to the Hobbesian view, he calls laughter:

> . . . a distorted passion, born
> Of sudden self-esteem and sudden scorn;
> Which, when 'tis o'er, the men in pleasure wise,
> Both him that moved it and themselves despise . . .

In *Guardian* (29) he makes the distinction between witty laughter, 'a constrained kind of half-laugh' and true laughter, which is 'a vent of any Sudden Joy that strikes upon the Mind'. In his own humorous writing Steele shows a clear preference for a tolerant, benevolent laughter which permits him to relish the richness and strangeness of things:

> Every Mechanick has a peculiar Cast of Head and turn of wit, or Some uncommon Whim, as a characteristick, that distinguishes him from others of his Trade, as well as from the Multitudes, that are upon a level with him . . . There is a Person of great Hospitality, who lives in a Plaistered Cottage upon the Road to Hampstead, and gets a Superfluity of Wealth, by accommodating Holiday Passengers with Ale, Brandy, Pipes, Tobacco, Cakes, Ginger bread, Apples, Pears, and other Small Refreshments of Life; and on workdays takes the Air in his Chaise, and recreates himself with the elegant Pleasures of the *Beau Monde*.

The portrait resembles a humours portrait or 'Character' of the seventeenth century, but here Steele has shifted the emphasis from the satire that humours portraits were designed for to a comedy of affirmation. Congreve had advocated just such a shift from 'humours' characterisation to humorous characterisation in his letter on comedy addressed to John Dennis in 1695.

There are plenty of examples, however, of this benign, amiable approach to the comic throughout the seventeenth century, though it was not much discussed. Cavalier humour, for instance, abounds in amiable comedy. Isaac Walton introduces the poems of his friend Alexander Brome by telling us the Cavaliers kept up their spirits singing them during the Civil War:

> Here's a collection in this book
> Of all those cheerfull songs, that we
> Have sung with mirth and merry-gle:
> As we have march'd to fight the cause
> Of Gods *anoynted*, and our *lawes*:
> Such songs as make not the least ods

> Betwixt us *mortals* and the Gods,
> Such Songs as *Virgins* need not fear
> To Sing, or a grave *Matron* hear.[16]

The burlesque that became popular from the 1650s is frequently non-satirical. Defending his own burlesque poem *Diarium* (1656) Richard Flecknoe makes the distinction in his introduction between his own good-humoured 'raillery' and the 'railing' of the satirists:

> Of this kind (Burlesque) is the Poem I present thee here, which when its figures are lively, and representation naturall, is one of the delightfullest of all; where note, that as nations grow more polite and witty, they fall upon this strain . . . yet to think to satisfie all objections, were to think to peel a *Bulbus* root to its last rinde, or sweep an Earthen floor to its last grain of dust, especially here, where they understand *railing*, farre better than *Raillery*.[17]

Davenant, in his play *Playhouse to Let*, has one of his characters describe stage 'burlesque or mock heroic' in a similar way as something:

> Which draws the pleasant hither i'the vacation
> Men of no malice who will pay for laughter.[18]

The wits of Charles's Court, men who were often accused of more than their fair share of malice, prided themselves on their good nature – a quality Prior singles out as especially characteristic of one of the most prominent, Charles Sackville, sixth Earl of Dorset. Wycherley, too, another prominent member of the witty Court circle and renowned as a satirist, declares in one of his poems (published in the *Miscellany Poems* of 1704 but written 'a good deal earlier') that: 'Good natur'd wit o'er t'other should prevail.' Although seventeenth-century divines like Isaac Barrow and George Morley made a clear distinction between opposing types of the comic, the first systematic account of laughter as essentially benevolent had to wait for Francis Hutcheson's three essays published as *Reflections on Laughter* (1728). Hutcheson's first essay disputes Hobbes's view of laughter by giving many examples (some of them taken from *Hudibras*) where we laugh without any feeling of superiority. In the second essay Hutcheson turns to the problem of finding an alternative to Hobbes's view. He is here rather more concerned with the comic – the cause of laughter, that is – than with laughter itself. The cause of laughter, he finds, is incongruity:

> the cause of laughter is the bringing together of images which have contrary additional ideas as well as some resemblance in the principal idea.

Among the numerous examples of this is the dirtying of a 'decent dress' belonging to a person 'of whom we have high ideas'. The association of the dress and the person is appropriate, the dirtying is inappropriate, so that it is the 'contrast, or opposition of ideas . . . which is the occasion of laughter'. Hutcheson also notes that the assessment of what is appropriate or inappropriate in any particular case will depend largely on the standards of the observer and that, therefore, what is laughable to one man may not be so to another. For instance, he says the frugal man will make a jest of the man of pleasure while the man of pleasure laughs at the frugal. For this reason people laugh at dress that is out of fashion or behaviour that is abnormal.

It is in the third essay that Hutcheson comes out most strongly against Hobbes's view that laughter is prompted by malice. Laughter, he says, is necessarily pleasant and we are more likely to laugh when we are in 'an easy and happy state':

> The implanting then, a sense of the ridiculous, in our nature, was giving us an avenue to pleasure, and an easy remedy for discontent and sorrow.

Hutcheson has moved to the other extreme from Hobbes in seeing Laughter as almost entirely benevolent: it is a sign of friendliness. Attempts to make fun of the truly wise and noble invariably fail, though ridicule has a useful part to play in pointing out inadequacy and, therefore, in helping us to a correct estimate of anything. If laughter is malicious it will generally excite contempt, not amusement, in the observer and so fail to be comic. This leads Hutcheson to ask what function laughter serves. Firstly, he says, it has a social function, helping to ease the relationship of man to man. Secondly, it helps us to acquire a sense of proportion when ridicule shows us the inappropriateness of strong emotions (an idea close to Shaftesbury's). Thirdly, laughter has a corrective function for small vices. Although Hutcheson does not ignore the satiric function of laughter, therefore, his main concern is to stress its benevolence and he leaves unexplained how it can be both satirical and benign, or what relationship there is between the two kinds of the comic implied in this view of laughter.

In addition to these opposing views of laughter as destructive and of laughter as benign, there is a third view encountered throughout the period: that laughter and the comic are essentially trivial and important enough to be neither destructive nor benign. This is essentially Locke's view in the *Essay Concerning Human Understanding* where the comic is associated with 'wit', the faculty of making fanciful combinations of ideas and, in contrast to the judgement, which is concerned with measuring differences, is dismissed as unworthy of serious attention. In criticism, as we have seen, comic forms are commonly regarded as inferior to non-comic.

The three kinds of laughter are a response to three distinct kinds of the comic. Destructive laughter, whether malicious or reformative, is clearly prompted by satirical comedy. Benign laughter is induced by celebratory comic literature; while between these two extremes is the detached, sceptical comic literature that apportions neither praise nor blame. Each kind is represented in the poetry of the second half of the seventeenth century, but there is a general shift of preference from amiable to satirical comedy throughout the period. Satirical comedy became the most characteristic during the Restoration and the most successful; the benevolent, celebratory comedy, found in the Commonwealth anthologies, became less common until it re-emerged into favour with Steele and the dramatists at the beginning of the eighteenth century. The dispassionate, balanced kind of comedy, always difficult to achieve because balanced so nicely between praise and blame, is never common in any period. It is found, however, throughout these fifty years and is characteristic of some of the court wits of Charles's court, notably Rochester in some of his lyrics and Sir Charles Sedley. In addition to these three distinctive types of the comic there is also the curious, mixed form of burlesque, which was extremely popular. Burlesque can neither be called celebratory nor satirical, though it contains both elements. It purports to be debunking its subject matter, and, as such, would seem to be a version of satire, but it is not consistent in its viewpoint because it proclaims no consistent standards from which judgement can be made.

The difference between the various kinds of the comic can be gauged in terms of the reader's expectations. In comic satire we are led to expect high standards and the satire attacks those who have fallen away from these. The comic incongruity is created by juxtaposing the idea of what they should be against what they are. The movement is one of rejection and of disappointment. Our hostility is aroused by what is seen to be inadequate and we repudiate what is described. Comic satire presupposes an optimistic view of man's potential and could only succeed in the Restoration as confidence came to be restored in the possibility of orderliness in the state and in moral conduct. This is, no doubt, why the turmoil of the Civil War produced no distinguished comic satire. Burlesque is more characteristic of this period. Our expectations of burlesque are uncertain: we are thrown into a disorderly world in which sometimes things turn out better than we expect, sometimes worse. Writers had lost their bearings and had lost confidence in the traditional standards of their society. Satire is a social activity. It requires general agreement about what *ought to be*, against which what *is* can be measured. It was only when the traditional standards seemed to be re-established with the restoration of the King that actuality could be judged in terms of a set of widely agreed assumptions. Hence it was not until the late 1660s that the first major comic satire appeared; Marvell's *Last Instructions to a Painter*.

Earlier ages had had a similar, or indeed much greater, sense of stability, and this, when threatened, had occasioned, in the reign of Elizabeth and James I, a considerable amount of satire. But satire, and especially comic satire, is not characteristic of these earlier periods for a different reason. The Elizabethan age had, it is true, high ideals, but they also had a sense that those ideals were embodied in actuality. Elizabeth was not only the acknowledged symbol of orderliness in her

realm as Charles II was in his, she was also, in the view of
the majority of her subjects, the actual embodiment of orderliness. Few could have accused Charles of that. At the centre
of the nation's life in his reign there was a man whose symbolic
life as supreme monarch was ludicrously discrepant with his
personal life as roué and debauchee. To his hierarchically
minded subjects he appeared a living satire; and with the
centre awry all else seemed discordant. On the other hand a
centre actually existed again as it had not done, in the view of
many, for almost twenty years before the Restoration.

Celebratory comedy is more characteristic of Elizabeth's
reign than satirical comedy. For celebratory comedy starts with
a humble view of man's potential, but celebrates the transcend-
ing of his limitations. The Elizabethans had inherited the
medieval view of man as a creature dogged by evil and en-
feebled by inherited sin. Yet this puny creature, by God's grace,
had achieved miracles through his courage and perseverance.
The globe had been circumnavigated, the Armada defeated, a
general social stability and prosperity achieved unknown to
their fathers. Not surprisingly, then, the comic mode of
Shakespeare and his contemporaries frequently asks us to move
from the contemplation of our littleness to the surprising
discovery of our greatness. Falstaff, whose origin is in the vice
figure of the Morality plays, becomes a celebratory figure and
the cause of celebration in others. The mind is led from the
expectation of littleness and inadequacy to an unexpected
flourishing of energy and talent. Things that appear hostile or
unworthy, turn out to be friendly and valuable. The mood
began to change at the end of Elizabeth's reign. James certainly
was less impressive as the sun than Elizabeth had been as the
moon. None the less traces of the Elizabethan self-confidence
and gaiety are still to be found in Commonwealth poetry.

Although, as I say, satire was written under Elizabeth and
became common under James I it is most frequently non-
comic. For the comic is a register of and an accommodation to
disorderliness. To an age so concerned with order any serious
departure from it was seen as a serious breach of nature which
had to be dealt with sternly. But just because they had such
faith in the triumph of order, when they did admit laughter the
Elizabethans tended not to take it seriously as a disruptive

force. In Shakespearean comedy it is the unimportant low-life characters who carry the principal comic burdens. Shakespearean comedy nearly always ends in harmony and reconciliation, that is, with a repudiation of the comic, or with its assimilation into joy. By Restoration times the idea of an innate orderliness in the universe had weakened and there were some, though not many, like the Earl of Rochester, who regarded the incongruities detected by laughter as likely to be a true reflection of the human condition. If man was indeed a creature only temporarily excluded from chaos before he was swept back at death into the meaningless 'lumber of the world' (as he put it) then the comic provided a profound insight into the nature of things. Man's existence might, after all, be an absurd cosmic joke. Few people were willing to face up to this possibility as courageously as Rochester, but there were inescapable signs of disharmony in the life around them and these did not go unregistered. Not surprisingly, therefore, the Restoration tends, in fact, if not in theory, to take laughter seriously.

Of course, this summary involves a good deal of distortion. No age is wholly one thing, rather than another. Restoration comic literature will not be found consistently satirical, nor is Restoration literature exclusively comic. Exceptions abound. Individual attitudes, or the attitudes of small groups within the larger society, made themselves felt. But it is possible to think in general terms of what is peculiar to a period. And the comic satire along with the comic drama of the Restoration are certainly its most characteristic forms. Neither can it be a coincidence that between periods characterised by comic geniality on the one hand and comic satire on the other comes a period of uncertainty. Burlesque, which appears perhaps as early as the 1620s and becomes characteristic of the Commonwealth period, is just such a form as we would expect of a disturbed period. It neither presupposes a high potential for man, like satire, nor celebrates the transcendence of limitations. Instead it does something of both; now moving one way, now another. It does not consistently assert standards because there was no consensus about the social standards to be asserted. Nor, however, as the poet at mid-century looks about him, is there much to celebrate. Characteristically, therefore, burlesque looks both ways and never settles into any steady view of its subject.

Finally there is the comedy of disinterestedness. It is most characteristic of the sceptical minds, and these are rare at any time. There was, however, a tradition of courtly reticence, of gentlemanly diffidence, that had encouraged the development of what can only be called a literature of play, in which ideas were sported with for the sake of the ingenious or pretty patterns that could be made with them. Certainly this play poetry came to be common among the late so-called 'metaphysicals': the lyrical Marvell, for instance, or Carew, or even more Cleveland. This poetry, however, is only accidentally sceptical and it was not until the appearance of more thorough-going sceptics in the Restoration that such play poetry did more than provide its readers with pleasant and witty entertainments. In some of Rochester's poems the comedy of detachment comes near to being a metaphysical statement.

Comic literature is a response of the human mind to incongruity, and the kind of comedy evoked records the attitude of the individual writer and of his audience when confronted with incongruity. During the second half of the seventeenth century we can see a change in this response as the possibility of a metaphysic of incongruity comes to be taken seriously. At the beginning of the period there are still traces of that Elizabethan confidence in order that either seeks to obliterate the incongruous by repudiating laughter altogether or sees incongruity as more apparent than real. During the Civil War and the Commonwealth period, when social confusion was at its height, the confused form of burlesque came into its own; it is a confused response to a confused situation. Then, as the restoration of traditional forms of government and traditional ways of thought is achieved, a certain amount of confidence in the possibility of order is regained. This, however, is tempered by the experience of the Civil War and a deeper questioning of the metaphysical justification for a belief in order. Not surprisingly, then, Restoration literature finds its typical expression in comic satire. This reaffirms a belief in order, but questions its metaphysical basis or the possibility of achieving it in actuality. It is to explore the particular responses to incongruity that we now turn.

2 Comic Poetry
of the Commonwealth

Comic literature has presumably always existed, except, possibly, in Paradise. There was however a sharp and quite sudden increase in the amount of comic poetry published during the Commonwealth period. This appeared principally in a large number of comic anthologies. The increasing importance of comic poetry can be seen by tracing the course of successive editions of two anthologies, *The Academy of Complements* and *Wit's Recreations*, both first published in 1640. The first editions of these collections contain hardly any comic verse. The second edition of *Wit's Recreations* (1641) is already augmented by a considerable number of comic poems including a new comic section headed 'Fancies and Fantasticks'. New editions appeared in 1645 and 1650, and the edition of 1654 contains yet more comic verse. There were further editions in 1663, 1667 and under a different title, *Recreation for Ingenious Headpieces*, in 1683. *The Academy of Complements* also seems to have been very successful. The edition of 1646 is described as the seventh edition, this includes a great deal of new comic material and has a new section headed 'The Court of Venus, Songs of Love and Mirth'. Further editions are found in 1650, 1671 (with the title *Windsor Drolleries*) and 1684.

The dates covered by these editions are those within which the demand for comic poetry reached its height, but the rise and decline in the demand for it were not as sudden as seems to be suggested. The earlier anthologies very often included comic verse written much earlier, sometimes as early as the Elizabethan period, while comic anthologies remained popular into the eighteenth century. One of the most extensive of these is Tom Durfey's six-volume collection of 1719, *Wit and Mirth, or Pills to Purge Melancholy*. But still, these comic collections are particularly characteristic of the thirty years or so between the mid-1640s and the mid-1670s. The reason for their appearance immediately before and during the Commonwealth period is explained in the drolleries themselves. The introductory epistle of the 1646 edition of *The Academy of Complements* refers to 'these sullen dislaureating times'[1] and suggests that the comic poems will help to relieve the gloom, and in an earlier chapter we have seen Isaac Walton recording that Alexander Brome's comic collection of 1661 consisted of songs used to keep up the spirits of the Cavaliers as they marched to meet their Puritan foes. Hugh Crompton announces, in the dedication of his *Pierides or the Muses Mount,* that his comic verse is to be an antidote against 'these destructive times' when 'the concommittants of pride and envy are swollen up.'[2] In short, the drolleries played a part in the idealogical war in which the gaiety of the Cavaliers was seen to be an antidote to the sobriety of the Puritans.

Cromwell's puritan regime obviously regarded these lighthearted publications as a serious threat to the Commonwealth, for severe penalties were promulgated for publishers and writers of such seditious literature. Anthony Wood tells us that *Choyce Drollery* of 1656 gave 'great offence to the saints of the time' and was burnt by the public hangman.[3] He also tells the story of Thomas Weaver, whose collection *Songs and Poems of Love and Drollery* was published in 1654: 'being looked upon by the godly men of those times as seditious and libellous against the Government, he was imprisoned and afterwards tried for his life.'[4] The judge, however, seems to have had some sense of humour, for when the book was produced for him to inspect he let Weaver off with the comment that he appeared to be a gentleman of wit and learning. The collection, which still survives in rare copies, seems completely innocuous to a modern reader. The 'Address to the Reader' of an edition of *Wit and Drollery* of 1682 referring to the first edition of 1656 states:

This sort of Wit hath formerly suffered Martyrdom; for Cromwell, who was more for Policy than Wit, not only laid the first Reviver of these Recreations in the Tower, but also committed the innocent sheets to the mercy of the Executioner's Fire; as being some of them too kind, as he thought, to the Royal Partie.

In fact, there is very little satire against Puritans in these collections and what there is is usually good natured. There is not a great deal of satire of any kind though there is a wide range of comic attitudes which gradually shift towards satire, reflecting the changing attitudes of the Cavaliers. The situation is made more confusing, however, by the existence of a sophisticated, somewhat cynical, 'anti-platonic', comic poetry from much earlier. This is perhaps medieval in origin. It is strongly evident in Wyatt in poems like 'Ye old Mule' or it can be found in such Italian comic writers as Berni and in early seventeenth-century French anthologies; and it appears in Elizabethan poets from Gascoigne to Donne. The drolleries represent a coming together of this elite tradition with the broader popular humour of the ballad literature, and as time goes on the cynicism and disillusion seem increasingly to prevail. In Donne the cynicism of a poem like *The Indifferent* seems to be rather the result of a *jeu d'esprit* than an expression of settled conviction. In Suckling, in the next generation, such attitudes have become more an expression of a way of life. The same change appears in the drolleries. There is a movement away from the fanciful, the rich and strange, towards a disillusioned realism. As John Aubrey puts it: 'When the warres came, and with them liberty of conscience and liberty of inquisition, the phantoms vanished.'[5]

The range of drollery comedy is wide. There is the cheerful, good-natured humour of the old ballad literature at one extreme, a comedy that asserts the richness and strangeness of life and celebrates fecundity and well-being. There is a more detached humour that is balanced nicely between praise and blame; verse that sometimes seems to derive from the play of 'metaphysical' wit and sometimes takes the form of rhetorical exercises in such forms as the mock encomium or the mock song. Further towards satire there is burlesque humour, a denigratory comedy that is not satire proper because it has no consistent viewpoint from which judgement is made; and there is some true satire.

Not surprisingly the earliest comic collections show a preponderance of good-humoured comedy. *Wit's Recreations* of 1640 has a song called 'The Gypsies', which illustrates the delight in the rare and strange:

Knacks we have that will delight you,
Slight of hand that will invite you,
To endure our tawny faces,
Quit your places,
And not cause you cut your laces.[6]

This is an unusually clear example of the way benevolent
comedy reassures its listeners by moving from the strange to the
less strange. The potentially hostile is shown to be actually
friendly. Another poem from *Wit's Recreations* (though it is not
in the earliest edition) which illustrates the reassuring nature
of amiable comedy is a poem (actually by Waller) called 'On
the Two Dwarfs that were Marryed at Court not long before
Shrovetide'; it celebrates the marriage of the dwarf court
painter Richard Gibson to whom Marvell refers in *The Third
Advice to a Painter*. Waller's poem has affinities with metaphysical poetry in that it finds unexpected resemblances
between things apparently dissimilar. Like much of Donne's
poetry this little poem discovers harmonies where one would
expect only incongruity:

Thrice happy is this humble paire,
Beneath the level of all care,
Far o're their heads all Arrowes fly
Of sad distrust, and Jealousie,
Secured in as high extream,
As if the world held none but them.[7]

The sense of incongruity is not, of course, entirely absent or the
poem would not be comic, but as in Chaplinesque comedy the
little people are found to have unexpected advantages: the
laughter is benevolent, reassuring, because things turn out to be
better than we expect. Waller, like Donne mostly, still thinks
in terms of a basically harmonious world.

Often the good humour is more obviously celebratory, as in
a poem from *The Academy of Pleasure* (1656) called 'An In-
vitation to Mirth':

He that's contented lives for aye,
The more he laughs the more he may . . .

Tis mirth that fills the veins with blood
More than wine, or sleep, or food.

There are, as one might expect, plenty of drinking songs and
although sex is usually treated rather cynically, occasionally it
is made the subject of a genuinely celebratory poem; as for
instance, in a poem from *Merry Drollery*, which begins:

With my hands in her hair, and her fingers so rare,
And her playing with my face,
We reapt the most happy contentment
That ever two lovers did find;
What woman did see but my love and me,
Would say, that we use to be kind.

Weddings are sometimes celebrated in verse. A poem called
'The Ballad of Arthur Bradley' also published in *Merry Drollery*
of 1661, but obviously from much earlier, will serve to illustrate
the kind:

When all the swaines did see
This mirth and merry glee,
There was never a man did smutch her,
But every man kist his wench.
But Giles was greedy of gain,
And he would needs kiss twain:
Her lover seeing that,
Did rap him on the pate,
That he had not one word to say
For the honour of Arthur of Bradley
Oh fine, Arthur of Bradley! Oh fine, Arthur of Bradley!

Here the poet conjures up a picture of rough, peasant good
nature, a sweaty image of pastoral innocence. The coarseness
nonetheless conveys a general feeling of good humour, reassuring us that no harm will come of it.

This celebratory comedy does not provide the prevailing
mood of these collections, however. It cannot have been easy
to maintain a serene conviction of the benevolence of things in
the 1640s and 1650s, especially in the Royalist camp for which

these verse collections were made. Accordingly even the light-hearted comedy of the time sometimes takes on an air of ironic ambiguity. *Sportive Wit* of 1656 for instance has a pleasant poem called 'The Maid's Portion' where the young lady, with naive charm, expresses her surprise that a simple country girl can do so well for herself in London:

> This *London* is a gallant place
> To raise a lasses fortune,
> For I that come of simple race,
> Brave roarers doe importune,
> I little thought in Dorchester
> To find such high preferment here,
> For I have but a Mark a year,
> Which my good Mother gave me.
>
> One gives to me perfumed Gloves
> The best that he can buy me,
> Live where I will I have the loves
> Of all that doe live nigh me
> If any new toyes I will weare,
> Ile have them, cost they ne're so dear
> Though I have but a Mark a year,
> Which my good mother gave me.
>
> My fashion with the Moone I change
> As though I were a Lady,
> All quaint conceits both new and strange,
> Ile have as soon as may be:
> Your Courtly Ladyes I can jeere,
> In cloath, but few to me come neere,
> Yet I have but a Mark a year,
> Which my good mother gave me.
>
> French Gowns with sleeves like pudding baggs
> I have at my requesting,
> Now I forget my Country raggs,
> And scorn such plain investing
> My old acquaintance I cashiere,
> And of my kin I hate to hear,

Though I have but a Mark a year,
Which my good mother gave me.

My petticoats of Scarlet brave,
Of Velvet, Silk and Sattin,
Some students of my love do crave,
That speak both Greek and Latin;
The Soldiers for me domineere,
And put the rest into great feare,
All this is for a Mark a year,
And that my mother gave me . . .

Now if my friends were living still,
I would them all abandon,
Though I confesse they lov'd me well,
Yet I so like of *London*,
That farewell Dad and Mammy dear,
And all my friends in Dorsetshire.
I live well with a Mark a yeare,
And that my mother gave me.

I would my sister Sue at home
Knew how I live in fashion,
That she might up to *London* come,
And learn this Occupation,
For I live like a Lady here,
I weare good clothes, and eat good cheare,
Yet I have but a Mark a yeare,
And that my mother gave me.

Now blessed be that happy day,
That I came to the Citty,
And for the Carrier will I pray,
Before I end my Ditty.
You maidens that this Ditty heare,
Though means be short, yet never feare:
For I live with a Mark a year,
Which my old mother gave me.[8]

Another poem of *Sportive Wit* called 'A Charm', a poem that
first appears in an inferior version in Francis Beaumont's

Poems (1640)[9] but need not necessarily be by him, illustrates how Aubrey's fairies were quitting the land. Elizabethan fairy poetry is here used to get the old man asleep so that the young wife can find her own entertainment:

> Sleep, old man, let silence charme thee:
> Dreaming slumbers overtake thee:
> Quiet thoughts and darkness arm thee:
> Let no creaking door awake thee.
> *Phoebus* hath put out his light,
> And his shadows closing:
> Phoebe lends her horns to-night,
> To thy head's disposing.[10]

It is not surprising that the fairies refused to come after this. Neither of these poems could be called satirical because a nice balance is struck between the incongruous images: is it the young girl's ingenuousness or her cunning that make her so successful a prostitute? Is the lullaby genuinely saying the old man is better unaware of what is happening, or is it suggesting that he is a credulous old fool?

An ambiguous attitude to such situations as this implies some uncertainty about standards. But one cannot help feeling that the poets are taking pleasure in ambiguity for its own sake rather than as a serious reflection of moral doubt. Certainly this love of ambiguity and paradox for its own sake frequently dominates the polite verse of the period. The tendency can be seen in Marvell's *Definition of Love* and *Dialogue between the Soul and Body* where displays of verbal ingenuity take precedence over the themes they might be expected to serve. Cleveland provides the best examples of this in his comic poetry. In a poem on the same subject as Milton's *Lycidas*, the drowning of Edward King, he seems to the modern reader to take ingenuity to the point of heartlessness:

> I am no poet here; my penne's the spout
> Where the rain-water of my eyes runs out . . .

In a poem called 'To Mrs. K. T. who askt him why he was dumb', he develops a version of Epimenides's paradox in a number of outrageous variations:

Stay, should I answer (Lady) then
In vaine would be your question.
Should I be dumb, why then againe
Your asking me would be in vaine.
Silence nor speech (on neither hand)
Can satisfie this strange demand.
Yet since your will throwes me upon
This wicked contradiction,
I'll tell you how I did become
So strangely (as you heare mee) dumb.[11]

Cleveland is not writing *about* anything, he is using his subject matter as an opportunity for creating clever intellectual patterns. The drastically simplified rhythms compared to earlier 'Petrarchist' poets (Donne, Herbert, Carew), with the constant and regular break at the end of each couplet, give an impression not of the passionate and complex unity achieved by Donne's sequaciousness, but of an essential discontinuity in which what really matters is the ingenuity of each isolated paradox, not the emotion through which the paradoxes are to be resolved. Again the inharmonious rhyming 'then/question', 'upon/contradiction' gives an impression not of a passionate wrestling with words, which it might if the rhythms had been more complex, but of a careless indifference that suggests that the poet/lover has an ironic, detached attitude rather than the passionate, committed stance he claims for himself. The language here reveals an incongruity between actual and proclaimed intentions towards the lady, which in part accounts for the comic effect of the lines. It would be wrong to dismiss this, however, as mere playfulness, if only because the game is played with such assiduity. It is partly escapism, but the same extravagance of ideas is found in Cleveland's satire. The Renaissance cult of disinterestedness is showing signs of developing into cynical uninterestedness.

One of the most intriguing aspects of Cleveland's verse here is the way in which, his (or the lover's) lack of any strong conviction leads him to adopt the rhymed couplet. What order there is has to be imposed on the language from outside by the adoption of a uniform metrical unit. A comic tension is created between the incongruous ideas and the regularity of the form in which they are articulated. Yet the end-stopping of the couplet gives the impression of discontinuity. Cleveland's contribution to the development of the Augustan pentameter couplet has already been noted[12] but here we can see that the urge towards a strict couplet is just as obvious in his octosyllabic verse and that its use is essentially comic in its implications. It is this, far more than any theoretical belief in the virtues of heroic couplets (shared anyway with Elizabethans such as Puttenham and Jonson)[13] that makes the end-stopped couplet the dominating metre from Marvell to Pope, and its use is nearly always more successful in comic rather than non-comic forms. Cleveland, like his friend Butler, is groping his way to a form which will be able to 'build a world on a point' in a more profound sense than Charles Batteau intended.[14] Only in Rochester's poetry is it made explicit that the isolated moment is the one known fact in a world where traditional coherences can no longer be relied on. But implicit in this fragmentation of rhythm is a similar awareness. Cleveland's approach in this poem marks a notable change in attitudes from the age of faith to a greater scepticism and uncertainty. The octosyllabic couplet in the hands of Cleveland and Butler and the deca-syllabic couplet in the hands of Marvell, Rochester and eventually Pope, especially in the later satire (the *Dunciad* is the most telling example), often comes to be not only an image of the discontinuity of the world they see about them, it provides a comic contrast between extreme, but arbitrary, regularity of form and the chaotic nature of what they describe.

These detached comic attitudes often reveal nothing more than a light-hearted unconcern with the problems of the day; they are often simply a form of play. Many serious-minded people could stomach paradox and witticism so long as it was not meant to be taken seriously. Thomas Fuller writes in his *Church History*:

> For mine own part, I confess it no heresy to maintain a paradox in history, nor am I such an enemy to wit as not to allow it leave harmlessly to disport itself, for its own content, and the delight of others . . . But when men shall do it cordially, in sober sadness, to pervert people's judgements,

and therein go against all received records, I say, singularity is the least fault can be laid to such men's charge.[15]

Rhetorical exercises, like the mock *encomia* that abound in the drolleries, playfully invert conventional attitudes. Mock encomia could be used, as Erasmus uses the form in his *Praise of Fools*, for serious satirical purposes, but the most popular in these anthologies are verses in praise of an ugly mistress, and these have generally no satirical intention. In origin the mock *encomia* seems to have been a sophisticated form. Thomas Wilson recognises it in his *Arte of Rhetorique* (1553) and defines it as 'a pleasant dissembling when we praise that which otherwise deserveth dispraise.'[16] Examples in English go back at least to the fourteenth-century poet Hoccleve.[17] They seem to have been just as popular on the continent. Berni has a famous poem addressed to his beloved beginning, 'A mop of fine silver hair, bushy and untidily twisted around a fair yellow face'[18] and examples can be found in seventeenth-century French anthologies. A typical example is 'Lackwit's Ironicall praise of his Mistress', in *The Academy of Complements*, which includes the lines:

> Her nose surmounts three inches in degree,
> In shape and colour like a Lobster's claw . . .

There were a large number of subjects available to these comic encomiasts. *Wit and Drollery* has a poem 'On the Praise of Fat Men' and as late as 1685 Samuel Wesley (the father of Charles and John) published a collection called *Maggots* in praise of such subjects as a shock bitch.

There were various other kinds of comic rhetorical exercise. The mock song for instance, in which a well-known song was parodied, or a comic song was written to a well-known tune, seems to have been popular, especially after the Restoration. A collection called *Mock Songs and Joking Poems* (1675) is largely devoted to the form. Henry Bold in his collection of poems of 1664 is good enough to print not only his mock songs, but the originals, presumably in case his readers could not recognise what he was mocking. A parody of Carew's 'Ask me no more' in *Westminster Drollery* (1671) discusses a subject with which we are now familiar, the relative merits of long and short hair for men. The opening stanza is:

> Ask me no more why I do wear
> My Hair so far below my ear:
> For the first Man that e're was made
> Did never know the barber's trade.[19]

Another rhetorical exercise favoured in the drolleries is the antithetical portrait, which I discuss in the chapter on Rochester's lyric poetry. In these again the 'metaphysical' habit of juxtaposing heterogeneous images has been developed for comic purposes by emphasising the disparity rather than by seeking an underlying harmony. Any of these forms of verse can be used satirically and it is not always easy to be certain whether satire is intended. There is one kind of verse, however, that by its very nature is non-committal – the nonsense poem. There are not many of these in the drolleries, but there are some. Rather more common is the kind of verse in which an apparently serious poem is turned into nonsense by a comic addition. An example is this stanza from a *Mock Song* from *Wit and Drollery*:

> Grant pity or I die,
> Love so my heart bewitches,
> With griefe I houle and cry,
> Oh how my Elbow Itches.[20]

It is rare for this uncommitted poetry to be anything but light-hearted play, though just occasionally it can have more serious implications, as it seems to when used by sophisticated poets like Cleveland and later, Rochester. A withdrawal into play poetry as an expression of scepticism is not as characteristic of Commonwealth as of Restoration and later Augustan poetry (John Gay's comic poetry is a good later example). In Cleveland's comic poetry we do not get the impression of *conscious* reflection of sceptical attitudes that we find in Rochester's *Song of the Young Lady* or *The Disabled Debauchee* or Sedley's *Knitting Song*. Cleveland's is not a sceptical mind, nor was scepticism ever an easy mode of thought for the seventeenth century except for a short period in the limited circle of the wits of Charles II's court. There is no surprise that even Rochester had a dramatic death-bed conversion and that Sedley became a respected member of Parliament.

Most characteristic of all the forms of the comic in the drolleries and in Restoration comic verse is neither pure comedy, celebratory comedy, nor satire, but that curious in-between form, burlesque. Burlesque became something of a disease throughout Europe in the second half of the seventeenth century. Spreading from Italy, where it had long been endemic, it took hold in France, notably in the work of Scarron, and arrived in England (though there are earlier native outbreaks) sometime in the 1620s or 1630s. It took the form of the parody of classical poems, the most famous of these being Scarron's travesty of the *Aeneid* which dates from 1648, translated by Cotton in 1664 as *Virgil Travestie*. The earliest of these burlesque poems on classical subjects that I have met in English is actually earlier than Scarron's travesty of Virgil: James Smith's *Meeting of Ulysses and Penelope*. This was not published until 1658, in *Wit Restor'd*, but was certainly written before 1640, for it has commendatory verses by Philip Massinger, who died in that year. Massinger describes it as 'a new strain' of writing. It was preceded in publication by the scatological *Loves of Hero and Leander* (1653, republished in 1667, 1672, 1682), and followed by a large number of similar efforts during the Restoration period. Butler's *Hudibras*, itself the subject of many imitations, is the most interesting of the kind.

Burlesque shares with satire the attempt to belittle and repudiate its subjects, but unlike satire and like the balanced comedy we have been discussing, it refuses to suggest consistent judgements because the satire is mixed with elements of celebratory comedy. A seventeenth-century account describes it as essentially uncertain both in its intentions and in the techniques it uses:

Its Nature is to Ridicule, Flatter, Huff, and Banter, by turns; to Scratch and Claw now, and anon to Grin and bite like a Satyr. I am ignorant of the true Reason why it is call'd *Doggerel*; but I know a witty young Gentlewoman, who has a small talent that way, and she calls her own *Burlesque*,

Bitcheral. It is wonderful to traverse its Arbitrary Power, how it proceeds without regard to *Periods, Colons,* or *Commas*: How sometimes it will change Accents for the sake of *Rhyme,* and accordingly to the most vulgar and careless Pronunciation, leave out what *Consonants* it pleases. It will end the verse with a Preposition, and make *Interjections* at its own *Libitum.* It often uses Grammar so ill, that it will baulk *Orthography* itself, rather than not assert its own Prerogative . . .[21]

The direction of the comedy is uncertain because there are no clear standards of reference. As I argued earlier, satire demands an overall movement from high expectation to low performance and celebratory comedy from low expectation to unexpectedly high performance. In both, one set of standards is measured consistently against another. Burlesque varies its viewpoint so that no overall impression is gained; this again differs from sceptical comedy where a precise balance is struck between two equally valid points of view. We are not sure in the end of burlesque, whether we are supposed to be laughing with the burlesque hero or against him. Frequently the uncertainty extends to the role of the poet himself, who appears in the role of clown-hero and the techniques used, imperfect rhyming, doggerel rhythms and slangy vocabulary, proclaim a loss of faith in the poet's calling. Burlesque reflects a loss of poetic nerve. The poet as clown becomes a common type in the Commonwealth and Restoration periods and the role is now assumed without the irony of that earlier neo-classical age, when Chaucer indulges in self-mockery or when William Langland assumes the part of mad prophet. The fondness for burlesque is clear evidence of the confusion of standards and attitudes that afflicts people at the mid-century.

Numerous examples are found in the poetry of the period, but perhaps burlesque is most appropriately illustrated from the work of the first translator of Scarron, Charles Cotton. Around 1670 Cotton wrote a poem he called *A Voyage to Ireland in Burlesque,* which illustrates the main features of the mode: the poet adopting the role of clown, the debunking of literary convention, the use of inelegant versification. Here, for instance, is the opening of the third Canto:

Instead it varies its stance between the alternative attitudes. In so far as it shares the corrective tendencies of satire, however, it reflects a common belief of the period that if only man's propensity for self-delusion could be removed he could arrive at some bed-rock of certainty from which everything would be seen as it really is. This quest for certainty inspires Hobbes's great achievements in *Leviathan*, and it is characteristic of the age that Hobbes's work should be as much concerned with destroying other people's illusions as in setting up his own version of truth. The last part of *Leviathan*, the attack on Catholic theology, is one of the great satirical works of the age. *Leviathan*, however, puts forward a constructive alternative to the world of illusion it tries to destroy. Burlesque is concerned with the surface, the appearance of things; like the play poetry, it is preoccupied with forms often in defiance of meanings. It leaves largely intact the general assumption of the age that there is an underlying certainty that commonsense will reveal once pretension, hypocrisy and all other kinds of delusion are removed. Such rationalism can be aimed even at poetry itself or at its more inspirational manifestations. There is clearly an inherent danger of throwing out the poetic baby with the rhetorical bath water in such outbursts as Hobbes's complaint to Davenant that poetic flights are 'a foolish custome, by which a man, enabled to speak wisely from the principles of nature and his own meditation, loves rather to be thought to speak by inspiration, like a Bagpipe'.[24] There is in general a suspicion of claims to experience beyond the usual. A frequent criticism of earlier poetry was that it transcended the bonds of common experience. Thomas Rymer writes in the preface to his translation of Rapin's *Reflections on Aristotle* (1674): '. . . it was the vice of those Times to affect superstitially the *Allegory*; and nothing would then be currant without a mystical meaning.' Debunking imaginative flights becomes a favourite occupation, witness the success of Buckingham's *Rehearsall* (1671) and George Lansdowne's 'Against Unnatural Flights in Poetry' (1701). Samuel Butler, in his satirical character of a 'small poet', compares him to a 'Fanatic, that inspires himself with his own whimsies'.[25] *Hudibras* is almost entirely concerned with destroying a wide range of illusions including the imagination itself, and in this it is not unique. Swift, the greatest English-

man to sit in Cervantes' easy chair, seems sometimes occupied
on a similar quixotic adventure, particularly in his poetry.
One inevitable casualty of this mood was that body of poetic
convention that had been painstakingly evolved over the
centuries: one by one the traditions were shed in the name of
'truth'. Artificiality becomes a word of reproof. By 1692
William Walsh was condemning the Petrarchist conventions
that held sway earlier in the century and were still practised by
his more outlandish contemporaries. He assumes a naturalistic
inspiration and purpose for love poetry: '. . . the end that
People propose in writing Love Verses, I take not to be the
getting Fame or Admiration from the World, but obtaining
the Love of their Mistress; and the best way I conceive to make
her love you, is to convince her that you love her. Now this
certainly is not to be done by forc'd conceits, far-fetch'd
similes, and shining Points, but by a true and lively Representation of the Pains and Thoughts attending such a Passion.'[26]
This goes considerably further than Dryden's objection to
Donne's love poetry for affecting 'the metaphysics',[27] for
Dryden is complaining principally against Donne's lack of
stylistic decorum. The demand that poetry shall be sincere and
from the heart rapidly gained ground. In 1696 John Oldmixon,
quoting Walsh for support, is even more forthright: 'You will
find nothing in this little Volume, but what was the Real
Sentiments of my Heart at the time I writ it, and he that will
not give himself a greater Liberty, has no need to fear being
thought forc'd, or unnatural, which is the Greatest vice in
Verses of Love and Gallantry'.[28] Contrast this with Giles
Fletcher's remark a century earlier: 'a man may write of love
and not be in love, as well as of husbandrie, and not goe to the
plough'.[29] For Fletcher the truest wit was the most feigning.
Not that all the conventions died at once. We shall see Rochester attempting to remain in touch with traditional modes, and
Pope can hardly be called an unconventional poet. None the
less the end of the old order was clearly in sight.

An excellent illustration of this desire to strip truth bare of its
outer fripperies can be found in a poem of Suckling's called
'Upon my Lady Carlisle's Walking in Hampton Court Garden'.
Suckling, who died in 1642, was an important influence on
Commonwealth and Restoration poetry. The poem is a

dialogue between J.S. (Suckling) and T.C. (Thomas Carew) and contrasts the response of the two poets to the appearance of Lady Carlisle. 'Carew' opens the poem with an elaborate conceit in which the garden is seen miraculously reacting to the lady's presence; the flowers start from their beds, music sounds when she talks and rare perfumes surround her. Suckling will have none of this however and replies:

> I must confess those perfumes, Tom,
> I did not smell; nor found that from
> Her passing by ought sprang up new:
> The flowers had all their birth from you.

This is the poetry of negative vision we meet frequently in the Restoration and in Swift, whose special characteristic as a poet it is. For here Suckling is denying any reality to the creative power of the imagination. Any product of the imagination is suspect, illusory. He adopts a deliberate simplification of rhythm in which spoken accents that fall out of place (like the unwanted stress on 'from' of the second line) suggest a derisory scorn of the balance and harmony of a cohering vision. The accent is on lack of harmony, incongruity, in short the vision of absurdity which is at the centre of the comic mode. The comic vision arises from the rational observation of the irrational creature, man.

After a reply from 'Carew' Suckling contributes a further stanza to the poem which shows the process of stripping literally as well as metaphorically:

> Alas! Tom, I am flesh and blood,
> And was consulting how I could
> In spite of masks and hoods discry
> The parts denied to the eye.

The desire to strip off surface 'unreality' (a familiar theme in Swift) leads to a suggestion of the disparity between the apparent and the real. Suckling's 'reality' underlying the clothes is that of the libertine rationalist and the contrast [between what man is, and what the imagination would like him to be, forms the basis of a comic satire on the 'platonic' idealisation of women. It is satire not burlesque because the 'platonic' standards which are being attacked are consistently presented and the two sets of standards are consistently juxtaposed. The assumption is that women are 'really' not beautiful creatures to be revered, but the objects of sexual desire; that the bed-rock of woman's reality is the bed. The comedy arises partly from the juxtaposition of the two attitudes to women, partly from the inherent absurdity of man's sexuality.

In the drolleries there is a good deal of this debunking, though the standards implied are frequently confused and it therefore generally takes the form of burlesque rather than satire. The collections of Sir John Mennis and Rev. James Smith consist principally of burlesque verse. These are *Musarum Deliciae* (1655, 1656), *Wit and Drollery* (1656, 1661, 1682) and *Wit Restor'd* (1658). One of the favourite subjects of these collections is self-mockery. *Wit Restor'd* opens with a series of verse letters in octosyllabic couplets in which the correspondents make fun of themselves and each other. This epistolary form of burlesque became popular during the Restoration; there is, for instance, a short exchange of verse letters between Etherege and Dryden. In method Smith and Mennis anticipate *Hudibras* and perhaps supplied Butler with his verse form. Here, for instance, is an extract of a letter from Mennis to Smith from *Musarum Deliciae* dated 1640. Mennis gives a ludicrous account of his plight in charge of a troop of Royalist soldiers in the North of England, complaining that he has no money and that none of the local innkeepers will give him credit:

> Judge, if thy Muse could soar so high,
> When pinion clip'd, what Bird can fly?
> No, no, good Wine and ease I'm bar'd of,
> Which makes my Muse to come so hard off; . . .[30]

Musarum Deliciae has quite a number of poems in which the poet presents himself as a clown. One called 'Upon a lame tired Horse' presents the poet as a Falstaffian figure:

> Now men observing, that I was so fat,
> And durst ride on a Horse so lean as that
> Did scoff and jeer me, as I pass'd the way . . .[31]

There is another poem called 'A Poet's Farewell to his Thread-bare Cloak' in which the poet makes fun of his own poverty and another called 'Upon a Fart Unluckily let' in which the poet indulges in some scatological humour at his own expense.

Once belief has been lost in one's own importance as man and poet, the step to complete scepticism is a short one. That step was sometimes taken later, in the Restoration period. But it was not easy in an age of faith like the seventeenth century to accept a completely sceptical view of the world. The general belief in a meaningful world, in spite of the widespread disagreement about the precise meaning of it, explains why satire was ultimately a more congenial mode than burlesque; why satire flourished when farce failed. Not surprisingly it was left to the sceptical twentieth century to turn farce into a serious art. The farcical verse of Mennis and Smith remains unconvincing, local, not a general expression of the absurdity of things. Very often it operates at the level of the private joke; not seldom as a comedy of private parts. Disconcertingly it will swing to nonsense like 'Hawkin's Heigh-ho' from *Musarum Deliciae* (p. 23), a parody of a love-song duet between a cook and a laundress:

> Oft have I perboyl'd been with grief,
> Season'd and saus'd with brine of bitter tears,
> With Salads sliced, and lettuc'd up with Beef,
> With Vinegar and sugar, hopes and feares
> Undone like Oysters, pepper'd with despair,
> 　　All for this Laundress fair.

Typically the nonsense has no suggestion of a general scepticism, it is entirely at the level of play. At the other extreme even the comic verse can become quite solemn as it expresses sentiments dear to Royalist hearts, as it does in a mock heroic poem called 'Upon Chesse Play' from the same collection:

> . . . now dares a martial Queen
> Check her foe King, when straight there slips between
> A vent'rous Soldier, or a Nobleman
> Who cares not for his life, so that he can
> From danger keep his King; he feares not death
> In Prince's cause, that gives each Subject breath.

It is from such humble beginnings that Augustan mock heroic was developed. The inconsistency of these collections is a mark of their confusion of outlook. On the one hand they are still wishing to affirm standards that they are wedded to by Royalist tradition, on the other hand their hostile attitude to the actual Puritan authority gives them an opportunity to express a desire to subvert authority that goes beyond the immediate political situation, though it never becomes, as with Rochester, an attack on Authority as such. Had they believed as firmly in the Royalist order as opponents like Milton believed in their reforming principles these collections would presumably have been devoted not to burlesque, but to satire, of which Milton was the supreme exponent during the Commonwealth period. Had they, on the other hand, been able to believe in nothing they would have been able to achieve a balanced, sceptical comedy. It was not easy to believe in the inviolability of a Sun King who had been decapitated, yet they could not bring themselves not to believe. There was of course a considerable amount of non-comic satire against the Commonwealth regime, because they knew well enough what they did not like in their opponents, and non-comic satire does not need to present the alternative standards. Comic satire requires a sharp and precise contrast between what is deplored and what is advocated. Attack by itself is not enough because the true standards being defended must provide one element of the double vision necessary to the comic. It was notably the opposition in Charles II's reign that developed comic satire as a serious poetic form, because the opposition had a precise idea of what it wanted as well as what it hated. Establishment of comic satire was made possible by the increasing authoritarianism of Charles's government, which made a defence of traditional monarchist standards once again capable of carrying some conviction.

It is at first sight surprising that there is little outright satire in the comic collections of the Commonwealth, though understandable when the bewilderment over traditional standards is understood. Satire needs a clear vantage point of belief in order to make its judgements convincing. When satire does occur in the collection it is usually couched in personal terms, dealing with the private morality of the Puritans, not with the regime in general. The favourite subject is Puritan hypocrisy, characteristically described in *Musarum Deliciae*, 'A poet's Farewell to his Threadbare Cloak' in terms of appearance masquerading as reality:

> The only Cloaks that are now in fashion
> Are Liberty, Religion, Reformation.
> All these are fac'd with Zeal, and button'd down
> With jewels dropt from an imperiall Crowne.
> He that would Cloak it in the new Translation
> Must have his Taylor cut it Pulpit-fashion;
> Do not appear within the City; there
> They mind not what men are, but what they weare.

The Swiftian imagery of clothes usurping the status of the man who wears them shows us again this desire to distinguish appearance from an underlying reality. But the satire consorts rather oddly with such baroque images of kingship as the 'jewels dropt from an imperiall Crowne'. This suggests a very different kind of order, based on religious concepts, from the rational order asserted by the desire to strip the Puritans of their fanciful coverings. Standards are confused, and the comedy moves fitfully from non-comic affirmation to satire, from imperial crown to Puritan tailor.

The best satire in these collections is less far-reaching. There are some particular attacks on Cromwell and other recognisable members of the Puritan establishment, but the most successful are those that create typical characters in typical predicaments. There is a pleasant, almost benign satire in *Merry Drollery* (1661), for instance, called 'The Way to Wooe a Zealous Lady', which makes not ungentle fun of the discrepancy between Puritan solemnity and Puritan lubricity. The use of Puritan cant is well handled and the result both amusing and good-tempered:

> Quoth I, dear Sister, and that lik'd her well;
> I kist her and did pass to some delight.
> She, blushing, said, that long-tail'd men would tell;
> Quoth I, I'll be as silent as the night;
> And less the wicked now should have a sight
> Of what we do, faith, I'll put out the light.

At the level of social intercourse the writer obviously still has great confidence in his own values. In terms of social accomplishment the Cavalier can still afford to treat his enemies gently and so depict them with satirical precision. The uncertainty lies at a deeper level.

Not that the Puritans are always treated quite so gently. Thomas Weaver, for instance, who has already been mentioned for getting into trouble with the Puritan authorities, has a poem in his collection *Songs and Poems of Love and Drollery* (1654) called 'The Rotundas' where a preacher of a Puritan sect of that name is castigated with scathing ridicule:

> Gainst humaine learning next he enveys,
>   And most boldly says,
> Tis that which destroyes inspiration,
>   Let superstitious sense
>   And wit be banisht hence . . .

Weaver has another anti-puritan poem in this collection called 'Zeal Overheated'.

The Puritans were fair game in these Royalist collections and the only surprise is that they were not more often attacked. Less expected are the attacks on their own kind. In some of the collections, for instance, there are clear signs of a generation gap, where the older Cavaliers object to the newfangled cynicism of the younger people. *An Antidote against Melancholy* (1661) is particularly concerned with the innovation in manners, for this was the time when the old Royalists were beginning to feel that the new regime was not quite what they had fought for. A poem called 'An Old Song of an Old Cavalier and a New' is a revamping of a ballad that had appeared earlier in the century, perhaps, as C. H. Firth suggested,[32] around 1630. It is particularly appropriate for the Restoration, however, because it contrasts the courtier of the old regime with that of the new. The old courtier is represented as neighbourly, jovial, generous, mindful of his function in the social order, a Sir Roger de Coverley. The new courtier, who is clearly not approved of, is indifferent to his social responsibilities, to his religion (to judge from his Chaplain) and has epicurean tastes:

With a new study stuff'd full of pamphlets and playes,
With a new Chaplin that swears faster than he preyes,
With a new buttery hatch that opens once in four or five days,
With a new French cook to make kickshawes and tayes,
    Like a young Courtier of the Kings.

and later:

Like a young gallant newly come to his land,
That keeps a brace of creatures at's own command
And lieth drunk in a new tavern till he can neither go nor stand;
    Like a young Courtier of the Kings.[33]

That this poem is a revival from the earlier part of the century
reminds us that the generation gap is always with us, but it does
point to a general change in the course of the century from the
old hearty bonhomie of a self-confident feudal culture to the
much less certain, more brittle and perhaps more brilliant
cosmopolitan culture that succeeded it. The comedy in this
poem is of a contrast in the generations, but because the writer's
preference is clear and consistent, because the complaint is of a
falling off, it is unmistakably satire.

Sometimes particular habits are excepted against. A poem
called 'The Drunken Humours' from *Wit's Recreations* in the
edition of 1654, satirises, surprisingly enough, the vice of
drunkenness with a realism that is vehement enough perhaps
to be classed as non-comic satire:

So this most sordid beast being drunk, doth misse
The chamber pot and in his hose doth pisse.
Nay, smell but near him, you perhaps may find
Not only pissed before, but shit behind.[34]

Even more solemn in its admonitions is a poem in Weaver's
Poems of Love and Drollery which states:

Tis crime enough to be o'retane with wine,
But to be drunk with purpose and design
Admits no pardon.

Weaver, of course, was an Anglican clergyman, which might, though does not necessarily, explain the preference for sobriety. Or possibly it was a matter of mood; for Weaver, like most of the drollery versifiers, is willing to try his hand at drinking songs.

Women, of course, provide a welcome subject for satire, as they always have, and it is for this subject that the drolleries reserve their best invective. Poems like 'The Baseness of Whores' of *Choyce Drollery* (1656) (pp. 90–1) or 'Upon the Naked Bedlams and Spotted Beasts of Covent Garden' of *Wits Interpreter* make the prostitute their target. More general anti-feminist satire is found in poems like 'The Curse' of *Sportive Wit* (1656) or 'To a Lady vex'd with a Jealous Husband' of *Musarum Deliciae*, which has a vehemence unusual in these collections:

> Debar her Lord, she, to supply his room,
> Will have a Horse-boy, or a Stable-groom.
> Keep her from youth of lower rank and place,
> She'l kiss his Scullion, and with knaves embrace;
> Suspect her faith with all mistrust,
> She'l buy a Monkey to supply her lust:
> Lock her from Man and Beast, and all content,
> She'l make thee Cuckold with an instrument.

You could hardly blame her in the circumstances; but at least the heart of the poem is in the right place, for it demonstrates the futility of repression.

We have now moved to the very edge of the comic spectrum and this intense satire is very rare in the drolleries. The picture they give in general is of an age in transition. Attitudes are becoming less certain, but still remain linked with the past. Comedy is moving away from the good-natured, coarse humour of earlier generations but has not yet acquired the detached sophistication of the more sceptical age about to start. Where the comedy is detached, as it is among wits like Marvell or Cleveland or Waller, it is largely a play comedy in which little of real concern is stated. But one thing is certain: in the drolleries there are already signs that comedy is becoming a more serious business.

3 *Hudibras*

No work better illustrates the confusions inherent in the form
and the confusions of outlook characteristic of the period than
Samuel Butler's *Hudibras*. As the best of the myriad burlesque
poems of the Restoration it illustrates best the weaknesses of
the genre. For like all burlesque it is an uncertain mixture of
comic modes, being part satire and part celebratory comedy.
This might seem an odd assertion as it has generally, though not
invariably, been regarded as a satire. An early editor, Zachary
Grey, had no doubts about it: 'nor can scarce any one be so
ignorant, as not to know, that the chief design thereof is a
satire against those incendiaries of church and state, who, in the
late rebellion, under pretence of religion, murdered the best of
kings, to introduce the worst of governments; destroyed the best
of churches, that hypocrisy, novelty, and nonsense, might be
predominant amongst us; and overthrew our wholesome laws
and constitutions, to make way for their blessed anarchy and
confusion, which at last ended in tyranny.'[1] Earlier than this
John Dennis had discussed it as satire in his preface to *Miscellanies in Verse and Prose* (1693).[2] Most modern critics follow
the eighteenth-century lead: Coleridge describes it as 'rather a
series of satires than a comic poem'[3] and its most recent editor,
John Wilders, assumes it to be satire without discussing the
point.[4] None of the title pages of the early editions, however,
of which there were many, describe the poem as a satire; in
most it is simply called 'Hudibras . . . written in the time of the
Late Wars', which, as John Wilders has pointed out, is not even
helpful in telling us when it was written, for Wilders has shown
that the first part was probably started about 1656 and finished
shortly after the Restoration of May 1660. Of course, the poem
contains satire on a variety of topics. It is much less concerned
with political topics and much more concerned with attitudes
of mind than Zachary Grey's account suggests, but the point at
issue is whether there is a consistent satiric perspective; whether,

that is, the poem as a whole can be described as a satire. Earlier commentators seem often to be inconsistent in their remarks on the poem. Dryden in his *Discourse on Satire* describes *Hudibras* as *varronian*, that is, mixed comic satire, but his qualification of this description shows that he is uneasy about its status. Discussing its burlesque style, for instance, Dryden writes:

> . . . It turns earnest too much to jest, and gives us a boyish kind of pleasure. It tickles awkwardly with a kind of pain, to the best sort of readers: we are pleased ungratefully and, if I may say so, against our liking. We thank him not for giving us that unseasonable delight, when we know he could have given us a better, and more solid. He might have left that task to others who, not being able to put in thought, can only make us grin with the excrescence of a word of two or three syllables in the close. 'Tis, indeed, below so great a master to make use of such a little instrument. But his good sense is perpetually shining through all he writes; it affords us not the time of finding faults. We pass through the levity of his rhyme, and are immediately carried into some admirable, useful thought.[5]

This passage bristles with Dryden's prejudices against the comic and is characteristically preoccupied with stylistic decorum. Yet his need to resort to paradox to describe the poem and his acute awareness of a conflict between an element of knock-about comedy in the language and an underlying seriousness of purpose shows an equally characteristic sensitivity of response to the quality of the verse. Elsewhere he paradoxically refers to Butler's 'bufooning grace'.[6] The conflict is not simply a matter of a discrepancy between style and subject matter. Dryden had himself exploited such a discrepancy in *Mac Flecknoe*, though the seriousness there inhered in the style. A gap between style and subject, whichever way round, is the essential requirement of mock heroic and clearly Dryden is not dismissing mock heroic as such in this passage. The conflict goes deeper, for the knock-about comedy is frequently a feature of the subject matter of the poem, which the style helps to represent and reinforce. It is a conflict between a farcical, benevolent comedy and a satirical moral and philosophical intention.

This conflict is to some extent inherent in the choice of a narrative structure for the poem. The very structure of comic narrative, as Susanne Langer points out, asserts continuity and therefore tends to be reassuring. This is even truer when the action is centred on the exploits of a single hero. It is not accidental that *Don Quixote* and *Joseph Andrews* are, in spite of considerable satiric content, examples of a benevolent, re-assuring comedy that flatters the reader into a sense of the ultimate rightness of the world. Even with Fielding's elaborate alienation techniques we cannot avoid identifying ourselves to some extent with characters as full of vitality as Parson Adams and Tom Jones. Butler's hero is not so obviously sympathetic as Fielding's; if he were, we would not be so tempted to describe *Hudibras* as a satire, but he has an invincible vitality that wins our sympathy almost certainly against the initial intention of the author.

Again, earlier criticism records this discrepancy. There are those critics who see in Hudibras nothing but an object of Butler's disgust. Dr Johnson, for instance, writes in the *Life of Butler*:

> But for poor Hudibras, his poet had no tenderness; he chooses not that any pity should be shown or respect paid him: he gives him up at once to laughter and contempt, without any quality that can dignify or protect him.[7]

Hazlitt adopts a similar view, though rather paradoxically he concludes that Butler created characters in the poem who immortalised him.[8] Other critics, however, have responded to *Hudibras* differently. George Gilfillan, the poem's nineteenth-century editor, considered that Butler had 'a lurking fondness for Hudibras amid all the contempt and ridicule which he showers around him; beginning, perhaps, with a little spite at him, not on his own account, but as the representative of his class, he has ere the end, fairly laughed himself into good humour with his hero.'[9] Certainly Hudibras, especially at the outset, is described as a rather repellent creature and Butler's use of epithets guides our response (i i 33–40):

. . . his Brain
Outweigh'd his rage but half a grain,
Which made some take him for a tool
That Knaves do work with, call'd a Fool,
And offer to lay wagers, that
As Montaigne, playing with his Cat,
Complaines she thought him but an Ass,
Much more she would Sir Hudibras.[10]

The physical description of the hero is certainly no more
savoury (1 i 285–98):

His Back, or rather Burthen, showd
As if it stoop'd with its own load,
For as Æneas bore his Sire
Upon his shoulders through the fire:
Our knight did bear no less a Pack
Of his own Buttocks on his back:
Which now had almost got the upper-
Hand of his Head, for want of Crupper.
To poize this equally, he bore
A Paunch of the same bulk before;
Which still he had a speciall care,
To keep well cramm'd with thrifty fare;
As Whitepot, Butter-milk, and Curds,
Such as a Countrey house affords . . .

This is an example of the association of physical deformity with
what is evil and to be repudiated, for we have already learnt
that Hudibras is a representative of the Presbyterian sect that
Butler attacks directly in an earlier passage (1 i 205–16):

A Sect, whose Chief Devotion lies
In odde perverse Antipathies;
In falling out with that or this
And finding somewhat still amiss:
More peevish, cross, and spleenatick,
Than Dog distract, or Monkey sick
That with more care keep holy-day
The wrong, then others the right way:

Compound for Sins, they have inclin'd to,
By damning those they have no mind to:
Still so perverse and opposite,
As if they worshipp'd God for spight.

This is an impressive piece of invective and so strongly satirical
that it could hardly be called funny at all. At this early stage
in the poem Butler's aims seem to be almost entirely satirical
and as the attack continues on Hudibras and then on his
Sancho Panza, Ralpho, representing the Anabaptists, it seems
clear that a consistent attack on various kinds of 'enthusiasm' or
fanaticism is developing from the implicit standpoint of common sense. It seems as if this is to be that familiar Restoration
exercise of the stripping away of illusion already discussed in
connection with Suckling and Hobbes, the Drolleries and
Swift, in which illusion and imagination are identified and
the assumption is that there is a bed-rock of truth available to
the unillusioned man.

There is much in Butler that would justify such a reading of
Hudibras. Like Suckling and Hobbes he was clearly highly
suspicious of the imagination, and indeed of poetry; an
example of that paradoxical, but not uncommon seventeenth-
century phenomenon, the poet who despised the poetic. The
notebooks abound in comments on the need to subordinate
imagination to reason: 'Fancy is . . . an excellent servant to
reason and judgement but the most unfit thing in the world to
govern.'[11] . . . 'Wit and Fancy are light and Airey, but Judgement weighty,'[12] . . . 'Reason is the only Helm of the understanding, the Imagination is but the Sayle, apt to receive, and
be carry'd away with every winde of vanity, unless it be
stear'd by the Former'[13] . . . 'Wit and Fancy are but the Cloaths
and ornaments of Judgement, and when they are stollen by
those whom they will not fit, they serve them to no purpose, or
that which is worse than none, to make them Ridiculous'[14] . . .
'Those who imploy their Studies upon Fancy and words, do
commonly abate as much in their Reason, and Judgements,
as they improve the other way; For unless they make Truth
and observation the Ground and Foundation, or rather the end
of their Studys, and use Fancy, and Stile only as Instrumentall,
to express their conceptions the more easily, and Naturally,

they are noe wiser than an Artificer that mistakes his Tooles, for that which they only serve to worke upon. For those who propose wit, and Fancy for their end, and take in sense and Reason only as circumstantiall and on the by, judge as extravagantly as those who believe themselves Rich, because they can cast up ever so great Sums of Money, but have not one Penny. And that is one Reason why such men are commonly the most unapt in things that require Judgement and Reason.'[15]

The last excerpt is the most thoroughgoing indictment of poetry, for having required the poet to centre his attention on reason and judgement he then goes on to show why 'those who imploy their Studies upon Fancy and words' (that is, poets) are the least likely to be rational. The trend of the argument is to relegate those elements that distinguish poetry from other writing into mere excrescences on the body of thought that should be as much the primary concern of the poet as of any other kind of writer. Poetry is reduced to decoration, and decoration which mainly serves to get in the way and obscure the substance of what is said. Butler's 'Character of a Small Poet', a series of jottings among the satirical prose 'characters', one feels, is at least as much about the poet as about the small poet, and it is consistently hostile:

I shall not need to say anything of the Excellence of Poetry, since it has been already performed by many excellent Persons, among whom some have lately undertaken to prove, that the civil Government cannot possibly subsist without it, which, for my Part, I believe to be true in a poetical sense, and more probable to be received of it, than those strange Feats of building walls, and making Trees dance, which Antiquity ascribes to Verse.[16]

– a passage of irony not unworthy of Swift. An earlier part of the same 'character' attacks the pretensions of the poet to be a legislator of the world or a justifier of the ways of God to men:

The antient Magicians could charm down the moon, and force Rivers back to their Springs by the Power of Poetry only; and the Moderns will undertake to turn the Inside of the Earth outward (like a Jugler's pocket) and shake the

Chaos out of it, make *Nature* shew Tricks like an **Ape,** and the
Stars run on Errands; but still it is by dint of **Poetry.** And if
Poets can do such noble Feats, they were unwise to descend
to mean and vulgar: For where the rarest and most common
Things are of a Price (as they are all one to Poets) it argues
Disease in Judgement not to chuse the most curious. Hence
some infer, that the Account they give of things deserves no
Regard, because they never receive any Thing, as they find
it, into their Compositions, unless it agree both with the
Measure of their own Fancies, and the Measure of their
Lines, which can very seldom happen: And therefore when
they give a Character of any Thing or Person, it does
commonly bear no more Proportion to the Subject, than the
Fishes and Ships in a Map do to the Scale.[17]

He often seems to be equating poetry with fanaticism: 'Gifts
and wit are but a kind of hotheadedness . . . and this is why
Poets are ill masters of reason.'[18] In *Hudibras*, Ralpho's fits of
inspiration are likened to the poet's sibylline utterances:

> This Light inspires, and playes upon
> The nose of Saint, like Bag-pipe-drone,
> And speaks through hollow empty soul,
> As through a Trunk, or whisp'ring hole,
> Such language as no mortall Ear
> But spiritual Eaves-droppers can hear.
> So *Phoebus* or some friendly Muse
> Into small Poets song infuse;
> Which they at second-hand reherse
> Through reed or bag-pipe, verse for verse.[19]

We are not surprised to find him expressing a preference for
prose over poetry in the notebooks[20] and saying that the sole
virtue he claims for his writing is 'plain downrightness of sense'.[21]
He has no sympathy at all for his contemporaries' belief in the
godlike nature of the poet, and pours scorn on the mystique of
symbolic utterance favoured by that pedantic Renaissance
tradition currently being unearthed by modern scholars:

As for *Altars* and *Pyramids* in Poetry, he [Benlowes] has outdone all Men that Way; for he has made a *Gridiron,* and a

Frying-Pan in Verse, that, beside the Likeness in Shape, the very Tone and Sound of the Words did perfectly represent the Noise, that is made by those Utensils, such as the old Poet called *sartago loquendi*.[22]

and elsewhere:

> I wonder . . . why I cannot as well understand there are five senses, when I am told so; as by seeing them written upon Cross-Triangles, which are no more to be regarded than Pyramids and Altars in verse. But these images are but the conceptions of wearyd Melancholy, like the Images which a Sick or Idle Fancy will observe in the fire.[23]

It is reassuring to find such commonsense remarks in a seventeenth-century writer now that we are being persuaded to find hidden pyramids even in Shakespeare's sonnets. Not surprisingly Butler defies the accepted hierarchy of poetic kinds,[24] esteeming satire above heroic poetry and panegyric – 'Satyrs that are only provok'd with the Madnes and Folly of the world, are found to conteine more Wit, and Ingenuity then all other writings whatsoever, and meet with a better Reception from the World, that is always more delighted to heare the Faults and vices though of itself well described, then all the Panegyriques that ever were, which are commonly as Dull as they are false.'[25] He never tires of mocking the pretentiousness of heroic verse and of parodying it in his own verse. *Hudibras* contains a certain amount of literary parody and in *Repartees between Cat and Puss* he is possibly, as De Beer has suggested, parodying Dryden's *Conquest of Granada*.[26] Heroic poetry, he writes, 'handles the slightest and most Impertinent Follies in the world in a formal, Serious and unnaturall way.'

His preference for satire over panegyric on the grounds that it is more realistic reveals the cynical attitude to mankind that inspires much of his writing. Even the most optimistic Christian text can take on a sinister implication:

> The Scripture says God made Man in his own Image, and therefore every man makes God as like himself as he can. And fashions him according to his own naturall Temper, or

the Custome of the Place where he has been bred and not the
true Reasons of his essence and being.[27]

In the same way those qualities that are usually seen to justify
an optimistic view of man get turned into evidence against him:

The best parents, who are commonly the worst men, have
naturally a tender kindness for their Children, only because
they believe they are Part of themselves; which show's that
self-love is the Originall of all others; and the Foundation of
that great Law of Nature self-Preservation, for no man ever
destroyed himself wilfully, that has not first left off to Love
himself. And therefore a man's self is the proper object of his
Love, which is never so well imployd, as when it is kept
within its own Confines and not sufferd to Straggle. For every
man is just so much a Slave as he is concerned in the will,
Inclinations or Fortunes of another . . .[28]

In the same jotting he goes on to remark cynically that the
dominance of self-love is seen clearly in the behaviour of
friends, who are only around when they are not needed. This
dark view of human nature receives its most extended ex-
position in the *Satyr upon the Weakness and Misery of Man*, a poem
that catalogues the depravity of man with the single-minded-
ness of a medieval *de contemptu mundi* tract:

> Our holy'st Actions have been
> Th' Effects of Wickedness and Sin;
> *Religious Houses* made Compounders
> For th' horrid Actions of the *Founders;*
> *Steeples,* that totter'd in the Air,
> By Letchers sin'd into Repair;
> As if we had retain'd no Sign,
> Nor Character of the divine
> And heav'nly Part of human Nature,
> But only the coarse earthy Matter.
> Our universal Inclination
> Tends to the worst of our Creation,
> As if the *Stars* conspir'd t'imprint
> In our whole Species, by Instinct,

A fatal Brand, and Signature
Of nothing else, but the Impure.[29]

The poem reaches a climax in denouncing the worst of all
man's inanities, his tendency to rely on what Rochester called
the 'whimsies, heaped in his own brain'. But it is the contrast
with Rochester's *Satyr against Mankind* that is more illuminating
than the similarity. For whereas the effect of Rochester's
ordering techniques is to 'place' the carping at humanity in a
context that examines it, modifies it and eventually makes fun
of it, Butler's drollery technique makes the poet a part of the
disharmony of which he complains. The notebooks and the
minor satire give the reader after a time the uncomfortable
feeling that he is reading the work of a crank whose judgement
is as unreliable as the world he describes. There are some
indications, for those who like to make Freudian conjectures,
that this crankiness was not simply a literary pose. Aubrey
records that Butler made many enemies and few friends[30] and
James Younge writes that he was in his old age 'an old paraly-
tick claret drinker, a morose surly man, except elevated with
claret.'[31] Charles II, though he greatly admired the poetry,
seems not to have had much affection for the man. Butler seems
to have been by nature a solitary, unfriendly man (who had,
however, some distinguished friends). To encourage further
Freudian speculation, he seems to have married somewhat late
in life and there are indications that his attitude to women (who
feature in *Hudibras* almost exclusively as virago or shrew) is
unusually frigid, even when we take into account the anti-
feminist conventions he exploits in such verse as the *Satyr upon
Marriage* and the *Marriage* and *Women* fragments.[32] This couplet
from *Marriage* for instance, though it plays on a traditional
association of sex and death, asks to be interpreted at the level
of dream:

A married Man com's nearest to the Dead
And to be Buryd but to go to Bed.[33]

In another jotting from the notebooks he writes:

The Antients did wisely to describe
the *Furies* in the Persons of *Women*.[34]

B.O.L.—C

What could the analyst make as evidence of sexual frigidity of such a remark in the *Miscellaneous Observations* as:

> The Femals of Human Creatures are allways ready to generate, and the Males seldome, contrary to all other Animals, whose Males are allways ready and femals seldom . . . ?[35]

Even leaving aside the cloudy regions of psycho-analytical astrology there is such a consistent note of denigration, so obstinate a refusal to see any pleasures or graces in life, that we inevitably see the poet himself as his own Morose as he forces his absurdly one-sided attitudes down our throats:

> Our *Pains* are real things, and all
> Our *Pleasures* but fantastical . . .

he writes in the *Satyr upon the Weakness and Misery of Man*[36] and in the notebooks, somewhat illogically:

> The world is so vile a thing, that Providence commonly makes Fooles and Knaves happy, and good men miserable in it, to let us know, there is no great Difference between Happiness and misery here.[37]

And the effect of this constant, almost unrelieved emphasis on man's depravity is to start us off at such a low ground base of expectation that we welcome all signs of relenting, however small, as an unexpected concession to human feeling. This relief comes in the minor satire most often from the exuberance of Butler's clowning with words. The sheer outrageousness and ingenuity of:

> Steeples, that totter'd in the Air,
> By Letchers sin'd into Repair;

has both the unexpectedness of true comedy and the reassurance that there is humanity behind the scowling mask. Strangely enough, the effect of Butler's poetic technique is the very opposite of the declared intentions: it ends by reassuring us that things can't be quite as bad as he says they are. The comedy is frequently not, therefore, satirical, but benevolent moving from bad to better not bad to worse. Nor is it only the verse techniques that give this impression, for there are inconsistencies in Butler's attitudes which suggest that he does not take his condemnation of mankind quite as seriously as he pretends. In the passage of the *Satyr upon the Weakness and Misery of Man* quoted earlier, for instance, the phrase 'as if' which occurs twice within six lines (it occurs three more times in this poem of 228 lines and is a recurring phrase of *Hudibras*) could imply that it is not actually the case that we are as depraved as we look. We behave 'as if' we had retained no sign of the divine element in our nature and it is 'as if' the stars conspired to bring out the worst in us. One possible implication is that we *have* a share in the divine nature and that the stars do not conspire against us. The tone hardly seems to justify this interpretation; the passage remains ambiguous. Butler doesn't seem himself to be ready to accept the implication of what he is saying.

Butler's denigratory tone has frequently led to a misunderstanding of his basic outlook. Commentators have assumed a much more thoroughgoing pessimism and scepticism than seem justified by what he actually says. Dan Gibson for instance, in a largely admirable summary of Butler's ideas,[38] suggests that Butler had doubts about an afterlife and there are a few jottings that could in isolation be taken to have this implication, though there is at least one excerpt that explicitly states his belief in a future life.[39] More recently Wilders has described Butler as a 'sceptic' concerning human affairs and seems to suggest he might also have extended his scepticism into religion.

> He regarded the intellectualism of the old philosophy and the experimentation of the new science as equally unprofitable. Moreover, he allied himself to no religious party, since he believed all sects to be misguided and intolerant . . . His outlook on human endeavour was therefore that of a sceptic and his scepticism found its natural expression in satire.[40]

But this is to take Butler's tone of voice for the substance of what he is saying. It is true that there is a consistent anti-clericalism in Butler's remarks on priestcraft, but this is not uncommon in Christian writing; it is found as strongly in Dryden's work. Both poets write from an Anglican viewpoint (in Dryden's case up to the time of his late conversion) which tended to identify priestcraft with Roman Catholicism. Butler can occasionally come out with a blanket attack on all priests:

> Clergymen are like Scavangers that pollute and Defile their own Soules and Consciences in clensing those of other men.

– and he was not the first, nor the last, Anglican to make such allegations. More characteristic is his objecting to what he regarded as the extremes of Puritanism and Catholicism, with the implication that the Anglican *via media* is the correct path:

> There is nothing in Nature that has so great a Power over the Minde of man and governs there so like a God as conscience rightly qualifyd, nor anything so like the Devill as that which is false, and mistaken, and erroneous, for then it is worse than the Possessions of evill spirits, which are seldom observed to do much to others, but there is no Mischief and Distruction which wicked, and Deluded Conscience is not always ready to attempt. For as there is no Folly so extravagant as that which believes itself to be wise and knowing, so there is no impiety so horrible as that which supposes itself to be Godlines and Christian Duty: for then of a Spirituall Calenture, and hot Fit of Zeal it turns to the Plague and destroys all that come neare it. This is that Devill that assume's the Shape of an Angell, and having Disguisd its Nature, indeavors to change its Name too, and calls it selfe Tenderness, and Feare, and holy Jealousy, instead of Obstinacy, Pride and Insolence, as all Imposters use to change their Names to Disguise their cheates, as well as Popes do it to Declare and profes their Holiness. Conscience is like the Magistrate's sword that protects in a Good man's hand, but destroys in a Bad man's.[41]

This is far from a sceptical passage, it lashes out at the corrupters of truth, whether Puritan or Catholic, on the assumption that truth itself is easily discernible to those disposed to recognise it. Truth indeed is equated with simplicity itself in another passage from the notebooks, where it is contrasted with the ingenuity of priestly falsehoods:

> The Law has not so many nice and Curious Subtleties to furnish with Perpetuall Disputes and wrangling as Priests have found out, to debauch and Corrupt the native Simplicity of the Christian Religion.[42]

The idea of the 'native simplicity' of Christian truth reflects the Anglican stress on the need to simulate the primitive church (as in article twenty-four of the thirty-nine articles). Swift reflects this emphasis in the *Tale of a Tub*. Both adopt Hooker's view of Anglicanism as the *via media* between Puritan and Catholic extremes. Butler's main theme in religion is summed up by his dictum: 'Those that Use *Excess* in any Thing never understand the Truth of it, which always lies in *the Mean*.'

Butler is neither sceptical about the existence of God nor – at least in his theorising – sceptical of man's ability to discover God's intentions. He is as vehement in attacking the Atheist and Sceptic in the two portraits he gives of those subjects[43] as he is in attacking the Fanatic and the Popish Priest. In the *Satyr Upon the Licentious Age of Charles II* he attacks both the irreligion and the scepticism of the age:

> For Men are grown above all Knowledge now,
> And, what they're ignorant of, distain to know.[44]

In his portrait of the sceptic he could hardly make his opposition to scepticism plainer, concluding as he does with the sentence:

> He [the sceptic] is a worse Tyrant than *Caligula* wished himself, for in denying Reason, Sense, and Demonstration he cuts off the best Heads of Mankind at a Blow.[45]

This is not only a rejection of theological scepticism but a rejection also of the limited scepticism, so common among his Restoration contemporaries, which doubted man's ability to arrive at rational conclusions about the world. In contrast to Swift

and even to Dryden, Butler's intellectual position is that of a
rational optimist. His notebook is full of jottings that show how
consistent his belief was in God and in man's ability to know
God. Unlike many of his contemporaries he did not believe
that mankind was steadily going to the dogs: 'They that say
the World grows worse and worse, are very much mistaken'.[46]
He argues that the moderns are generally superior to the
ancients.[47] He believed man capable of understanding the
divine wisdom: 'There are Infinite evident Demonstrations of
the Prodigious wisdom and Ingenuity used in the Creation and
Fabrique of the World', he writes, although he goes on to admit
greater difficulty in understanding God's 'providential' government and concludes: 'there is reason enough for some men to
suppose, that all those affares that fall out in the Civill manage-
ment of it [the world] are but the Effects of its own Nature'.[48]
In another jotting he writes: 'There is nothing that can improve
Human Nature so neare to Divinity as knowledge'[49]; a remark
that hardly justifies Wilders' assertions that Butler 'had little
faith in human progress'.[50] Man may not always act rationally,
but Butler certainly sees him as a rational animal and not merely
an animal capable of reason: 'Men without Reason are much
worse than Beasts because they want the end of their Creation
and fall short of that which gives them their Being'.[51] As
Wasserman points out, Butler held that man's rationality was
his distinguishing feature as a direct consequence of the Fall,
before which time, like the rest of the animals, he needed only
instinct to guide him.[52] In the notebooks he frequently returns
to the subject of the value and efficacy of reason. Under the
heading 'reason' in the 'Miscellaneous Observations' he writes:

> The Original of Reason proceedes from the Divine wisdome,
> by which the Order and Disposition of the Universe was
> immediately contrived, every Part of which ha's so rationall
> a Relation to every other in particular, and the whole in
> generall; That though it consist of innumerable Pieces and
> Joynts, there is not the least Flaw imaginable in the whole
> ... This Booke of Nature, Man only of all Mortall creatures,
> has the Honor, and Priviledge to read, which lead's him
> immediately to God, and is the greatest demonstration he
> hath given of himself to Nature; and the nearest visible Access

to his Divine Presence Humanity is capable of. For in the first Characters and single elements of the Creation, we cannot so perfectly read God, as we can where those letters are joyned together and become words and sense, as they do in the Rational Distribution of all the Parts of Nature. This order is the universall Apostle of the whole world that perpetually preaches God to mankinde (and to mankinde only) every where, and ha's hardly found any nation so Barbarous, where some have not become Proselytes; and for others, nothing but this can encounter with them upon their own groundes; This is the foundation of all Religion, for no man that is not certaine there is a God can possibly believe or put his trust in him.[53]

This is an extreme statement of rational optimism, for it suggests that man has the ability to reason himself into the true faith. This view is put forward even more succinctly in the next excerpt where Butler argues: 'Faith can determine nothing of Reason, but Reason can of Faith and therefore if Faith be above Reason, (as some will have it) it must be reason only that can make it appeare to be so . . . So that Faith is beholden to Reason for this Prerogative; and sure it cannot be much above that from which it receives its Credit.'[54] Man has the unique ability to deduce evidence via his senses by the use of reason and so obtain an understanding of God's intention. Butler is sufficiently Baconian to insist that it is by induction, not deduction that he can achieve this result: 'It has pleasd Almighty God to allow Man no meanes of knowledge but by Sense, and Reason collection, Consequence and Demonstration'.[55] Equally, abstract speculation is delusive for man because it is spun 'out of his own Bowels',[56] and is thus subjected to the disturbing influences of the passions which Butler, in accordance with traditional Christian psychology, finds the chief source of disorder in our nature.[57] 'Those who have attempted to deal in universalls, never perform anything, as universalls.'[58]

Given this extremely optimistic account of man's potential it might seem strange that Butler is so preoccupied in much of his work with satirising his fellow men. When we consider, however that satire asks us to judge man as he is by the standards of what we expect him to be, Butler's liking for satire becomes less surprising. Indeed it would be much more difficult to explain his satire if he were, as Wilders would have him, a sceptic, because, as we have seen, scepticism leads typically to a detached, balanced comedy. Part of the reason for Butler's sour view of humanity is certainly to be found in his orthodox view of the disruptive nature of human passion. In spite of his theoretical optimism, when he looks about him he sees little to make him rejoice. Man may have been given the divine gift of reason at the Fall, but he did not thereby abandon his animal nature. On the contrary, that nature had become corrupted, and reason was simply the means by which man could assess and mitigate the consequences of the Fall (a position not dissimilar to Hobbes's). Not surprisingly, therefore, Butler considered it rare for any man to overcome his corrupted nature:

> They that layd the first Foundation of the civill Life, did very well consider, that the Reason of Mankinde was generally so slight, and feeble that it would not serve, for a Reine to hold them in from the Ruine of one another; and therefore they judg'd it best to make use of their Passions, which have always a greater Power over them, and by imposing necessary Cheats upon their hopes and Feares, keepe them within those limits, which no Principles of Reason or Nature could do.[59]

There is nothing essentially contradictory in Butler's combination of theoretical optimism and practical pessimism. It is based on the aristocratic Renaissance notion that only a very few, unusual men are capable of controlling their passions by their reason. Indeed Butler's position is rather more logical than that of his friend Hobbes, with which it has much in common. For Hobbes seems to have assumed men more capable of reasonable conduct in the mass than as individuals, whereas Butler remains a staunch individualist:

> Every man is just so much a slave as he is concerned in the will, inclinations or Fortunes of another.[60]

Not surprisingly Butler was much less enamoured of absolute monarchy than Hobbes:[61]

From what biographical evidence we have, it seems (as I have argued) that Butler was not without his share of malice, and this remark seems more than likely to be a reflection of his own experience. But while malice is obviously the driving force it is only one of two essential elements of satire. The great verse satirists, Dryden, Rochester, Pope combine a considerable degree of personal animus with techniques of control and detachment that enable them, while they are attacking their targets, also to embody those ideal standards by which the victims are to be judged. Satire demands not only attack, it demands that what is attacked should be assessed and found wanting. The ideals are embodied either in explicit statement, or in panegyrical portraits (like that of Barzillai in *Absalom* or Martha Blount in the *Epistle on the Characters of Women*) or in the provision of a verse form that asserts faith in an orderliness that is not otherwise necessarily apparent. Such satire establishes a norm of righteousness from which we can judge to what extent the satiric targets have fallen away. Without that movement of the mind from what should be to what is there can be no satire. In Butler's verse there is little, if anything to embody that sense of the orderliness of the world that, as is clear from his notebooks, he certainly possessed. It is possible in fact, that Butler's temperament was too satiric for him to be a successful satirist, for he lacks that detachment which enables the great satirist to translate his own dislikes into general statements and convince the reader of the validity of his judgements. At first sight Swift would seem to be like Butler in lacking an idealising framework, but Swift's elaborate use of satiric *personae* and his controlled irony provide a detachment not provided by the techniques Butler adopts. And fundamentally Butler's failure is a failure of technique. In practically all his verse satire he appears to be speaking at us *in propria persona*, so that the singleminded insistence on the depravity or foolishness of men comes to be associated as much with the poet's *voice* as with the satirical targets. In *Hudibras* the poet and his hero talk with similar voices. Butler becomes Hudibras–Butler in a way he presumably never intended, sharing not only his crankiness, but his intellectual vigour as well. There is neither explicit statement nor verse embodiment of that sense of order which alone can allow us to make judgements on disorder. The poet, clowning with words, becomes part of the anarchic world he is meant to be guiding us through. The malicious narrator becomes his own fool. The world Butler creates in his poetry, and in *Hudibras* in particular, is a world of comic anarchy rather than of consistent satire.

I have already discussed the variety of responses caused by Butler's dichotomous treatment of his hero as satiric butt and *alter ego*. *Hudibras* is very much the poem of its hero and to understand how the poet treats him is to understand the poem. The confusions in Butler's attitude to his hero are well summed up in A. H. West's study of French influence on English burlesque. West argues that Hudibras is described as a brute, yet he does many good deeds:

> In fact the most odious traits of his Character do not seem to belong to him. Hudibras is often in contradiction with himself.[65]

As Gilfillan observed, what starts out as an attack on Hudibras ends by being something of a celebration of him. Not that Butler ever entirely abandons satire at any stage of the poem, ringing the changes on a variety of subjects from scholastic philosophy to astrology as examples of fanaticism. Rather the satire and the celebratory comedy tend to alternate in an uneasy coexistence, as can be seen in his treatment of the hero. The inconsistencies in Butler's treatment of Hudibras are already to be seen in one of the passages I quoted earlier, the account of the hero (1 i 285–98) where, having described his grotesque shape, Butler goes on to describe his extraordinary habits and accoutrements. He was, says the narrator, a great eater and kept his belly well supplied with such 'thrifty fare':

> As Whitepot, Butter-milk and Curds,
> Such as a Countrey house affords,
> With other Victual, which anon
> We further shall dilate upon . . .

When, a few lines later, the poet does come to dilate upon the victuals we learn that Hudibras kept a vast array of foods in his hose and breeches (1 i 311–24):

> Through they were lin'd with many a piece
> Of Ammunition–Bread and Cheese,
> And fat Black-puddings, proper food
> For Warriors that delight in bloud.
> For, as we said, He always chose
> To carry Vittle in his hose.
> That often tempted Rats, and Mice,
> The Ammunition to surprize:
> And when he put a Hand but in
> The one or th'other Magazine,
> They stoutly in defence on't stood
> And from the wounded Foe drew bloud
> And till th'were storm'd, and beaten out
> Ne'r left the Fortify'd Redoubt . . .

The comedy here has clearly got nothing to do with satire; it is farce, in which the hero has become the sympathetic little man, constantly battling against circumstances just outside his control. When, a few lines further, Butler goes on to contrast his hero's healthy appetite with the Romance hero's traditional superiority over such carnal considerations, it confirms our impression that we are dealing with real flesh and blood and not with romantic abstraction. The description wavers in fact between hostility and admiration; and this can be shown in small inconsistencies of detail. Dr Johnson observes that it is out of keeping to describe Hudibras's arms 'as ridiculous or useless' because the Presbyterians were at least good fighters, if nothing else. This objection smacks of neo-classical character decorum. Butler seems to be giving his hero the traits of the *miles gloriosus* at this point, suggesting his hero is a coward with 'undaunted heart' who would rather fight chickens than human foes (354–6) and whose sword had grown rusty through lack of use (318). When Butler moves on to describe the dagger, however, it turns out to be the agent of considerable aggression (377–80):

> It was a serviceable Dudgeon,
> Either for fighting or for drudging.
> When it had stabb'd, or broke a head,
> It would scrape Trenchers, or Chip Bread . . .

As we move into the action of cantos two and three, the heroic fight against Talgol, Orsin the bear keeper, the bear itself and then with the termagent Trulla, we find that Hudibras has indeed an 'undaunted heart' and performs miracles of comic heroism before he is finally fondly overcome by female arms and placed in the stocks. This is the best part of the poem, in which Butler for long stretches forgets that he is writing satire and gives us a farcical comedy. Hudibras performs the classic role of comic hero, constantly badgered and belaboured by his foes, but never giving up, never admitting defeat and always coming back for more. The climax of the fight is the final attack of Trulla, who turns on the apparently victorious Hudibras. Hudibras has just rushed to Ralpho's aid (one of the many good deeds West refers to) when Trulla turns from Ralpho to Hudibras himself (781–4):

> . . . for as he bow'd
>   To help him up, she laid a load
>   Of blows so heavy, and plac'd so well,
>   On the other side, that down he fell.

Trulla, having taken this ungentlemanly advantage, calls on Hudibras to yield. He retorts, in the best tradition of heroic romance, that she has attacked him unfairly and must give him a chance to defend himself (814–38):

> I scorn (quoth she) thou Coxcomb silly,
>   (Clapping her hand upon her breech,
>   To show how much she priz'd his speech)
>   Quarter or Counsel from a foe:
>   If thou canst force me to it, do.
>   But lest it should again be sed,
>   When I have once more won thy head,
>   I took thee napping unprepar'd
>   Arm, and betake thee to thy guard.
>   This said, she to her tackle fell,
>   And on the *Knight* let fall a peal
>   Of blows so fierce, and prest so home,
>   That he retir'd and follow'd's bum.
>   Stand to't, quoth she, or yield to mercy;
>   It is not fighting Arsie-versie

Shall serve thy turn – This stirr'd his spleen
More than the danger he was in,
The blows he felt, or was to feel,
Although th'already made him reel.
Honour, despight, revenge and shame
At once into his stomach came;
Which fir'd it so, he rais'd his arm
Above his head, and rain'd a storm
Of blows so terrible and thick,
As if he meant to hurt her quick.

This is certainly not the response of the coward we were led to expect in the first canto and the courage he displays throughout the fight goes on being displayed when he is finally taken prisoner and put into the stocks; for he shows as much mental resilience in his defence of his humiliating position as physical resilience during the fight. Even the defeat by Trulla is not the abject defeat by the weaker sex it might seem; not simply because Trulla is clearly an Amazon who is a match for any man, but also because Hudibras is defeated by his own zeal, lunging forward to strike the decisive blow and, in the best traditions of farce, missing his target and being sent off balance to the ground.

This excerpt shows how well Butler's verse technique reinforces the farcical action. The constant clowning with words, the bad rhymes (home/bum: mercy/Arsie-versie), the distortions of syntax (the opening lines), the use of a 'low' vocabulary to parody the heroic subject of battle, suggest a parallel with the unruliness of the characters. Nor is there any difference between the language of the participants and that of the poet. Trulla speaks with the same voice as the narrator of the scene. The passage is also interesting for its avoidance of a common feature of Butler's verse, distortion of accent. The rhythms here are much smoother, more harmonious than they are in more satirical passages and this helps place more emphasis on the action, reinforcing the impression of movement and vitality that the activity of the participants give. It is sparkling with energy in which action takes precedence over comment. We are being asked not to criticise, but to enjoy. At its best *Hudibras* gets the nearest to successful poetic farce in the language; an effect, however, that is dissipated by an obtrusive and distorting satirical element.

Butler's switch of allegiances in the course of the poem, if it sabotages the satire, adds to the interest of the hero. In the opening section of the poem, though Butler never establishes a consistent standard for judging his satiric world, the poem gets its vitality from the vigour of the critical analysis of that world. As poet and hero comes closer together the hero himself begins to take on the intellectual vigour of the poet. The philosophical Butler, with his delight in logical paradox, comes into the poem by the backdoor in giving Hudibras a dazzling ability to argue his way out of tight corners, as he does, for instance, in his defence of his honour to the widow as he sits in the stocks (ii i 217 f). Butler's ability as a comic writer comes from his willingness to mock those analytical qualities he himself possesses and which in the hands of the true satirist are his principal tools. Butler's malice extends to a willingness to take the ground from under his own feet and he exploits the comic spectacle of his own tumbling.

By the time we come to the episode of the wooing of the widow in part two Butler has fully established the classic comic pattern of the resurgent hero. The episodic structure Dr Johnson complains about is the perfect comic form for such benevolent comedy. In the love episodes the comic vitality stems not from the physical indestructability of Hudibras, as it has in cantos two and three of the first part, but in his stalwart refusal to take the widow's 'no' for an answer, and indeed his willingness to suffer trials and tribulations to win her. Hudibras' confession of love is literary parody, but it is also a demonstration of the hero's verve and self-confidence (ii i 343–54):

> Quoth he to bid me not to *love*,
> Is to forbid my *Pulse* to move,
> My *Beard* to grow, my Ears to prick up,
> Or (when I'm in a fit) to hickup;
> Command me to piss out the Moon,
> And twill as easily be done.
> *Loves* power's too great to be withstood,
> By feeble humane *flesh* and *blood*.

> 'Twas he, that brought upon his knees
> The Hect'ring Kill Cow Hercules;
> Reduc'd his *Leager-lion's* skin
> T'a *Petticoat*, and made him spin . . .

This is not just Butler destroying the absurd pretensions of the
courtly code, it is Hudibras revelling in his own downright
honesty. Far from being the symbol of hypocrisy for which
(with much justification) he is often taken,[66] Hudibras shows
here that plain speaking which is the property of all such comic
figures from the Wife of Bath onwards. What, for instance
could be less hypocritical than his reply to the widow's accusation that it is her property he's after (II i 47)?

> I do confess, with *goods* and *land*,
> I'd have a wife, at second hand;
> And such you are: Nor is't your person,
> My stomach's set so *sharp*, and fierce on,
> But 'tis (your better part) your *Riches*
> That my enamour'd heart bewitches . . .

This is the man whom Butler described in the beginning of the
poem (I i 233-4):

> As if Hypocrisie and non-sense
> Had got th'Advouson of his Conscience.

Hudibras is nearly the one great farcical poem of the language.
In some sections – the fight with the travelling players in part
one, the wooing of the widow in part two – it does seem just
that. The over-all effect of the poem is unfortunately less
satisfying. 'We admire it a while as a strange thing; but when
it is no longer strange, we perceive its deformity'.[67] For Butler
never quite understands how good he is as a comic writer. His
temperamental preference for satire, and perhaps the tendency
of his age to understand the comic in terms of satire, leads him
to blur the comic effect and gets in the way of the farcical
action. Passages of satire are constantly being allowed to
intrude, but succeed ultimately in alienating us from the writer
more than from his material. The comedy of the poem is

therefore neither consistently satirical nor consistently benevolent. At the root of the failure to make the poem fully coherent may lie Butler's own temperament: on the one hand a refusal to accept the benevolent implications of his own philosophy (which could have led to consistent satire), on the other an unwillingness to plunge himself entirely into the sea of doubt which would allow full reign to his sense of comic anarchy. As important I think was Butler's failure to evolve a technique that could deal adequately with this contradiction between his temperament and his intellectual convictions. Butler adopts the techniques of burlesque, which were readily to hand because of the success of the drolleries, but burlesque encouraged just that confusion of comic modes that proved Butler's chief temptation. It was left to Andrew Marvell to establish a verse form that could bring the gap between feeling and idea into a proper comic focus. *Hudibras* remains, in the words of George Gilfillan, 'more a problem than a poem'.

4 *Last Instructions to a Painter*

Among his contemporaries Marvell's political satires were his chief, almost his only, claim to poetic fame. Looking back at the Restoration period Gilbert Burnet, in his *History of his Own Time* (1724), describes Marvell as:

> the liveliest droll of the age, who writ in a burlesque strain, but with so peculiar and entertaining a conduct that, from the King down to the tradesman, his books were read with great pleasure (1 260).

In stark contrast, modern critics, at least until very recently, have condemned the satires as without poetic merit and have devoted most of their attention to the lyrics, which were not published until after Marvell's death and then almost completely ignored. Bradbrook and Thomas describe the satires as doggerel, 'writ well to the purpose he intended, but that was not a poetic purpose', and T. S. Eliot describes them as 'random babbling' compared to Dryden's. The attention that they have received has been largely for their historical interest.[1] There are, however, signs in very recent criticism that these attitudes are being revised.[2]

It is always dangerous to ignore contemporary estimates of a writer, not because these are invariably right, but because it is just as likely that we are indulging in our prejudices as they were in theirs. A brief look at modern judgements on the satires shows to what extent the poetry itself has been ignored and the prejudices indulged. The principal objections can largely be dismissed as critically irrelevant. That they are 'too occasional to be of permanent interest' (Bradbrook and Thomas, p. 23) begs a large question about founding poetic insight on the particular. That they suffer because 'they contain so many allusions that they require a great deal of annotation' (Macdonald) is a polite way of saying that the writer is not prepared to take the trouble to acquire the necessary background information; on these grounds *Absalom and Achitophel* or the *Dunciad* might be equally unacceptable. That the satires are 'formless' (Davison, Eliot, Sutherland) will not bear close investigation. That they are biased in their political comment (Cruttwell) is as true as it is of Dryden's satires and as equally irrelevant for criticism. That they are 'coarse' (Davison, Cruttwell) begs too many critical questions to be a serious critical comment (Aristophanes is coarse, so is Rabelais, so is Swift, so often is Shakespeare).

If we were to guess at Marvell's own attitudes to his satirical poetry (we have fortunately some direct comment) it would be that they are much more likely to be those of his contemporaries than of ours. Even in his Nun-appleton days, when he was celebrating, if somewhat ambiguously, the virtues of retirement, he seems (to judge from Milton's attempts to get him a government appointment) to have longed to be back in the hurly-burly of London, where most of his adult life was spent. Moreover, the few poems that he had had published before 1660 were mostly of a political nature and he had been writing satire from his early days. Few Renaissance poets regarded poetry as purely an end in itself and Marvell was no exception. He seems to have looked on himself as primarily a public man whose gift for verse was an extra and valued talent in a political career. It is likely therefore that he would think of his political verse as more serious than his lyrics and regard its topicality as a guarantee of this. We need not quarrel with this view. Indeed one of the few comments we have from Marvell on his verse would seem to be making just this point, that it is poetry of an inferior sort that neglects its public functions. At the end of the *Last Instructions to a Painter* he excuses his satire, in a direct address to the King, claiming that it is the duty of the poet to speak out on public affairs (957–64):

> Blame not the Muse that brought these spots to sight,
> Which, in your splendour hid, corrode your light:
> Kings in the country oft have gone astray
> Nor of a peasant scorn'd to learn the way.
> Would she the unattended throne reduce,
> Banishing love, trust, ornament and use,

> Better it were to live in cloister's lock
> Or in fair fields to rule the easy flock.[3]

Both in the serious tone and in his insistence on the moral duty of guiding the King, Marvell is here assuming the solemn role of *vates*, of prophet, a role fully recognised in Renaissance views of the function of the poet in society. It is the muse's responsibility to see the throne is not 'reduced', that the civilised, moral standards in the state (and I think in verse itself) are maintained in 'love, trust, ornament and use'. 'Ornament' I take to refer not only to the decorum of court ritual, but to the rhetorical duties of the poet himself. It would be better, he says, for his muse to retire altogether from public life than for him to neglect his political duties as a poet of upholding the monarchy. This is a far cry from the usual assumption that the satire (or this poem at least) was written casually and without a serious poetic intention. A close study, I believe, will show with what seriousness Marvell took his satiric responsibilities in this poem.

Nor is it only in *Last Instructions*, generally acknowledged as the best of these satires, that a serious artistic purpose is revealed. The first of two earlier 'painter' satires, *The Second* and *Third Advice to a Painter*, like *Last Instructions* published anonymously, but considered by their latest editor, George Lord (I think rightly) to be by Marvell, received a detailed reply by Christopher Wase that Lord has printed for the first time.[4] In this Wase rebuts the ascription of the *Second Advice* to Denham and goes on to emphasise the skill and art with which the actual author has written by contrasting him with an earlier versifier, George Wither (43–52):

> Against the court this [poet], with worse-meaning art,
> Levels a polish'd but a poison'd dart,
> Suggest[s] the work of well contrived and high,
> A master-builder speaks in poetry . . .
> This sober malice is not Denham's rage . . .[5]

This last line refers to a fit of madness from which Denham was suffering. The *Second Advice* is neither so polished nor so well constructed as the *Last Instructions*, with which Marvell seems to have taken special pains, but it is a work of considerable poetic skill, fully justifying Wase's praise and all the more impressive in coming from an adversary. Wase, incidentally, was himself a classical scholar, a friend of Denham and Waller and had been a fellow of King's, Cambridge. This estimate differs markedly from the views of most modern scholars, of whom this comment of J. R. Sutherland is typical: 'so far as construction is concerned, that is almost non-existent'.[6] Even more recently A. S. Fischer has described *Last Instructions* as 'a collection of shorter satirical pieces'.[7]

In *Third Advice*, too, Marvell shows a serious purpose. In the address to the King at the end of the poem Marvell writes (p. 87):

> What servants will conceal and couns'llors spare
> To tell, the painter and the poet dare;
> And the assistance of a heav'nly Muse
> And pencil represents the crimes abstruse.
> Here needs no sword, no fleet, no foreign foe:
> Only let vice be dam'd and justice flow.
> Shake but like Jove thy locks divine and frown –
> Thy sceptre will suffice to guard thy crown.
> Hark to Cassandra's song ere Fate destroy
> By thy own navy's wooden horse, thy Troy.

Here, quite explicitly, Marvell is assuming a vatic role, which he associates, as did Milton and Dryden, with Divine inspiration. The muse is 'heavenly' because the poet speaks with direct authority from God. Milton describes it as 'divine song, the work of the poet, than which there is nothing that more commends his ethereal origin and heavenly birth'.[8] Marvell assumes the role of prophet typified by the Trojan Cassandra – hardly an indication of a casual approach to his satire. It is very clear that Marvell took his role as comic satirist seriously; more so, one would guess, than he did his earlier role as lyric poet.

In this chapter I shall be exclusively concerned with *Last Instructions*, a work which justifies even more than the *Second*

Advice Wase's description of 'polished, well-contrived and high'. It is a comic work of almost epic proportions and arguably, I think, Marvell's finest poetic achievement. If we are looking for the lyric grace, the witty detachment of the earlier poetry we shall be disappointed. *Last Instructions* is not easy reading and like most satire, before Dryden 'left it marble', it has some of the harshness and acerbity that was cultivated for the satirical genres in accordance with the principles of poetic decorum.[9] It is usually assumed that its main theme is political, but essentially it is a poem about morality and gets its coherence from its moral theme. From its concern with contemporary events it obtains a vitality that makes the earlier lyrics look fragile and dilettante by comparison. The nervous wit that is so much a feature of the lyrics is still in evidence, but it is now indulged in less for its own sake than to reveal a moral uncertainty that the poem as a whole 'places' and ultimately repudiates. There is, in other words, a marked increase in the maturity of outlook in the satire compared to the earlier poetry. Marvell, like his contemporaries, moves some way from the tortured ambiguities of mannerism to the orderly assertions of baroque. The movement away from 'sheer wit' is in the same direction, though much less marked, as Milton's development from the comic 'clenches' of the Hobson poems to the dismissal of 'metaphysical' language by giving it to Satan in book six of *Paradise Lost*.

   The comment of Gilbert Burnet with which I opened this chapter rightly stresses Marvell's ability as a comic poet.[10] Marvell's concern is with the comic incongruities arising from the breakdown of moral order, and the apparent fragmentariness of the poem derives from the picture it gives of a society where moral order is in danger of complete collapse. Its ultimate purpose, however, is not to envisage the rule of chaos, but to re-establish a faith in order. The comic incongruities arise both from the inconsistencies that ensue when moral standards are ignored and from the juxtaposition of actual and ideal standards of conduct. Broadly speaking, Marvell's attitude to the comic resembles Dryden's in *Absalom and Achitophel*. For both of them, as for Milton, the comic is primarily a measure of disorder. They were poets of virtually the same generation and unlike some of the younger men of the Restoration, such as Rochester, held on firmly to their belief in an orderly universe. Marvell's attitude to the comic, however, is more equivocal than either Milton's or Dryden's. Wylie Sypher has described several of the earlier lyrical poems as 'mannerist' because they express that sense of non-comic incongruity common in the art of the earlier seventeenth century. The sense of uncertainty, though it weakens in the satires, is never entirely absent. It is worth recalling incidentally, that Marvell was at least twice censured for disorderly conduct in the House of Commons. Marvell rarely saw anything in terms of simple black and white, and while the comic butts in *Last Instructions* can be treated at times with some sympathy, the element of laughter is not entirely absent from the more solemn parts.

Disorder is assessed and kept in check by means of the poem's overall structure. Marvell makes use of a double structure, a mimetic structure derived from the imitation of the actual world and a 'tectonic' structure by which the actual world is assessed. The clash between the mimetic disorderliness and the imposed 'artificial' structure is a principal source of comic disharmony. A further complication, however, is added by the use of what must be called a false structure to symbolise the breakdown of order in the world of the poem. The false structure is provided by the painter convention, which purports to be a way of giving artistic order to the chaos of the subject matter. It is in fact a way of demonstrating just how far the disorder has caused a breakdown, not only in life itself, but in the means of communication through which a remedy might be sought. In effect, therefore, the structure comprises three elements: there is a narrative and descriptive level in which the doings of the actual world (the immoralities of the courtiers, the proceedings in Parliament, the negotiations with Holland, the Dutch war) are described. These are presented in a some-what fragmentary way, as befits Marvell's theme. Secondly, upon this material Marvell pretends to be trying to impose his 'instructions' that will allow the painter (and by analogy, the poet himself) to give artistic coherence to his recalcitrant material. This attempt, however, is shown to be impossible and the breakdown of the attempt emphasises the difficulties in the way of the artist in his attempts to restore order. At the same time it emphasises in the clearest way possible the inadequacy of the old forms to represents the new situation. It is the clearest example in the whole period of a poet abandoning the traditional forms to 'stoop to truth and moralise his song'. The 'forward youth' is now once and for all leaving 'his Muses dear' to deal with a world that demands something sterner. Marvell, however, does not allow his poem to break up into fragments to 'shore against his ruins' as Eliot does in his waste land poem. Rather he attempts what Pope is later to do in the *Dunciad*, to assert his faith in order by presenting his satiric world in an orderly medium. The 'tectonic' structure (the third structural element) is part of that orderliness.

The poem is supposedly made on that analogy between poetry and painting, 'ut pictura poesis', much honoured in Renaissance poetry and used by Marvell himself in the non-comic *The Gallery*. In particular it follows a convention going back to classical literature[11] of giving instructions to a painter to compose a picture. As hostile critics have noticed, however, the instructions given to the painter are somewhat cursory and for long stretches of the poem Marvell seems to lose sight of the convention he has chosen to adopt. Marvell's cavalier treatment of the convention is intentional and carefully calculated. The point is not, as Gearin-Tosh argues, that a low style is appropriate to both poet and painter because the subject is low, but that any conventional method will be inappropriate to this chaotic, unconventional situation. Like his previous two poems to a painter, *Last Instructions* has as its starting point a parody of Waller's non-comic *Instructions to a Painter*, a panegyric celebrating the indecisive Battle of Lowestoft, in 1665. Like many comic and satirical works, therefore, it derives (if remotely) part of its structure parasitically from a non-comic work, because the disintegrating world described is itself structureless. As parody, therefore, the content of the poem runs counter to this arbitrary form and the main use Marvell puts this structure to is to show its inadequacy. The poem opens, for instance, with a series of instructions to the painter which, paradoxically, suggest the subject is virtually unpaintable (3–4):

> But ere thou fall'st to work, first Painter see
> It be'nt too slight grown or to hard for thee.

In the second line there are contradictory suggestions: that Lady State (the subject of the portrait) might be dissolving altogether, or that the political situation is becoming so obscure that it is unportrayable. Even if the painter does attempt this nearly impossible task he will have to find a uniquely bizarre method to do it and Marvell makes a further series of sometimes contradictory suggestions. It will have to be a portrait without colours because the subject is to be a sea battle without a fleet (5–6):

> Canst thou paint without colours? Then 'tis right:
> For so we too without a fleet can fight.

The word 'colours' here is a pun; it was used to describe the rhetorical arts of the poet as well as the literal colours of the painter. The confusion of methods is equally appropriate to painter and poet. Alternatively it will have to be like a crude sign-post of an inn to suit the crudity of the subject, or better still, be done in lamp black in the way obscene drawings are made on inn ceilings, for the subject is 'this race of drunkards, pimps and fools'. Even the type of picture suggested has changed from a single portrait to a group subject now. Still more bizarre, it should not be a painting at all, but a montage of feathers, like the pictures done by American savages. A savage medium is needed for a savage subject. Changing tack yet again the poet asks the painter to use a microscope on a subject that is so insignificant; and again Marvell suggests that perhaps the subject is too difficult and unpleasant to tackle at all (19–20):

> Else shalt thou oft thy guiltless pencil curse,
> Stamp on thy palette, nor perhaps the worse.

Finally in this opening passage Marvell suggests that the only way to represent the chaos is in the manner of the classical painter Protogenes, by using chaotic methods. Protogenes ended by smashing his canvas and so provided an early example of action painting (25): 'Chance finish'd that which art could but begin'. The chaos of state affairs defies method and can only be portrayed by a chaotic technique, which is to say it cannot be described at all – one is reminded of Mallarmé's 'un coup de dés jamais n'abolira le hasard'. Thereafter Marvell's use of the painter convention is spasmodic.

The opening section of the poem (1–104) and the last section (excluding the epilogue), both largely consisting of satirical character portraits, have the most references to the instructions. The parliamentary sections (105–396, 761–862) largely ignore the convention, indeed at line 117 the painter is asked to 'rest a little' and instead, the proceedings in Parliament are given a literary, mock-heroic treatment. The central section (397–760) uses the painter convention only for satire, while the account of De Ruyter's heroic expedition to destroy the English fleet, although presented in vivid pictorial terms, does not involve the use of the 'instructions' convention at all. Clearly the 'instruction' technique is a satirical device. Marvell's use of the painter convention is as much to defy the analogy of painting and poetry as it is to observe it. And rightly so. For the usual purpose of the analogy was to give poetry an epic breadth, dignity and stability that the more volatile verbal arts did not naturally have.[12] Marvell therefore suggests, in the very impossibility of painting the subject, its unsuitability for dignified treatment. Conversely, it is noticeable that when he does portray heroic action in the middle of the poem, the poetic technique becomes markedly painterly, although, as I say, he drops the 'instruction' convention altogether. Throughout the satiric parts of the poem there is a deliberate confusion of media to suggest the difficulty of pinning the subject down.

As often in Renaissance poetry the medium becomes a symbol for the message. The opening lines of the first portrait, for instance, the portrait of Henry Jermyn, Duke of St Albans, requires the impossible of the painter (27): 'Paint then St. Albans full of soup and gold.' The violent juxtaposition of images here recalls the satirical Eliot more than the 'metaphysicals', for the purpose is to stress discord, not to reconcile opposites.

This confusion of media reaches its height in the magnificent scene at the end of the poem. Outside the door of the King's bedchamber the painter must (909–10):

> With cannon, trumpets, drums, his door surround,
> But let some other painter draw the sound.

This is not, as Earl Miner suggests,[13] a casual joke thrown in to break an otherwise consistent use of the painter convention, but the culmination of the decorum of confusion. There is confusion between painter and poet, and even between painter and musician, so that we are constantly having to switch from one medium to another (864): 'Where pencil cannot there my pen shall do't'. There is also confusion between art and life, most dramatically when Charles mistakes the allegorical figure of Peace for a real-life woman, but also earlier when the painter is reminded that even Rubens on occasions changed roles (119–20):

> For so too Rubens, with affairs of state
> His lab'ring pencil oft would recreate.

In the portrait of Lady Castlemaine, too, the painter is asked to transfer his skills from art to life and paint the lady herself, not her portrait (79–80). In the cacophony of Charles's moral world sight is confused with sound, abstract with concrete, metaphorical with literal, art with life. By a stroke of genius Marvell sums up this chaos in a brilliant last scene in which the libidinous King stretches out his arms to receive the naked allegorical figure of Peace into bed with him (901–4):

> And with kind hand does the coy vision press
> (Whose beauty greater seem'd by her distress),
> But soon shrunk back, chill'd with his touch so cold,
> And th'airy picture vanish'd from his hold.

Here the chaos is as much a moral as an aesthetic one; indeed the two are inseparable. We are back to the point that art cannot opt out of life without ceasing to be art. Charles is moved not by the distress of the lady, but by the beauty which is heightened by her distress, as well as being deceived into mistaking her allegorical status. The painter convention is brilliantly used to show a world that is in complete confusion. The chaos is primarily a moral one, making the orthodox seventeenth-century assumption that there can be no good government (or good art) unless the rulers are good men.

Marvell is not content, however, simply to make the negative point that the government is corrupt. It was the duty of the serious satirist, according to seventeenth-century views of satire, not merely to rail, but to instruct. The satirist had to state, or at least clearly imply, the standards from which his criticisms were being made. In Milton's words, the satirist had to combine 'jest and reprehension'; in Dryden's, there must be 'majesty finely mixed with venom'.[14] Marvell touches on this view in the poem itself (390–2), but also discusses the subject at length in a passage of part two of the *Rehearsall Transpros'd* (1673), arguing that when evil doctrines are being spread it is the duty of the satirist to counter them.[15] One of the chief ways of countering evil was stylistically. Both Dryden and Pope, for instance, are fond of measuring the chaotic actuality they are satirising against the orderliness and dignity of their highly controlled verse form: the method of mock-heroic. To some extent Marvell does this, but like Rochester (who, one suspects, learnt many of his satirical techniques from Marvell) his use of the heroic couplet is much freer, less orderly, than it is in the work of the two later poets. To judge from his lines on *Paradise Lost* where he pokes fun at Dryden's 'jingling rhime' and praises Milton's rejection of rhyme (45–54) he shared Milton's distaste for that 'Invention of a barbarous age' as it was called in the preface to the second edition of *Paradise Lost* (1674). With his usual delight in contraries, however, Marvell used this barbarous invention both as appropriate for the needful barbarities of satire and also in accordance with the alternative view that the rhymed decasyllabic line was, as Puttenham had written earlier, a 'very stately and heroicall' metre.[16] Clearly there had been two views of this metre throughout the seventeenth century going back at least to the debate on the matter between Campion and Daniel at the beginning of the century. Marvell, typically, adopts both attitudes. At times the couplet is contorted into a grotesque reflection of its grotesque subject matter. Here, for instance, is Marvell's account of the instructions sent from London to the English peace negotiators with the Dutch at Breda (449–56):

> Two letters next unto Breda are sent:
> In cipher one to Harry Excellent;
> The first instructs our (verse the name abhors)
> Plenipotentiary ambassadors

> To prove by Scripture treaty does imply
> Cessation, as the look adultery,
> And that by law of arms, in martial strife,
> Who yields his sword has title to his life.

All the Hudibrastic tricks are used here: false accent (the first line reads almost like a dactyllic line), bad and over-ingenious rhyme, absurd analogy, the deliberate calling of the reader's attention to the technique in the aside 'verse the name abhors'. The purpose, as in *Hudibras* and Commonwealth burlesque, is to throw ridicule on the subject from the way it is described. Marvell is ridiculing the Government's assumption that because they want peace with the Dutch they can act as if they have obtained it.

Sometimes the air of grotesque moral or political derangement is conveyed as much by the content as by the method. The character portraits that feature strongly in the poem illustrate this well. Here, for instance, is an 'antic' passage from the description of Anne, Duchess of York (57–64):

> Hence Crowther made the rare inventress free
> Of's Highness's Royal Society –
> Happiest of women, if she were but able
> To make her glassen Dukes once malleable!
> Paint her with oyster lip and breath of fame,
> Wide mouth that 'sparagus may well proclaim;
> With Chanc'llor's belly and so large a rump,
> There (not behind the coach) her pages jump.

Here the grotesque, crabbed verse is the appropriate medium for a grotesque portrait of a woman who epitomises the moral corruption of the governing class. This is not, of course, a real life portrait or necessarily a fair one, any more than Dryden's Mac Flecknoe is a fair portrait of Shadwell or Zimri of Buckingham. Its status in the poem is mythic not representational. For the seventeenth century there was something more important than being fair-minded about individuals and that was being clear about moral principles. For this reason the scurrility that allows Marvell to refer mockingly to Anne Hyde's cancer of the breast (74), or allows Dryden to refer to Shaftesbury with scorn because he is a cripple (*The Medal*, 272), or after his death make fun of his memory in *Albion and Albanius* by recalling that he had a running sore in his side caused by an internal abscess, seemed legitimate to the seventeenth-century reader. It is the *moral* not the *literal* significance that is important in the serious poet's intentions and for Marvell Anne Hyde symbolises the general corruption of morality among the ruling clique. The doggerel expresses exactly the disorderliness epitomised by her portrait and so casts reflection on the state of affairs which permits the wife of the heir to the throne to act like a fishwife. Characteristically, too, it emphasises her sexual immorality because throughout the poem it is the nation's sick sexuality and Charles's in particular, as we shall see, that explains the national malaise. The comedy is fiercely denigratory, moving from the starting point of what we naturally expect of courtly conduct to the barnyard actuality.

There is, however, a rather different use of the couplet in other parts of the poem to embody more openly those standards against which people like Anne Hyde are to be judged. Ironically enough, but not unexpectedly in this topsy-turvy world, the most extended of these passages is the description of the enemy's fleet sailing up the Thames to destroy the English fleet in the Medway (537–46):

> Their streaming silks play through the weather fair
> And with inveigling colors court the air,
> While the red flags breathe on their top-masts high
> Terror and war but want an enemy.
> Among the shrouds the seamen sit and sing,
> And wanton boys on every rope do cling.
> Old Neptune springs the tides and water lent
> (The Gods themselves do help the provident),
> And, where the deep keel on the shallow cleaves,
> With trident's lever and great shoulder heaves.

This is a fine example of the sensuous baroque grand style, possibly, as Lord suggests, echoing Enobarbus's speech in *Antony and Cleopatra*. Commentators have tended to misunderstand the sensuality of the scene as a sign of Marvell's disapproval. Toliver, for instance, in a sensitive analysis,[17] suggests that the sexual imagery earlier, in which the Dutch admiral, De Ruyter, is described as 'an amorous victor' about to rape the naked nymphs of the Medway, is meant to reinforce the general theme of sexual depravity in the poem. But it is a commonplace of baroque art, as Hagstrum has pointed out,[18] to express heroic qualities through sensuous and especially sexual imagery. Of the portraits of women by such painters as Rubens (mentioned in the poem) and Guido Reni Hagstrum says: 'Whether saint or sinner there was a combination of sexual and religious exstacy, of Ovidian voluptuousness and Christian sweetness.' Wylie Sypher, in a similar account of Baroque, points out the importance of sexual imagery in those poets like Crashaw and Milton who cultivated the grand style.[11] And Marvell himself had used sexual imagery as a metaphor for spiritual ecstasy in *The Garden*, as does Donne in the *Holy Sonnets*. In *Last Instructions* Marvell makes his intentions quite clear by his consistent use of sexual imagery at the climax of the poem's heroic action, the lines on the heroic death of 'the loyal Scot' Archibald Douglas (649–54):

> . . . Brave Douglas, on whose lovely chin
> The early down but newly did begin,
> And modest beauty yet his sex did veil,
> While envious virgins hope he is a male.
> His yellow locks curl back themselves to seek,
> Nor other courtship knew but to his cheek.

This imagery is highly appropriate in the poem because it both echoes and, at the same time, provides a vivid contrast with the sordid sexual licence described in the satirical parts of the poem. There is considerable irony in its use. It is only in a country where standards have become inverted that the poet must seek heroic standards among his country's enemies or foreign allies, so that even these non-satirical passages have in fact a satirical purpose. Again, however, it is the mythic qualities rather than the actual qualities that Marvell is most concerned with, hence the baroque paraphernalia of tutelary Gods and the presentation of war as love – as Toliver suggests, an ironic inversion of Charles's courtiers poets' view of love as war. Marvell's grand style has not the resonance of Milton's or Dryden's, and in a predominantly satiric poem this is not inappropriate. At the end of the poem, however, in the un-equivocally non-comic address to King Charles, his verse attains a sonority that reminds us of Dryden (955–8):

> And you, great Sir, that with him [the sun] empire share,
> Sun of our world, as he the Charles is there,
> Blame not the Muse that brought those spots to sight,
> Which, in your splendour hid, corrode your light . . .

Appropriately the poem ends on a note that asserts the positive standards of which the satire is also an expression. There is some very effective use, too, of mock heroic heightening in the account of the excise debate in Parliament, especially lines 257–76.

I have described the account of De Ruyter's expedition up the Thames and of the death of Douglas as 'baroque', and certainly in its sensuous magnificence the term is appropriate. But in the context of the poem as a whole the central passage is undercut by an irony that gives a nervous quality to the description closer to Mannerist attitudes. This element of uncertainty appears in some of the details. It is ironic for instance that De Ruyter finds himself rejuvenated by the magical qualities of the English landscape (529–30):

> The sun much brighter, and the skies more clear,
> He finds the air and all things sweeter here . . .

Marvell's fervent patriotism had led him in an earlier poem, *Upon Appleton House*, to describe England as the 'paradise of four seas/Which Heaven planted us to please'. Here he makes a trenchant criticism of the 'scratching courtiers' that undermine this realm (978). Toliver may be right, too, in suggesting that the homely image of De Ruyter shaving himself as he prepares to attempt his rape is intended to throw doubt on the heroic status of the scene, though I think it more likely in this case that Marvell has made the kind of miscalculation in a daring use of sensuous imagery to which the later 'metaphysical' poets were prone; in any case the effect is to add to the uncertainty of the passage. Again in the loyal Scot passage there is an intentional irony in the stress on Douglas's apparent effeminacy and actual virility (649–52), which inverts the 'female' Stuart's much publicised virility, but actual effeminacy. We will return to this theme of sexual inversion later.

The use of an heroic style is not Marvell's chief method for asserting the sense of moral order from which the actual world of English government has lapsed. I spoke earlier of a double structure in the poem. Against the chaotic actual world described in the instructions to the painter there is juxtaposed a formal, 'tectonic' structure by which the poet-seer provides us with a measure for ordering and judging actuality. The contrast between this idealising orderliness and the actual disorderliness of society, between what society ought to be and what it is, is the chief source of the comedy in the poem. And it is satiric because the actual world is seen as a falling away from an earlier ideal. It is the overall sense of orderliness that prevents the poem from ever sliding into burlesque.

This formal structure is made up of five major sections symmetrically arranged, plus a prologue introducing the painter convention (7–28) and an epilogue (the address to the King, 949–90) which gives an explicit account of the order that is envisaged in political terms. Like the painter instructions this formal structure has a metaphorical function. In this case it represents Marvell's underlying faith in God's orderly providence and asserts the belief in the sun-king Charles (even though he might be momentarily eclipsed) as the centre of a divinely given order. In his address to the 'great Sir', the 'Sun of our world' (956), who shares his power on earth with the other sun, that is, God himself (955), Marvell asserts that his purpose in the poem has simply been to expose the obscurities that impede a full appreciation of the divine order. This is expressed by the king in his true relation to his people (973–4):

> But Ceres Corn, and Flora is the Spring,
> Bacchus is wine, the country is the King.

It is a commonplace of seventeenth-century thought that the health of the nation depends directly on the health of the king.[20] This religious concept of the divinity of kingship is, as

John Wallace has well shown, at the heart of all Marvell's political poems:

> The religious rather than party basis of a political satire will seem odd only to those readers of Marvell who are unpersuaded by the Christian feeling that permeates all his political poetry.[21]

Even comparatively trivial political events are seen as of direct concern to divine providence. So much so that Marvell can thank the 'propitious heavens' (237) for defeating the excise bill, which would have undermined the power of Parliament. Conversely it is a sign of the moral bankruptcy of the English when they address their prayer for protection against the Dutch not to God, but to an iron chain (591).

The formal organisation of the poem, obscured as it seems to be by the chaos of actuality, is an assertion of the underlying universal order, which it is the purpose of the poem to have reasserted in the nation. At the centre of the poem (397–760) is the account of De Ruyter's heroic expedition up the Thames and of the British reaction to it. In this section Marvell can not only assert the true standards of courage and selflessness (epitomised above all in the heroic death of Archibald Douglas) at the same time he can maintain his satiric purpose by contrasting this foreign heroism with the immoral and frivolous behaviour of his own countrymen. It is no accident that the positive values of the poem inhere principally in two foreigners, a Dutchman and a Scot. In this the poem is an inversion of the great national epic that Renaissance writers such as Spenser sought to write to celebrate the best values of their own societies. A contrast with Spenser's epic is made explicit in the contrast between Spenser's heroic treatment of Medway and Thames (*F.Q.* IV 11) and that forced on the satirist (747–8).

By contrast to De Ruyter's daring and enterprise the English defenders are shown as absurdly incompetent. The wars against the Dutch had inevitably been fought out at sea, yet the English before the peace agreement was signed had drastically cut back their navy. Marvell depicts this incompetence in a series of incongruous land-sea images. Clarendon orders the militia to meet the Dutch threat and Marvell comments: 'As if, indeed, we ships or Dutch had horse' (482). During the battle itself Spragge, the commander at Sheerness, a seaman given a land command, is described as panting 'like a fish on land' (562). The 'sick' ships stranded on land are 'like molting fowl' (573). The only hope of saving the ships in the Medway is by a protective chain that 'fitter seem'd to captivate a flea'. The courtiers who came down 'to be spectators safe of the new play' are described as 'feather'd gallants' (597–8). The imagery of 'play', the comic equivalent of war, is taken up from the earlier section of the poem and suggests further the theme of art usurping the function of life. What is serious with our enemies is treated as trivial by us. The first glimpse we have of the court makes the contrast (373–4):

> The Court as once of war, now fond of peace,
> All to new sports their wanton fears release.

The sport we find them indulging in is said, ironically, to be a 'pastime martial and old' (376). This turns out to be the Skimmington ride (a traditional punishment for hen-pecked husbands and hen-pecking wives) which Pepys records the court watched at Greenwich.[22] Marvell allegorises the event to point the moral that in this war England is the effeminate husband and Holland the unnatural wife and goes on to develop a parallel between this traditional mode of satire and his own (390–2):

> So thou and I, dear Painter, represent
> In quick effigie, others' faults and feign,
> By making them ridiculous, to restrain.

To bring out the full irony of these contrasts Marvell juxtaposes on either side of this heroic and satiric core of the poem, mock-heroic passages describing the sordid proceedings of Parliament in terms of a war-game (105–396, 761–862). The English Parliamentarians, like the English courtiers, are more concerned with play than war. At first sight it might seem surprising that a parliamentarian like Marvell should present the proceedings in Parliament in this way, but his purpose is again not to do justice to the actual situation, but to present a clear artistic pattern which will convey his moral purpose

exactly. Even the parliamentarians of whom he approves and
with whom he must have voted are treated as comic figures
(257-77):

> Then daring Seymour, that with spear and shield,
> Had stretch'd the monster Patent on the field,
> Keen Whorwood next, in aid of damsel frail
> That pierc'd the giant Mordaunt through his mail,
> . . . Each thinks his person represents the whole
> And with that thought does multiply his soul,
> Believes himself an army, theirs one man
> As eas'ly conquer'd; and, believing, can;
> With heart of bees so full, and head of mites,
> That each, though duelling, a battle fights.
> Such once Orlando, famous in romance,
> Broach'd whole brigades like larks upon his lance.

This really is an astonishing treatment of Marvell's own side
in the dispute, but its purpose in the poem is clear. The
chicanery of Parliament, described in terms ranging from a
game of trick-track (108) to a comic military procession (157f)
is part of Marvell's consistent attempt to depict a society at the
point of disintegration. Marvell is not suggesting that Parliament as an institution is worthless, but that this particular
parliament, like everything else in England, is corrupt and
therefore inefficient and ridiculous. There is also some pru-
dential concern to absolve Charles from any direct blame for
the conduct of affairs which leads Marvell to distort the facts:
it was Charles himself, for instance, who addressed the New
Militia, not Clarendon as Marvell has it (484);[23] and to
increase the pathos Charles is made to beg Parliament for
money to conduct the war when in fact he addressed Parliament
after the land tax had been granted (327-8).[24] Again Marvell's
cavalier treatment of the facts (when it suits him) points to an
over-riding artistic purpose. By artistic purpose, of course, the
seventeenth century would understand primarily a moral
purpose and it is the over-riding moral purpose that links the
various sections of the poem together.

This is most clearly evident in the two outer sections of the
poem, the passage preceding the first 'parliamentary' section

and the passage succeeding the second debate in Parliament (29–104 and 863–948). Both these sections are devoted to a series of satirical character portraits that seem to bear little direct relationship to the political concerns of the three central sections of the poem. Marvell had used the portrait series in *The Gallery*, which might itself have been influenced by Marino's *La Galeria*, a poem that includes a series of satirical portraits. Like Rochester in *Tunbridge Wells* and even more brilliantly, Pope in the *Epistles*, Marvell here discovered that the portrait series could not only, by the strong element of discontinuity, suggest comic fragmentation, but also by its illustration of a moral theme contribute to the overall thematic unity of a poem. In the earlier section (29–104) there are three portraits: Henry Jermyn, Earl of St Albans, Anne Hyde, Duchess of York and the King's perennial mistress Barbara Villiers, Lady Castlemaine. These three people seem to have little in common and even less to do with the excise debate in Parliament or De Ruyter's attack on the Thames. It is true that they all had political influence, the two ladies in a somewhat indirect fashion, but their real purpose in the poem and the prominent position Marvell gives them in placing them in the first major section of the poem, is to define the moral state of the nation. Each of these characters symbolises the moral sickness from which England must be cured before political health can be restored. Lady Castlemaine in particular is given such prominence because, as the King's principal mistress, she has infected the core of the nation's moral health. When the King is sick, the country is sick, for 'Bacchus is wine, the country is the king' (973). The disease is venereal. That the poem is enacting the fisher-king myth is made clear in a brilliant passage later in the poem in connection with yet another of the King's mistresses, Frances Stuart. The climax of De Ruyter's triumph is the capture of the 'Royal Charles', the flagship of the navy. The capture of the 'Charles' of course images King Charles's own captivity to his evil courtiers, and when Marvell compares the ship's fate to that of Samson, we are expected to see the full implication (733–6):

Then with rude shouts, secure, the air they [the Dutch] vex,
With gamesome joy insulting on her decks.

Such the fear'd Hebrew, captive, blinded, shorn,
Was led about in sport, the public scorn.

The comparison with Samson, absurd for a ship, is highly
appropriate for the King. The King, too, has been 'fondly
overcome with female charms', blinded by his enemies, humiliated by defeat: but like Samson he too can find strength in
the divine will and has the strength to topple his enemies. It
is also appropriate that the 'Royal Charles' can be referred to
as 'she' for, like Samson and the ship, King Charles has
become unmanned. England therefore complains most for her
'daring Charles' (755), who has been dishonoured by the
'ravisher' De Ruyter (758). The epicene Royal Charles/King
Charles comparison is brought to a climax in four brilliant lines
at the end of this passage (761–4) where Marvell's audacious
witticisms link together all the complexities of the theme:

> The court in farthing yet itself does please,
> And female Stuart there rules the four seas,
> But fate does still accumulate our woes,
> And Richmond her commands as Ruyter those.

This is a superb example of the ingenious way literal detail is
made to serve the fundamental moral concern of the poem.
When the De Ruyter disaster struck we have already seen that
the courtiers are represented as concerning themselves with
trivial games. Here Marvell reminds his audience of the new
coin (appropriately, the trivial farthing) which on one side
had the image of the King's mistress, Frances Stuart, dressed
up to play the part of Britannia and on the other side the
legend 'Quatuor maria vindico' (I rule the four seas). But,
unfortunately for the King, says Marvell ironically, neither
Frances Stuart nor the four seas are easily accessible to Charles,
for the lady is ruled by her husband the Duke of Richmond, the
seas by De Ruyter. The farthing is therefore a token of Charles's
impotence. As the phrase 'female' Stuart suggests, the King
has lost his manhood (the fisher-king's complaint) and his
country is accordingly laid waste by its ravisher, De Ruyter.
        The relevance of the earlier portraits should now be clear.
There is a profound malaise throughout the kingdom. It is a

malaise caused by the gross immorality of the governing class represented by these three figures. Suitably enough for this petticoat government, two of them are women. The poem as a whole, therefore, is one of the many attacks of the period (and the most subtle) on the immorality of Charles's court. Pepys expresses the general feeling that the poem articulates (*Diary* 29 July, 1667): 'the nation in certain condition of ruin, while the King they saw was only governed by his lust and women and rogues about him'. The solution to these troubles is not a political but a moral one, to get rid of corruption (975–8):

> Not so does rust insinuating wear,
> Nor powder so the vaulted bastion tear,
> Nor earthquakes so an hollow isle o'erwhelm,
> As scratching courtiers undermine a realm . . .

With typical economy of means, Marvell sums up the two related problems of embezzlement and sexual immorality in the word 'scratching'. The courtiers scratch each other in the rat-race for preferment and its emoluments, and scratch themselves to relieve the itch of the pox. So throughout the poem there are constant references both to speculation and sexual depravity, which are seen as two aspects of the same general moral corruption. From the opening words, where the appropriate technique for the poem is said to be that used by dawbers sketching lewd graffiti on ale-house ceilings (11), to the final bedroom scene, sexual immorality and political corruption are everywhere associated. Sometimes the one is made an analogy of the other, as when the English negotiators at Breda, Coventry and Holles, persuade themselves to assume the Dutch want peace because they both are making money by running down the navy. They prove to themselves 'treaty does imply/ Cessation as the look adultery' (453–4). Or when Clarendon is forced to recall Parliament, his reluctance is compared to the reluctance an old lecher feels in having to face castration to cure a rupture (473–4).

In the character portraits political and sexual immorality are inextricably intertwined: St Albans, our ambassador in Paris, is open to French bribes; he is a notorious lecher. Anne Hyde and Lady Castlemaine are notorious for their sexual immorality

and have a considerable political influence. Often the distortion of moral standards is indicated in a Jonsonian substitution
of real values for money values: St Albans is full of 'soup and
gold' (28). Anne Hyde's sexual experiments are compared to
Archimedes assessing the base metal in Hiero's crown (51–4);
Lady Castlemaine's affair with her lackey is revealed to the
world by the extra gold in his trouser pocket (98) replacing the
bulge in his trousers that had attracted her in the first place
(81).[25] The money nexus prevails. The government party in
Parliament operates not by rational argument, but by buying
votes; the English seamen defect to the Dutch because there is
no money left to pay them after the politicians have embezzled
it all (583–4):

> Our seamen, whom no danger's shape could fright,
> Unpaid refuse to mount our ships for spite,
> Or to their fellows swim on board the Dutch,
> Which show the tempting metal in their clutch . . .

We have seen, too, how the court are more interested in the
farthing than in the collapse of moral standards, the English
soldiers readier to pray to an iron chain than to God. The
governing party in Parliament consists of embezzlers and
perverts. Sir Stephen Fox, a man without talents, bribes his
way to power, 'for always he commands that pays' (172);
Progers 'gentlest of men' and Brouncker, 'love's squire', are
two of Charles's procurers; Clarendon's troupe are described
as (179): 'Gross bodies, grosser minds and grossest cheats'.
Sir Richard Powell enters 'welt'ring in his stride' because of his
venereal disease (214). The list anticipates the technique of the
Dunciad, giving the impression of a vast hoard of deformed,
inhuman creatures. And yet this is a more Christian world than
Pope's. Marvell cannot treat these creatures as quite worthless.
Corrupt and depraved they may be, but they retain human
individuality, which holds out hope for a cure.

The portrait of Lady Castlemaine illustrates Marvell's
attitudes clearly. As Charles's mistress she is one of the 'spots'
that hide his sun. She is also very much part of that petticoat
government that has unmanned Charles and so the nation.
Yet she is not portrayed as totally evil, but as someone whose

essential goodness has become corrupted in grotesque ways. She is a comic not a frightening figure, an incongruous mixture of good and bad. Her sexual depravity is the chief subject of the portrait and Marvell recounts an affair she has with her lackey – an affair inspired by her anticipation of his sexual prowess (81–2):

> She through her lackey's drawers, as he ran,
> Discern'd love's cause and a new flame began.

It is a spiritless, sordid affair in which she is described 'washing his sweaty hooves . . . lest the scent her crime disclose', a grotesque Magdalene. But it also has its pathos (87–90):

> Poring within her glass she readjusts
> Her looks and oft-tri'd beauty now distrusts,
> Fears lest he scorn a woman once assay'd,
> And now first wish'd she e'er had been a maid.

The regret for innocence lost holds out the hope that it might be regained. Even the lackey retains something of the pristine glory of an unfallen world, for the sweaty feet are 'feet formed for a smoother race' (86). So the hope is that in Charles's wasteland the poet can point the way to a time when the King will no longer be 'islanded from his isle' (968):

> Kings in the country oft have gone astray
> Nor of a peasant scorned to learn the way.

It is fitting too that in the second series of portraits (863–948) the principal figure to sit should be the King himself, for in a sense the whole poem has been about the King. This portrait of Charles is preceded by a short portrait of Sir Edward Turner, the speaker of the House of Commons and a particular enemy of Marvell. Turner is described in the most grotesque terms used in the poem (877–80):

> When grievance urg'd, he swells like squatted toad,
> Frisks like a frog to croak a tax's load;
> His patient piss he could hold longer than
> An urinal and sit like any hen . . .

He, too, is presented as politically corrupt, and as a lecher: 'than Chanticleer more brisk and hot'. In this portrait the feeling of moral perversion and corruption reaches its climax and we move directly to the description of Charles's unfortunate encounter with the naked Lady Peace. Clearly Charles himself cannot be described in the harsh terms meted out to Sir Edward Turner. This would neither be consistent with the theme of Charles as a victim of bad advisers, nor decorous for a poet who maintains an explicit reverence for Charles throughout the poem. But the association of Charles's portrait with Turner's, by its proximity, leads us to the inescapable conclusion that in Charles's bedroom we have arrived at the place from which the general corrupting influence spreads. And the scene is deliberately made to convey the air of the sick bed. The sun-king is found enveloped in a darkness (886–8):

> Only dispers'd by a weak taper's light,
> And those bright gleams that dart along and glare
> From his clear eyes . . .

Again there is a glimmer of hope in the darkness. He retains the divine glimmer of kingship just as the satire retains the divine glimmer of moral order. The King is presented as if in a serious but not hopeless fever (889–90):

> There, as in th' calm horror all alone
> He wakes and muses of th' uneasy throne . . .

And Marvell does not for long retain the solemn, macabre atmosphere. Charles's illness may be serious, but Marvell's laughter as he introduces the Lady Peace, clearly diagnoses the illness and helps us to 'place' it, indicating the possibility of a cure.

The careful structure of *Last Instructions*, then, reveals the full theme of the poem. The opening address to the painter, with its suggestion of a general chaos in English society, is countered by the final section, the address to the King, where the poet spells out the rational solution to the chaos that the poem has defined and 'placed'. The two portrait sections which underpin, as it were, the main narrative structure of the poem, reveal the basic moral causes of the disorder in personal depravity. The three central sections of the poem, the description of the two sessions of Parliament and the account of De Ruyter's attack on the English fleet, spell out both the political consequence of the moral corruption and suggest (in Douglas's heroism in particular) the positive standards which are the alternative standards to the moral disorder. The very fact that this moral chaos has been shaped into a coherent framework is a demonstration of Marvell's faith in the ultimate triumph of orderliness.

Last Instructions to a Painter, then, in the last analysis does not make a comic statement about life: it does not aim to reveal a sense of life's essential incongruity. Rather the comic is a device for revealing and eventually exorcising those incongruities that arise from moral disorder, and the purpose of the poem is to get us to repudiate what we laugh at (389–91):

> So thou and I, dear Painter, represent
> In quick effigie, others' faults and feign,
> By making them ridiculous, to restrain.

This is a Jonsonian, clinical view of satire, in which laughter is meant to cure the victims and to re-establish a non-comic orthodoxy to which the reader is expected to accede. What is laughable is diseased (occasionally, as with Anne Hyde, literally so) and laughter is the cure. Yet Marvell's laughter is at times too pervasive, his sense of the irony of things is too acute for us to see the poem in a simple satiric light. It is not surprising that Charles himself should have enjoyed Marvell's satire,[28] for in this poem the bedroom scene, and especially the attempts of the lecherous King to get Lady Peace into bed with him, has something of a Falstaffian quality which asks our admiration for such fully human pertinacity. In the heroic scenes, too, Marvell's sense of incongruity never quite deserts him, allowing him to present a rejuvenated sixty year old as his Achilles, in defiance of the facts; for the squadron that destroyed the English fleet was not commanded by De Ruyter – who remained at the mouth of the Thames – but by the younger Van Ghent. After everything has been considered, *Last Instructions* must be rated a major comic achievement and the first of

5 John Dryden

John Dryden's attitude to the comic, throughout his life, was a curious one. In common with his contemporaries he could neither ignore the predominance of the comic mood nor, as a professional poet, refuse to comply with it. Indeed a good deal of his work is comic, and in *Mac Flecknoe* and *Absalom and Achitophel* he achieved two of the finest comic poems in the language. Yet he always seems to have been less than at ease in the comic mode and his contemporaries, though conceding his superiority as a poet in his generation, frequently expressed reservations about his abilities as a comic writer. Neither his own views on the matter nor his practice are entirely consistent. He was writing stage comedy fairly regularly throughout his working life from his earliest play *The Wild Gallant* (1663) to his last, the tragi-comedy *Love Triumphant* (1694), and although several of these were popular he seems to have been a reluctant contributor to the genre. He writes in the preface to *An Evening's Love* (1668):

> Neither, indeed, do I value a reputation gained from comedy, so far as to concern myself about it, any more than I needs must in my own defence; For I think it, in its own nature, inferior to all sorts of dramatic writing. Low comedy especially requires, on the writer's part, much of conversation with the vulgar, and much of ill nature in the observation of their follies. But let all men please themselves according to their several tastes. That which is not pleasant to me, may be to others who judge better: And, to prevent an accusation from my enemies, I am sometimes ready to imagine, that my disgust of low comedy proceeds not so much from my judgement as from my temper; which is the reason why I so seldom write it; and that when I succeed in it (I mean so far as to please the audience), yet I am nothing satisfied with what I have done; but am often vexed to hear

the people laugh, and clap, as they perpetually do, where I intended them no jest . . . That I admire not any comedy equally with tragedy, is, perhaps, from the sulleness of my humour. (Watson ed. i 145).

There are two important points in this passage which will help us later to understand his use of the comic in his poetry; that he felt he had no personal taste for the comic, that humour was not something spontaneous with him – and that he thought of the comic, as orthodox comic theory tended to do in the seventeenth century, as a sign of ill nature, that is, as essentially satiric. In the *Essay of Dramatic Poetry* he refers to the comic in Hobbesian terms as 'that malicious pleasure in the audience which is testified by laughter'. His personal distaste for the comic he expresses on several other occasions. In the *Defence of the Essay of Dramatic Poesy* also written in 1668 he remarks:

I know I am not fitted by nature to write comedy: I want that gaiety of humour which is required to it. My conversation is slow and dull; my humour saturnine and reserved. (Watson ed. i 116).

He returns to this opinion in his old age, for as late as 1695 he can write in *A Parallel Betwixt Painting and Poetry* in a passage which begins as a defence of the comic:

Laughter is indeed the propriety of a man, but just enough to distinguish him from his elder brother with four legs. 'Tis a kind of bastard pleasure too, taken in at the eyes of the vulgar gazers, and at the ears of the beastly audience. Church painters use it to divert the honest countryman at public prayers and keep his eyes open at a heavy sermon. And face-scribblers make use of the same noble invention to entertain citizens, country-gentlemen, and Covent Garden fops. (Watson ed. ii 190).

That a writer who felt like this should have gone on writing comic literature throughout his long career is a measure of the popularity of the mode. Dryden says in the *Defence*, on writing comedy, 'my chief endeavours are to delight the age in which I live'.

Yet it would be an oversimplification to take these expressions of distaste for the comic too much on their face value. It is clearly not true that he had no relish for the comic, and certainly not true that he had no comic talent. T. S. Eliot finds it characteristic of Dryden's satire that in it 'wit . . . becomes pure fun' (essay on Andrew Marvell). In these outbursts Dryden is partly indulging in the usual theoretical prejudices against comic literature, partly failing to distinguish between kinds of the comic. It is true, I think, that he had little aptitude for good-natured comedy, as will appear when we look at his attempts at non-satirical comic verse: his wit is rarely 'pure fun'. On the other hand he had an acute sense of the ridiculous so that his best comedy invariably takes a satiric form. This bias was not occasioned by any personal qualities: he was by all accounts a not unamiable man, though a tenacious enemy. Rather it stems from his deepest convictions about the importance of orderliness and propriety. The comic was essentially to Dryden what it was to a lesser extent in Marvell and Milton, a measure of disorder, and he was sharp both in his analysis and exposure of disorder and in his condemnation of whatever caused it. He was therefore a natural satirist, and like many satirists, used laughter to repudiate the comic. Both by temperament and intellectual training he was taught to fear the disruptiveness of which laughter was a symptom, but he was also taught to see in laughter the opportunity for exposing disorderliness and by the exposure curing it.

It is not surprising, then, that his two best stage comedies *Secret Love* (1667) and *Marriage a la Mode* (1672) should both have as their main theme the repudiation of moral disorder and the triumph of romantic values. In both plays the comic subplot associates the comic with disorderly, libertine views and in both cases these views are rejected in favour of the romantic values of the non-comic main plot. This is clearest in *Marriage a la Mode* where the 'wife'-swapping of the comic plot quartet is contrasted with the idealism of the romantic hero's love for the heroine, Palmyra. The resolution of the play vindicates Leonidas, the romantic hero, but demonstrates that the comic cynicism of Palamede and Rhodophil, the comic heroes, is self-defeating. At the end they agree to lead an orderly sexual life and, through their defence of Leonidas, are admitted into the heroic non-comic world of the main plot. Comedy is exorcised along with the disorderliness of which it is a sign and the comic heroes end the play speaking (except for a short excursion into comic prose by Palamede at the very end) in the orderly cadences of the heroic pentameter. *Secret Love* also contrasts the platonic attitudes towards love of the characters of the main plot with the anti-platonic love of the comic plot. In this case, however, while the romantic love of Philocles for Candiope is vindicated, and the comic hero, Celadon, is made to conform by agreeing to marry, the two opposing sets of values are left largely intact, though opposed, with Celadon and his future bride, Florimell, agreeing to a truce in the libertine sex war only on carefully prescribed conditions. The tendency in both plays is to seek the resolution of comic tensions in a return to social orthodoxy. So the comic plot of *Marriage a la Mode* ends by an explicit resolution of tension (v i 319–23):

Rhodophil: . . . we had as good make a firm league not to invade each other's propriety.

Palamede: From henceforth let all acts of hostility cease betwixt us; and that in the normal form of treaties, as well by sea as by land, and in all fresh waters.

Comic tensions for Dryden are tensions of disorder. As in medieval art they signify deprivation, a disabling lack, and the comic is therefore the symptom of a disease that has to be cured by laughter.

With this view of the comic it is not surprising that Dryden finds it difficult to express benevolent laughter; hence his tendency to reject signs of comic abilities in himself. When he writes plays that are more comic than romantic, such as *An Evening's Love* or *Limberham*, though not always unsuccessful, they are markedly coarser-grained. There is some substance therefore in the charge of such enemies as Rochester and Shadwell that Dryden's sense of humour was coarse and heavy-handed. It is obviously only a half-truth, for the satiric comedy that was to come could hardly be defter. Rochester makes the

distinction with his customary fire and with accuracy, in his
Allusion to Horace, when he contrasts Dryden's coarse humour
with the refinement of his non-comic work, for when this was
written Dryden had not as yet showed his mastery of satirical
comedy:

> Dryden in vain try'd this [Sedley's] nice way of wit,
> For he to be a tearing *Blade*, thought fit,
> But when he wou'd be sharp; he still was blunt
> To frisk his frollique fancy, he'd cry Cunt,
> Wou'd give the *Ladies* a dry Bawdy bob,
> And thus he got the name of *poet Squab*,
> But to be just, 'twill to his praise be found,
> His *Excellancies* more than faults abound,
> Nor dare I from his sacred Temples tear,
> That *Lawrel*, which he best deserves to wear . . .

This passage, though not unfair, gave great offence, for Dryden
attacks the *Allusion* bitterly as the work of one of Rochester's
'zanies' in the preface of *All for Love* (1678), though he must have
known the real author. One of Rochester's 'zanies', Thomas
Shadwell, makes a similar but more extended charge in *The
Medal of John Bayes*, a 'Whig' reply to Dryden's satirical poem
The Medal, which attacked the opposition leader, the Earl of
Shaftesbury. Shadwell also made the (for him) disastrous
charge that Dryden's satirical is as inept as his comic sense and
received for his pains the publication of one of the most
devastating satirical replies ever penned, a poem that had
already been circulating some years in manuscript, *Mac
Flecknoe*. From this Shadwell's reputation has never recovered.
The cause of the publication of this onslaught is worth examin-
ing, however, because it seems to reflect a general opinion of
Dryden's sense of humour and gives some fresh evidence:

> As far from Satyr does thy Talent lye,
> As from being cheerful or good company.
> For thou art *Saturnine*, thou dost confess;
> A civil word thy dullness to express.
> An old gelt Mastiff has more mirth than thou,
> When thou a kind of paltry mirth wouldst show.

Good humour thou so awkwardly put'st on,
It sits like Modish Clothes upon a Clown;
While that of Gentlemen is brisk and high,
When Wine and Wit about the room does flie,
Thou never mak'st, but art a standing Jest;
Thy mirth by foolish Bawdry is exprest,
And so debauch'd, so fulsome, and so odd,
As–
"Let's Bugger one another now by God."
(When ask'd how they should spend the Afternoon)*
This was the smart reply of the Heroick Clown.
He boasts of Vice (which he did ne'r commit)
Calls himself *Whoremaster* and *Sodomite*;
Commends *Reeve's* Arse and says she buggers well,
And silly Lyes of vitious pranks does tell.
This is a sample of his Mirth and Wit,
Which he for the best Company thinks fit.
In a rich soyl, the sprightly Horse y'have seen,
Run, leap, and wanton o're the flow'ry green,
Prance, and curvet, with pleasure to the sight;
But it could never any eyes delight,
To see the frisking frolicks of a Cow;
And such another merry thing art Thou.[1]

The third line is a reference to that passage in the *Defence of the Essay of Dramatic Poesy* I have quoted, while the asterisked line is glossed by Shadwell: 'At Windsor in the Company of several persons of quality, Sir G(eorge) E(therege) being present'.

A look at examples where Dryden is writing amiable comedy does to some extent bear out these charges. He finds it difficult to separate the idea of the comic from satire and equally difficult at the other end of the comic spectrum to separate satire from the comic. He tends to think of the bad in terms of the ludicrous and the ludicrous in terms of the bad. He is therefore supremely successful at comic satire, but much less so at both non-satirical comedy and non-comic satire. If we look at a passage of his translation of the largely non-comic satirist Juvenal, for instance, we can see how he increases the comic element and so loses the earnest note of scorn that characterises the original. A certain coarsening of effect is the result, because the moral depravity that Juvenal presents is not funny but frightening. In the tenth satire, the poem that inspired Johnson's entirely non-comic imitation, *The Vanity of Human Wishes*, Juvenal lists the various objects of human desire and demonstrates their worthlessness. When he turns to the desire for longevity he describes the affirmities of old men:

> Their voices are as shaky as their limbs, their heads without hair, their noses drivelling as in childhood. Their bread, poor wretches, has to be munched by toothless gums; so offensive do they become to their wives, their children and themselves, that even the legacy hunter, Cossus, turns from them in disgust. Their sluggish palate takes joy in wine or food no longer, even copulation has been long ago forgotten, or if you try it the mean limb flops with its blood vessel and it will remain limp, although it is stroked all night long. For should this grey-beard be able to hope anything of this weak crutch? What perversion is deservedly suspected which attempts to copulate without the power?

This attempt at a straight translation fails to convey the clinical, frightening language Juvenal uses. Johnson's 'imitation', though it decorously reduces most of this passage to the two lines:

> Now pall the tasteless meats, and joyless wines
> And luxury with sighs her slave resigns,

none the less conveys, in the whole, the essential grimness of the Latin. Dryden on the other hand, turns the passage into bawdy comedy and, though his translation remains strongly satirical, he clearly relishes the absurdity of the situation, suggesting, as Juvenal does not, the simultaneous relish of sex itself and the ludicrous sexual incompetence of the old man. The juxtaposition of a multiple standard required by comedy, the ideal (sexual enjoyment or alternatively chastity) and the real (sexual incompetence), is maintained throughout. There is greater detachment, greater scepticism, but also greater vulgarity, because the moral standards are compromised. Is the old man really being condemned for sin or merely being laughed at for incompetence?

> His taste, not only pall'd to Wine and Meat,
> The limber Nerve, in vain provok'd to rise,
> Inglorious from the Field of Battel flies;
> Poor Feeble Dotard, how cou'd he advance
> With his Blew-head-piece, and his broken Lance?
> Add, that endeavouring still without effect,
> A Lust more sordid justly we suspect.

If Dryden's intention here is to reproduce the effect of the original, as he himself implies in the Dedication,[2] it would be difficult to imagine a more complete failure. His Christian optimism refuses to let him see men in the degradation imagined by Juvenal. His sense of God's order is too strong to allow such a stark view of a creature made in the image of God. So the old man becomes, not a menacing warning, but a figure of fun; someone who has fallen from the norm of healthy robustness which the passage implies. Dryden's method is, therefore, that favourite mode of the Augustans, mock-heroic; a contrast between an approved norm (expressed through the dignity of the treatment and the heroic associations) and aberration from it. Juvenal's straightforward 'hairless head' (*leve caput*), for instance, becomes the hyperbolic and absurd: 'The skull and forehead one Bald Barren plain'. For Juvenal's clinical, factual account of the impotence of old age, with the biological terminology of words like 'coitus', 'ramex', 'nervus', 'inguen', Dryden substitutes the comic euphemisms 'nobler treat', 'limber Nerve' (nerve, unlike 'nervus', being used in a sense remote from its normal meanings, as a poeticism). The starkly realistic, like Juvenal's 'quamvis tota palpetunt nocte' ('although stroked the whole night'), becomes the mock heroic, 'in vain provok'd to rise', and to complete the mock-heroic effect Dryden adds a line of which there is no hint in Juvenal: 'Inglorious from the field of battle flies', following it with the equally unsolicited mock-heroic of the 'advance' of 'blew-head-piece' and 'broken lance'. Here Dryden has been led by his Christian sense of the ludicrousness of evil to turn a fierce non-comic satire into mock-heroic. The complementary sense of the evil of ludicrousness similarly accounts for his tendency to turn amiable comedy into comic satire.

A good example of this can be found in his Chaucer translations. One of them is *The Nun's Priest's Tale*, which Dryden calls *The Cock and the Fox*. Chaucer's sense of humour is perhaps the most subtle and sophisticated of any poet in the language and most attempts at translation, like Coghill's popular translation today, only succeed in vulgarizing their original. Dryden's does not entirely escape this fault. The essence of Chaucerian humour in *The Canterbury Tales* is that it moves dextrously towards satire by occasionally tilting a delicate neutral balance. It is satire at the nearest point to pure comedy. Take, for instance, the description of the poor widow at the opening of *The Nun's Priest's Tale*. This achieves the subtlest of balances, neither celebrating the mythic joys of poverty nor using the widow as a device for satirising urban luxury. There are perhaps some slight hints tending in that direction countered by the occasional hint going the other way; the hint that there is something slightly ridiculous in poor contentment. The comic incongruity is developed from these two contradictory ideas: that poor means good and poor means bad:

> Ful sooty was hire bour and eek hir halle,
> In which she eet ful many a sklendre meel.
> Of poynaunt sauce hir neded never a deel.
> No deyntee morsel passed thurgh hir throte;
> Hir diete was accordant to hir cote.
> Repleccioun ne made hire nevere sik;
> Attempree diete was al hir phisik,
> And exercise, and hertes suffisaunce.
> The goute lette hire nothyng for to daunce . . .

The passage starts with the unpleasantness of the sooty bower, the irony of the ambiguous equation (if that is what it is) of 'bour' and 'halle', the paucity of her diet. This is an alienating description that is followed by a series of ideas contrasting the life of the 'narrow cottage' with the tribulations that attend the life of luxury, redressing the balance towards a sympathetic assessment of the widow. There are other levels of comedy in the relationship of tale to teller and the relationship of the tale

to the work as a whole that are important to the total complexity of Chaucer's comedy but are not relevant to the comparison with Dryden's isolated translation of the tale. Dryden's
treatment of this passage completely changes the emphasis both
by idealising the widow – making her into a figure from the
bucolic golden age, and in increasing the satirical implication
of the contrast with urban life. The movement from good to
bad makes it much more unambiguously satiric:

> Her Parlor-Window stuck with Herbs around,
> Of sav'ry Smell; and Rushes strew'd the Ground.
> A Maple-Dresser, in her Hall she had,
> On which many a slender Meal she made;
> For no delicious Morsel pass'd her Throat;
> According to her Cloth she cut her Coat:
> No paynant Sawce she knew, no costly Treat,
> Her Hunger gave a Relish to her Meat,
> A sparing Diet did her Health assure;
> Or sick, a Pepper-Posset was her Cure.
> Before the Day was done her Work she sped,
> And never went by Candle-light to Bed:
> With Exercise she sweat ill Humors out,
> Her Dancing was not hinder'd by the Gout.
> Her Poverty was glad; her Heart content,
> Nor knew she what the Spleen or Vapors meant.

The sooty bower has disappeared in favour of a clean, sweet-
smelling hall, the irony of 'bower and hall' has been dropped.
Chaucer's specific 'Hir diete was accordant to her cote' (diet
and dress were alike simple) becomes the generalised proverb
of the temperate man in Dryden: 'According to her cloth she
cut her coat', suggesting the typical, idealised status of the
widow. The contrast, therefore, with the luxury of the town takes
on much more clearly the nature of a contrast between bucolic
innocence and urban corruption. Dryden is 'classicising' his
medieval text by using the conventions of pastoral. The
effeteness of urban life is strongly suggested by the use of
fashionable cant words like 'spleen' and 'vapours' which develop
the slight hint in Chaucer's words 'goute' and 'apoplexy'.
    This shift of Chaucer's intention towards the urban satire

of the classical pastoral tradition is even more clearly seen in the
passage a little later where Chaucer describes his hero, Chauntecleer:

> This gentil cok hadde in his governaunce
> Sevene hennes for to don al his pleasance,
> Which were his sustres and his paramours,
> And wonder lyk to hym, as of colours . . .

This becomes in Dryden's imitation:

> This gentle Cock for solace of his Life,
> Six Misses had beside his lawful Wife;
> Scandal that spares no King, tho' ne'er so good,
> Says, they were all of his own Flesh and Blood:
> His Sisters both by Sire, and Mother's side,
> And sure their likeness showed them near ally'd.
> But make the worst, the Monarch did no more,
> Than all the *Ptolomeys* had done before:
> When Incest is for Int'rest of a Nation,
> 'Tis made no Sin by Holy Dispensation.
> Some Lines have been maintain'd by this alone,
> Which by their common Ugliness are known.

Although by now Chaucer's own lines are becoming more
unequivocally, if still only mildly, satirical, Dryden's lines are
far more emphatic satire. He cannot resist embroidering the
passing reference to incest in Chaucer into ten lines on the
morals of kings (indeed, though written some time after
Charles's death, it reads like some earlier anti-caroline satire),
moving again from Chaucer's particularity to a generalised
moral. Whereas to Chaucer Chauntecleer is an object of fun, to
Dryden he is an opportunity to demonstrate the viciousness of
the comic. The result in Dryden's version is superb, incisive
satire, which has little to do with Chaucer's subtly mocking
tone. In this case Dryden's lines are totally different in effect
from Chaucer's but they are not poetically inferior. Within his
satiric range Dryden's comic powers are unsurpassed.

Dryden's use of the comic in his purely original poems is
equally successful in satire. Very little of his original comic

poetry is non-satirical and that almost entirely confined to the songs for his stage comedies. Here again, as for example in the song 'Whil'st *Alexis* lay prest' from *Marriage a la Mode*, Dryden's treatment of non-satiric comedy justifies Rochester's and Shadwell's charge of coarseness. This particular song, for instance, exploits the single bawdy joke that the more often Alexis and Celia copulate the easier it is for her and the harder for him. The idea itself is essentially satirical because it downgrades sexuality to the purely physical sensation. It is, however, without the moral assumptions of satire proper, even if we take into account the general disapproval of libertinage of its setting within the play. As with the Juvenal translation the comic categories have become confused and we are given the bastard burlesque form of denigration without disapproval, a kind of toothless satire. Dryden's achievement when his intention is straightforward comic satire is in a different category altogether.

Both *Mac Flecknoe* and *Absalom and Achitophel* are described by Dryden as 'Varronian satires' in his *Discourse Concerning Satire*[3] and Varro is described as 'studious of laughter . . . his business was more to divert his reader than to teach him'. Dryden clearly intends us to see both works as comic satire. In both, the comedy arises from what is seen as ridiculous and to be repudiated. In both, what is funny is bad. There is, however, this important difference between the two works: while *Absalom* deals with the ethically bad, evil, *Mac Flecknoe* is primarily, if not wholly, concerned with what is aesthetically bad, the ugly and unpleasant. Dryden writes in the address to the reader of *Absalom* that his purpose is 'the amendment of vices by correction'. *Absalom* therefore is more concerned with serious instruction than *Mac Flecknoe*, for aesthetic matters were not generally considered as matters of high seriousness in the seventeenth century if they were divorced from morality. Throughout his working life Dryden held the belief, that he derived from Horace's *Ars Poetica*, that poetry should both teach and please, that art had both an ethic and hedonic function. He tended to waver about which was the more important. Most of his earlier pronouncements emphasise the importance of giving pleasure. In *The Defence of the Essay of Dramatic Poesy* he writes of verse:

I am satisfied if it cause delight; for delight is the chief, if not the only end of poetry; instruction can be admitted but in the second place for poetry only instructs as it delights. (Watson ed, i 113–4).

This was not an unprecedented view at the time, for even the moralistic critic Thomas Rymer writes in his *Tragedies of the Last Age* (1677) 'I believe the end of all poetry is to please . . . some sorts of poetry please without profiting'.[4] In later comments Dryden tended to insist on the priority of moral instruction, though the debate over the relation between instruction and pleasure went on into the next generation, to judge from Gildon's remarks in *The Laws of Poetry* (1721): 'it has been a dispute, whether the end and aim of poetry be to give pleasure only, or to convey to us likewise by that pleasure profitable instructions'.[5] Generally speaking in Dryden the two aims are seen as complementary; a good poet must have something to tell us, but he must also be able to instruct us in a way that will give us pleasure. *Mac Flecknoe*, however, is almost entirely about pleasure, and the lack of it. The idea of pleasure is used in two ways. It is both a demonstration of Dryden's ability as a poet to give pleasure, and of Mac Flecknoe's (Shadwell's) total failure in the art of giving pleasure. The primary contrast is between poetic wit and poetic dullness. Shadwell is 'Born for a scourge of wit and flayle of sense' (89) and Flecknoe's blessing to his 'son' is 'be thou dull'. Hence Dryden's contention that his purpose in this poem was 'more to divert his reader than teach him'.[6]

The poem sets up high expectations about poetry and the poet in presenting the heroic ceremony of the crowning of the bard; expectations which are justified by Dryden's skill in handling his theme, but which contrast ludicrously with Mac Flecknoe's abilities as a poet as they are described in the poem. The central device of the poem, therefore, is bathos. As a judgement of the actual Shadwell the picture presented is grossly unfair. Shadwell's was not a major talent, but his best comedies have a liveliness and a thematic coherence that justifies his contemporaries' assessment of him as the best of the professional writers of stage comedies in the period. Dryden was no more interested in the actual Shadwell than Marvell in the actual people pillorized in the *Last Instructions* or than Pope in the actuality of his Dunces. Dryden's purpose is mythic: to make of Shadwell the archetype of all incompetent poets.

Shadwell, then, is a falling off from the ideal poet. He is depicted in terms of inadequacy, as someone lacking the essential spiritual qualities that make the poet. He is an aesthetic equivalent of Augustine's evil man: a man lacking his full attributes as a man. The Shadwell of the poem lacks above all what Dryden so adequately exhibits in the poem, inventiveness, the ability to create life, 'like the rational creatures of the Almighty Poet' – as he says of the characters of Roger Boyle's plays[7] – while the true poet by his art imitates the creative impulses of nature, which Dryden demonstrates by having his comic creation, Mac Flecknoe, come so superbly to life. Shadwell's poetry is pastiche, an inorganic conglomeration of other poets' work. So 'Flecknoe' addresses his 'son', Shadwell: 'What share have we in Nature or in Art?' Shadwell purports to be a disciple of Ben Jonson, but 'Flecknoe' contrasts Jonson's creative method with Shadwell's:

When did his [Jonson's] Muse from Fletcher Scenes purloin,
As thou whole Eth'ridg dost transfuse to thine?
But so transfus'd as Oyl on Waters flow,
His always floats above, thine sinks below.

The mechanical image of sinking, the idea of Shadwell's own gross material separating out from the lighter more spiritual material he has purloined from Etherege, emphasises the heavy, uninspired quality of Shadwell's work. Whereas true art is of the spirit, everything about Shadwell is coarse, materialistic. And the poem ends suitably with 'Flecknoe' sinking out of sight through a mechanical contrivance (a trap door) Shadwell had required for his play *The Virtuoso*. The idea of Shadwell's physical qualities pervades the poem. He is 'A tun of a Man in [his] large bulk'. In contrast, his wit is but a small barrel, a kilderkin. The setting provided for his coronation is among the brothels of Barbican, suitably in the commercial part of the city, the part devoted to earthly pleasures. At the coronation in place of the spiritual symbols of orb and sceptre, he is found with a mug of ale in one hand and Flecknoe's play *Love's Kingdom* in the other:

His Brows thick fogs, instead of glories, grace,
And lambent Dullness plaid around his face.

The opposition of the idealistic 'glories' and the material fogs
reminds the reader of the aesthetic and spiritual values which
Shadwell is traducing. Throughout the poem true aesthetic
standards are kept before us as a contrast to Shadwell's 'Genuine
night'. In its verse, the poem maintains the harmony and dignity of poetry against the gross improprieties of its subject. The
opening lines, for instance, are an impressive sounding *sententia*
on the transitoriness of things, which only turns to bathos when
we know that this particular monarch, 'Flecknoe', is absolute
ruler of 'all the Realms of Nonsense'. The action of the poem,
too, the crowning of the bard, is an action reminding us of the
true dignity of the poet and recalls the high status of poetry in
civilised lands. Also reminding us of the classical dignity of the
poet is the constant allusion to the poetry of the past; to the
Aeneid, to the *Bible* (Flecknoe is described as Shadwell's John
the Baptist, 32), to recent epic achievement: Cowley's *Davideis*,
Davenant's *Gondibert*, Waller's panegyric *Of the Danger to his
Majesty*. All these allusions to heroic literature inevitably become perverted in their application to Shadwell and so become
a measure of the difference between the true and the false in
poetry. Above all there is Dryden's own play of wit in which
unexpected juxtapositions are constantly revealing the enor-
mous gap between reality and 'actuality':

> Shadwell alone, of all my Sons, is he
> Who stands confirm'd in full stupidity.
> The rest to some faint meaning make pretence,
> But Shadwell never deviates into sense.

This is panegyric superbly adapted for the art of sinking, the
sound and form of panegyric without its content. *Mac Flecknoe*,
then, in its constant movement from high expectations to low
actuality is consistently satirical and the constant juxtaposition
of the exalted and the debased maintains the element of
surprise essential to comedy. It is essentially a comic poem
because it shows us a world where the two incompatible views
of the poet, the image of the poet as he should be and the image

of Mac Flecknoe as he actually is, are continually juxtaposed
and finally left unreconciled.

Absalom and Achitophel, on the other hand, is not essentially
a comic poem at all but rather a non-comic poem which makes
use of comic devices. These devices, however, are so important
and so subtly handled that the poem as a whole must rank as
the most convincing refutation of Dryden's contention that he
was 'not fitted by nature to write comedy'. Certainly Dryden
emphasises the importance of the comic element in the poem
both in the *Discourse Concerning Satire*, in describing it as 'Varronian' satire, and in the *Address to the Reader*, where he singles
out for comment the comic element in the satirical portraits:
'I have but laught at some mens Follies; when I coud have
declaim'd against their Vices'. And he is right to do so; for the
subject of the poem is the dangers of disorder and the comic is
throughout one of the main measures of disorder. Dryden is
once again in this poem equating the comic with evil. The
humours he depicts, as in Jonsonian comedy, have to be
purged of the eccentricities and restored to health. The movement of the poem is therefore from the disorder of the opening
lines to the orderliness of David's assertion of kingly power and
dignity in his long final speech. The reader is taken through the
process of the restoration of order from chaos. Comedy is
exorcised through the ceremony of ridicule. The poem ends
by asserting a faith in a coherent, non-comic world reflecting
the divine harmony.

The poem opens in comic confusion:

> In pious times, e'r Priest-craft did begin,
> Before *Polygamy* was made a sin;
> When man, on many, multiplied his kind,
> E'r one to one was, cursedly, confin'd:
> When Nature prompted, and no law deny'd
> Promiscuous use of Concubine and Bride;
> Then, *Israel*'s Monarch, after Heaven's own heart,
> His vigorous warmth did, variously, impart,
> To Wives and Slaves: And, wide as his Command,
> Scatter'd his Maker's Image through the Land . . .

Ostensibly Dryden is here expressing the kind of libertine
sentiment we find in Donne's *Elegy 17* (38–49), his *Progress of the*

Soul (*Metempsychosis*) (191–203) and in 'The Relique' (30), and which is constantly echoed in the poetry of Charles's courtier friends like Sedley and Rochester. Freedom from sexual restraint is seen apparently as a lost pleasure of the innocence of the golden age; pleasures of pre-lapsarian pious times, lost 'cursedly' by the fall. As Rochester expresses it in *The Fall* of Adam and Eve:

> Naked beneath cool shades they lay
> Enjoyment waited on desire;
> Each member did their wills obey,
> Nor could a wish set pleasure higher.

But Dryden's intention is not at all what it appears; for the whole purpose of the passage is to undercut the libertine sentiments which he appears to be favouring. References to the fall of man are common in the poem and it is clearly a post-lapsarian society that he is describing. As the *Address to the Reader* has it: "'tis no more a wonder that he [Absalom] withstood not the temptation of Achitophel, than it was for Adam, not to have resisted the two Devils; the Serpent, and the Woman'. The fall of man is the event that prefigures the whole poem. Dryden's chief device in these opening lines is to confuse his two allegorical levels. For Israel's monarch is not, of course, the Old Testament David, at the allegorical level which gives the poem its principal significance. The real hero of the poem is not David but Charles, and Charles (unfortunately for him) was born after the 'pious times' have ended, and since the laws that confined one to one were promulgated. By confusing past and present Dryden has provided us with a topsy-turvy world, in which the fallen Charles has not even the benefit of the fruit of knowledge. Charles, the Christian King, in his notorious lechery, is behaving like a pre-Christian without pre-Christian innocence.

But a further element of confusion in this brilliant opening passage stems from yet another confusion of the chronology. The libertine freedom from law is erroneously equated with Old Testament law. It is pagan libertinism not Old Testament law that permitted 'what Nature prompted'; nor was David's reign 'before priestcraft did begin'. The story of David and

Urias (2 Kings 11–12), for instance, in which David's adultery with Urias' wife, Bethsheba, and treachery towards Urias is recounted as 'displeasing to the Lord' makes it quite clear that David was not permitted 'promiscuous use of concubine and bride', while the reverence shown by Saul to Samuel, the priest, is ample evidence that priestcraft had begun. David's reputation for sinful promiscuity became a byword in Christian apologetics. He is almost invariably included in lists of those who have sinned on account of women, as he is in *Sir Gawain and the Green Knight* (2418).[8] Thomas Fuller had written a long poem on the subject of David's sinfulness in 1631 called *David's Heinous Sin* in which David 'bold in sin' (III, 21) is exhibited as a prime example of sexual depravity:

> Thus hee that conquer'd men and beast most cruell
> And lay'd the giant groveling on the ground:
> He that of Philistines two hundred slue
> No whit appalled at their gridly hue
> Him one frayl woman's beauty did subdue.[9]

David's 'heavie punishment' is to see his son slain for even more heinous sexual transgressions, Amnon's adulterous intercourse with Thamar, which Fuller rather quaintly describes:

> He for the cook not for the cates did care
> Shee was the dish on whom he meant to feed.[10]

A more intentionally witty reference to David and Amnon's sinfulness is found in an anti-puritan satire of Bishop Corbet published in the Commonwealth collection *Parnassus Biceps* (1656), where the Puritan brethren are warned of the dangers of reading that portion of holy scripture that contains the account:

> Brother and Sister in the field may walk
> Beginning of the holy word to talk,
> Of David and Uriah's lovely wife,
> Of Thamar and her hurtful Brother's strife,
> Then underneath the hedge that is the next
> They may sit down and so act out the text.[11]

Dryden is deliberately confusing three chronologies: the pre-lapsarian time as interpreted in libertine literature, before there was a need for priests and before man was aware of sexual guilt; the Old Testament Law which allowed considerable, but not complete, sexual freedom and the New Law which included the Pauline strictures on sexuality. The picture conjured up is not unlike that magnificent satire on the Earl of Mulgrave's sexual vanity in Rochester's *Very Heroical Epistle addressed to his mistress Ephelia*:

> The boasted favour you so precious hold
> To me's no more than changing of my gold:
> Whate'er you gave, I paid you back in bliss;
> Then where's the obligation, pray of this.

Like Mulgrave, Charles is presented as the 'happy sultan' for whom 'womankind's thy whore'. And like Rochester, and Marvell in the *Last Instructions*, Dryden suggests the Jonsonian substitution of moral for money values in the picture of Charles scattering his maker's image through the land. The opening picture of Charles is therefore mock-heroic. It purports to be panegyric; but it puts Charles in an absurd light by showing him falling foul of two incompatible views of sexual morality. Bernard Schilling's view that Charles is made the origin of disorder in the poem is therefore correct.[12] As in *Last Instructions* Charles's immorality is the cause of disorder in the state. And directly so, for Absalom (Charles's bastard son, the Duke of Monmouth) at the centre of the plot against the throne, is one of God's images that Charles has been busy scattering about. As in *Last Instructions*, the King is sick and therefore the nation is sick. The poem sets out to cure the King by ridicule and divine aid. It is true, as Hoffman points out,[13] that even at the beginning of the poem there are a number of hints connecting Charles with God. Hoffman's suggestion, for instance, that line 418, 'God was their King, and God they durst Depose', refers to Charles I and therefore asserts the divinity of kingship, seems to me probable. But like Marvell, Dryden sees the kingly sun obscured by the spots not only of what Marvell describes as 'scratching courtiers', but of his own vices. So at the end of the poem Charles is made to appear dramatically in his true

nature: 'Tis time to show I am not Good by Force' (950) and
this sudden revelation presents us with the reality that the
appearances of the chaotic comic world of the earlier part of
the poem have obscured.

Dryden presents the conflict in the medieval terms of a
struggle between good and evil. And, as so often in the old
morality play, the evil is thought of as comic, and the good as
non-comic. But unlike the usual morality play depiction of the
psychomachia the defeat of evil is a foregone conclusion in
Absalom because the comedy of evil indicates deprivation and
deprivation is always ultimately compensated by God's
infinite goodness. The subject is not the war of good and evil
for the soul of man, but, as it is in *Paradise Lost,* the inevitable
defeat of evil by good; the elimination of negatives by the
presence of an infinite positive. Dryden is quite specific in his
association of his work with *Paradise Lost,* as Miss Brodwin's
article on the subject has amply shown.[14] Early in the poem
Achitophel and the mob that supports him are associated with
the diabolic (79–81):

> But, when to Sin our byast Nature leans,
> The carefull Devil is still at hand with means;
> And providently Pimps for ill desires . . .

Again, as in Marvell, the language of sexual immorality stands
as a type of immorality in general. A little later the Jebusites
(the Catholics), whose initial attempt to disrupt the State was
the immediate cause of the protestant backlash that Achitophel
(the Earl of Shaftesbury) is manipulating, are described as
allied with the Devil (130–3):

> Some thought they [the Catholics] God's Anointed
>   meant to Slay
> By Guns, invented since full many a day:
> Our Authour swears it not; but who can know
> How far the Devil and *Jebusites* may go?

And later those that respond against the Jebusites are described as 'like Feinds . . . harden'd in Impenitence' (145). The
description of the Jebusites quoted here is another excellent

example of Dryden's deliberate confusion of the historical and
the allegorical level of his poem. The incongruous introduction
of gunpowder into the biblical narrative is emphasised by the
reminder that gunpowder was not yet invented when it is
supposed to have been used. There are two specific reasons for
this pointed absurdity. Firstly, to link the Catholics as rebels
to the theme of the absurdity of disorder and make them, too,
an object of ridicule in the passage as a whole; and secondly to
suggest that the charges against the Catholics were preposterous
and throw further ridicule on those that made the charges
against them. These two intentions are to some extent contradictory but that only increases the muddle that plotters and
counter-plotters have got themselves into, where the truth of
accusation and counter-accusation has been lost in the welter of
recrimination. We are in a world of complete chaos in which
right and wrong can no longer be distinguished – a situation all
too familiar for those like myself who have had to suffer the
consequences of the breakdown of order in Northern Ireland.
The muddle is represented syntactically by the time sequences in
the passage. The phrase 'invented since full many a day' starts
by going backwards from the reader's time to some inter-
mediate point of time between the historical time of the poem
and the present. The time sequence then moves from the historical time forwards ('invented' is a past participle from our
point of view but expresses future time at the historical, that
is, literal level). A recent critic of this passage, incidentally,
takes it to task for being 'stiff and awkward' which, of course, is
exactly what it sets out to be.[15]

The reference to gunpowder is also one of the many comic
uses to which Miltonic allusion is put in the poem. The
anachronism recalls Milton's war in heaven in book six of
Paradise Lost where Satan and his men use cannon in their
absurd attempt to overthrow the invincible. Dryden's use of the
word 'invented' seems to deliberately pick up Satan's words
'not uninvented' (VI, 470). Milton's war in heaven is as farcical as
Dryden's political squabble because it is as futile. Satan cannot
win and his efforts to do so are merely the result of an absurd
delusion – the war in heaven is essentially a mock battle.
Unfortunately Milton does not exploit the comic material and
tries to pretend that the battle is genuinely heroic. The mock-

heroic element is thus obscured and the solemn tone runs counter to the logic of the action. Milton has not been able to face up to the comic implications of his theme.

Absalom and Achitophel might, therefore, be regarded as the great comic poem that Milton failed to write. Dryden frequently makes use of Milton's language for comic purposes in his poem. The description of the hysteria caused by rumours of the Popish plot, for instance, makes use of imagery that reminds the reader of Milton's description of the 'Stygian gulf' in book one of *Paradise Lost* (*Absalom and Achitophel*, 136–41):

> For, as when raging Fevers boyl the Blood,
> The standing Lake soon floats into a Flood,
> And ev'ry hostile Humour, which before
> Slept quiet in its Channels, bubbles o'r:
> So, several Factions from this first Ferment,
> Work up to Foam, and threat the Government.

Here Dryden is able to use the baroque materialism that characterises Milton's attempt to define the spiritual, much as he uses the physical properties in *Mac Flecknoe*, to exploit the absurdities inherent in treating psychological phenomena as physical objects. Again the emphasis is on confusion. Milton's lake is alluded to as part of a complicated mixed metaphor: the hysteria of the Popish plot is compared to a fever, then a flooding lake, then returns to a medical metaphor that compares the humours in the blood to raging fever and finally returns to the literal, political level in which the instigators of the accusations are compared to a fermenting liquid.

Many critics from, at least, Dr Johnson have noted a confused handling of the allegory of the poem. The status of the poem, as primarily historical or epic or satire, has long been a subject of discussion. Johnson argues: 'The original structure of the poem was defective: allegories drawn to great length will always break; Charles could not run continually parallel with David'.[16] But this structural muddle is exactly that comic device for depicting disorder which we have seen Marvell using so brilliantly in Charles's rape of Peace and indeed throughout *Last Instructions*. In both poems the confusion in levels of interpretation stands as a symbol of the confusion in the standards of the society depicted. The world of the poem switches disconcertingly and intentionally between biblical and contemporary history. Hoffman, for instance, illustrates the confusion very ably in discussing lines 437–40:

> He to his Brother gives Supreme Command;
> To you a Legacy of Barren Land:
> Perhaps th' old Harp, on which he thrums his Layes:
> Or some dull *Hebrew* Ballad in your Praise.

Hoffman points out that the brother refers to Charles's brother, the future King James, and is not applicable to David, while the harp and ballad seem far more appropriate for David than for Charles.[17]

As in Marvell's poem, the purpose is to depict a society where standards have become perverted, where appearance and reality are so confused that one cannot easily be separated from the other. It is only at the end of Dryden's poem, when Charles's grandeur as divinely appointed monarch is revealed, that David and Charles coalesce in an ideal image of Kingship. By then the poem has moved from the shadowy world of appearances to the reality of God's moral order.

The structure of *Absalom and Achitophel*, too, echoes *Paradise Lost*. Both poems begin in disorder and move towards order. The first half of Dryden's poem is devoted to a description of the comic world of Achitophel and the other 'Whig' rebels, just as books one and two of *Paradise Lost* show us Satan and his followers in hell. The first action of Dryden's poem, the attempt of Achitophel to corrupt Absalom, parallels Satan's conversation with Beelzebub in book one of *Paradise Lost*. This conversation is preceded by a portrait of Satan (27–80) just as Achitophel's temptation of Absalom is preceded by a portrait of Achitophel. Immediately after the temptation of Absalom we are given a series of portraits of Achitophel's cronies, just as Milton follows the Satan-Beelzebub conversation with the catalogue of Satan's chief supporters in hell. But again Dryden is not merely reproducing Milton. This is mock-heroic, not heroic poetry; and the purpose is not simply to draw parallels with Milton's heroic villains, but to suggest contrasts as well. The satirical portraits, therefore, exploit the comedy only latent in Milton, because Dryden writes to accentuate the absurdity of the rebels. Milton's rebels are, in fact, absurd because in challenging God they are challenging someone they cannot beat. Their actions are therefore ludicrous, pointless. Milton, however, does not treat them in the way they deserve, deliberately attempting to present them as heroic figures in order to retain the feared adversary of classical epic and so heighten the glory and prowess of the hero. Milton is forced into unintentional absurdity by pretending that the Satanic host are nobler and more formidable than they really are. And so successful has Milton been in this pretence that there is a long tradition of criticism which accepts Satan as the rightful hero of the poem. The result for Milton is unfortunate because it provides a double and contradictory vision of the adversary (as both serious and non-serious) which he is unwilling to exploit for comic purposes. From time to time the incongruity inevitably shows through in unintentional comedy like the slicing up of the angels or the use of mountains to silence Satan's guns in the war in heaven. Dryden exploits his similar material with much greater dexterity.

I have said earlier that *Absalom and Achitophel* moves from the comic world of disorder to a world dominated by divine orderliness. But this assertion needs to be qualified in two important ways. Firstly Dryden's poem is at all times a formal expression of that orderliness which is shown to triumph in the action of the poem. To a greater extent than Marvell, Dryden is asserting in the very orderliness of his couplets that order will prevail. This means, too, that throughout the comic first half of the poem there is the comic tension between form and meaning of mock heroic, while in the second half the form decorously embodies the literal meaning. Secondly the sequence of portraits in the 'comic' half of the poem instead of becoming less comic as they progress become more so, and this seems to contradict my contention that there is a progress from comic disorder to non-comic orderliness.

The first portrait, for instance, that of Achitophel, is scarcely comic at all, while the last of the portraits of the rebels, that of Corah (Titus Oates) is the most consistently comic. We should remember, however, that *Absalom and Achitophel* is a satire and that the comedy is throughout – as so often with Dryden –

a satirical device, not an end in itself. Comedy is from its very nature an expression of incongruity, a sensitive device for measuring disorder, but it is not the only way of depicting disorder. Indeed because comedy leads to contemplative detachment it is unable to express the kind of disorder that seems to endanger the very fabric of the society in which it appears. Fear casts out the comic. Milton's evil figures are comic in spite of their epic presentation because they cannot win and provide, therefore no real threat; even the successful temptation of Eve is only achieved by God's acquiescence and must therefore be supposed to have had his approval. Dryden's villains on the other hand have, it seems at first sight, terrestrial opponents and could conceivably win. It is only at the end of the poem that we realise that God has guaranteed Charles the victory; certainly we cannot be expected to realise it in the opening confusions of the poem. Milton, on the other hand, has already shown us Satan's defeat before he recounts the war. Achitophel and the other conspirators seem, therefore, to be potentially much more dangerous than Satan. For his arch-villain Achitophel, therefore, Dryden quite rightly borrows some of the heroic qualities that are given with less propriety by Milton to Satan.[18] Achitophel is given satirical treatment that is scarcely comic. The satiric portraits become more comic as their serious threat to society diminishes.

Dryden's use of comedy in the first half of the poem is extremely carefully modulated. The poem opens in comedy because society is seen, as a whole, ludicrously distorted from the norm implied by the orderliness of the poem; and later, in retrospect, with the explicit account of a balanced society described by the poet in the central balancing section of the poem (753–810). The rebels are placed in a comic setting, too, because ultimately we shall see they do not prevail. The perspective here is an ideal one against which actual manifestations of evil can pose no real threat. But as soon as the action of the poem moves to the actual intrigue of the 'Whig' rebels the perspective changes. We are no longer comparing ideal and actual, but seeing a real threat to the society of which the poet is a part. This gives cause for genuine fear, and Dryden's portrait of Achitophel and the account of Absalom's temptation are largely non-comic satire. The portrait of

Achitophel is a good example – fairly rare in Dryden – where the strength of repudiation has almost cancelled out the sense of incongruity. Achitophel is made to seem less futile than the rest of the conspirators, and more satanically menacing. Yet in this portrait there is a comic element, and indeed there has to be, because the poem, even while investing Achitophel in heroic attributes, is demonstrating his ultimate futility. For like Milton's Satan, Achitophel cannot win, because he is challenging divine omnipotence. Dryden exploits the absurdity of his position by presenting him in terms of grotesque incompatibilities: he is a fiery soul in a pigmy body, a man equally dissatisfied with power and without it, a man gifted to deal with trouble, yet risking self-destruction out of the perverse desire to seem clever, like Volpone's self-destruction out of mere wantonness (v vi 1–4).

The theme of purposeless heroism, energy without rational aim, is taken up again in the unequivocally comic portrait of Zimri. Now the incongruity is depicted more concretely and the juxtaposition of opposites is more obvious. So the comic impact is more apparent. Zimri is clearly a fool, a 'Buffoon', a 'blest madman', so that we are not likely to consider him as even a temporary danger. The essence of his absurdity is the great energy he expends to no purpose, and Dryden embodies this image of futility in verse that seems to turn round on itself (547–52):

> Stiff in Opinions, always in the wrong;
> Was everything by starts, and nothing long:
> But, in the course of one revolving Moon,
> Was Chymist, Fidler, Statesman, and Buffoon:
> Then all for Women, Painting, Rhiming, Drinking;
> Besides ten thousand freaks that dy'd in thinking.

Unusually for Dryden, this verse exploits the technique of heavy end-stopping we find in Cleveland, which Pope was so fond of using to break up continuity. Couplet is juxtaposed with couplet, half line against half line, and illustrates perfectly that Bergsonian concept of the comic where the organic imitates the movement of the inorganic.

In the last of the portraits of the rebels, that of Corah (Titus

Oates) the juxtaposition of incongruous physical images of the organic imitating the inorganic becomes even more marked. Corah is a 'monumental brass', he is a brass serpent, his birth is compared to the rise of 'Earthy Vapours'. At times Dryden adopts the medieval technique of *Physionomia*, the description of character by the enumeration of physical details, which was still a feature of the satirical 'Characters' popular in the seventeenth century. Dryden's Scottish contemporary, David Abercrombie, in his *Discourse of Wit* (1685) devotes the whole of section six of his treatise to describing 'how physiognomy can help indicate the wit of a person'. So Dryden writes of Corah (646–9):

> Sunk were his Eyes, his Voyce was harsh and loud,
> Sure signs he neither Cholerick was, nor Proud:
> His long Chin prov'd his Wit; his Saintlike Grace
> A Church Vermilion, and a *Moses's* Face . . .

Here Dryden is not only using the physical details ironically to suggest the character of a choleric man; he is also suggesting that his physical attributes are the most conspicuous thing about him; that he can best be defined, like Mac Flecknoe, in physical terms, because there isn't much spirituality about him. The parody of scripture, too, which is a feature not only of this portrait but of the earlier portraits of Shimei (Slingsby Bethel) and the lines on Nadab (Lord Howard of Escrick), indicates the widening gap between these absurd figures and the divine image in which they were made; whereas Achitophel and, still more, Absalom retain a little of that radiance of before the fall: 'his form had not yet lost/All her original brightness'. In contrast to the clarity with which the physical qualities of Corah are made to stand out, the spiritual qualities, such as they are, are shrouded in mystery: his memory is 'miraculously' great, exceeding man's belief, his wit exceeds human capabilities, he is subject to visionary flights and his spirit takes him 'the Lord knows where'.

The comic ambiguity of the phrase 'the Lord knows where' suggests both the purposelessness of the conspirators and, in parody, the genuine movement of the poem towards the divine. The effect of the general madness is seen directly after the portrait of Corah in the fall of Absalom (683–752). The element of scriptural parody reaches a climax in the 'celebration' of Absalom's fall, which in this topsy-turvy world is greeted in Messianic terms. Absalom is 'the young Messiah', he is 'like the sun' the symbol of Godhead; Christ-like he is heralded by 'the morning star', but all this in masquerade, in parody of the reality of David's kingship (751–2):

> Thus, in a Pageant Show, a plot is made;
> And Peace itself is War in Masquerade.

Dryden, having declared his hand in defining the comic insanity of Absalom's position, changes now to a rational declaration of the true position. The change to reasoned argument is extremely important, for it bridges the comic 'negative' world of the conspirators to its positive complement, the world of divine reality.

The forces of disorder are echoed and superseded by the real world that the comic world parodies. And the bridge is rightly presented as reasoned argument because it is through the exercise of reason that man can move from the chaos of a world of appearances to a transcendental world of reality.

The poem thus moves like a baroque painting from a naturalistic disorderly foreground into an idealised and exalted but remoter heavenly world in the top background of the picture. Baroque martyrdoms are frequently conceived in this way. Lodovico Cigoli's *Martyrdom of S. Stephen* (1597) in Florence shows a complex foreground of the stoning of the saint, and the murderers are represented as sardonically humorous figures enjoying their task. A clear association of evil and the comic. Above the martyr the lines of the saint's arm lead us to *putti*, one bearing a crown, and rather mistily painted above these, the eye led by one of the *putto*, are Christ, the dove of the Holy Spirit and the Father in radiant glory, drawn in much smaller perspective at the top of the painting but dominating and giving meaning to the action below on earth. This kind of pattern is frequently repeated with numerous variations. The famous Ferrabosco *Miraculous escape from Shipwreck* (1670) in Malamocco, Venice, shows in the lower right foreground, in naturalistic detail, the variety of expressions of relief on the faces of the

family saved from drowning. The eye is led upwards and back-
ward to the top of the picture where floating in clouds *putti*
surround the Virgin and child drawn to a smaller scale but
dominating the picture, in this case perhaps more in intention
than in pictorial effect. Guido Reni's *Madonna with the Patron
Saints of Bologna* (1630–1) in Bologna works on three levels. At
the bottom of the painting, in miniature, is a painting of the
outline of the city of Bologna; immediately above that the
Bolognese saints, painted realistically, form a semicircle at the
centre of which and above them is the Christ child held on his
mother's lap, painted in smaller perspective.

Even more remarkable is the combination of realism and
idealism in Reni's earlier painting *Samson* (1611) at Bologna.
Here the dead Philistines are shown scattered over a realistic
battlefield landscape in the lower half of the picture. The
nearest of the slain is shown in armour that is painted with
great care to detail, his sword lying on the ground near him.
Dominating the picture, however, and with a bare foot placed
on the dead Philistine is an idealised almost naked Samson, who
stands in a sensuous classical pose gazing into heaven.

I am not of course, suggesting that Dryden knew any of these
paintings or that there is any close parallel between Dryden's
poem and any particular baroque painting. Dryden's interest
in painting and knowledge of the *ut pictura poesis* tradition is
well known, but I am not wanting to suggest that Dryden was
actually following a pictorial method in *Absalom and Achitophel*.
My purpose is simply to show the similarity in the conventions
used by both painter and poet in working on different planes of
experience and that baroque art, whatever its medium, is
accustomed to move from the actual to the ideal not only by
means of allegory – which is common in painting as well – but
by shifting from one level of meaning to another temporarily
or spatially and within a single scale of reference, whether it
is a progression of the eye from one part of a canvas to another
or the narrative progression of a poem.

An even closer connection than baroque painting is perhaps
to be seen in the court masque, especially as it was developed
in the beginning of the seventeenth century by Ben Jonson and
Inigo Jones, where, as Stephen Orgel has pointed out, 'the
movement from disorder to order [is] central to its nature'.[19]

In Jonson's *Masque of Queens* (1609), for instance, we begin in a world of evil which is the negative image of the world of good that replaces it in the second half of the masque. The twelve witches of the 'anti-masque' represent the antitheses of the twelve virtues expressed at the end of the masque by the dance of the twelve court ladies headed by the Queen herself. The Queen, heralded by the abstract figure of Heroic Virtue, is presented not only *in propria persona* (she would herself have taken part in the masque) but as one of the twelve abstract virtues. She is described by Heroic Virtue as the incarnation of the Virtues singly represented by the other ladies. Moreover, her Virtue is celebrated and the homage is accepted by her not from 'self-love' but 'as humbling all her worth/To Him that gave it'. The association of actuality with abstract and divine is at the centre of baroque art. When we consider too that the 'anti-masque', with which most Jonsonian masques begin, was developed from the earlier 'antic' or comic prelude to the masque proper we get that link with the comic and evil that brings the masque parallel even closer to Dryden's poem. Jonson often presents the anti-masque in comic form as in *The Haddington Masque* of 1608, and in the *Masque of Queens* the witches are given a dance 'of preposterous Change and gesticulation'. The tendency to make the anti-masque comic becomes even stronger in the later masques. It was natural for Jonson to associate the comic with evil.

Dryden's poem moves from the chaotic mock-heroic world of the conspirators to the ideal world in which David is no longer the lecher, Charles Stuart, but a truly 'God-like' David, the embodiment of Divine authority, in whom: 'His train their Maker in their Master hear' (938). The transition from the actual to the ideal is made with considerable subtlety in the poem not only by the reason, for reason itself is only the beginning of wisdom, and we must follow the movement of the poem upwards beyond reason: 'So pale grows Reason at Religion's sight' (*Religio Laici*, 10). The function of sending the mind's eye upwards – the function given to one of the *putti* of Cigoli's painting – is given in the poem to the dead Earl of Ossory, son of Barzillai, the first of David's few friends. It has frequently been remarked, notably by Bernard Schilling, that the band of the faithful, unlike the conspirators, is very limited in numbers – indeed, Dryden makes this point explicitly (813, 817, 914) – and that this makes Charles's/David's victory all the more miraculous. It has been remarked rather less that much of the space given to David's supporters (thirty-three out of the forty-six lines) is given to a dead man. The purpose of the elegy on the Earl of Ossory (831–63) is expressed in lines that inevitably recall the upward movement of baroque painting (850–3, 860–1):

> Now, free from Earth, thy disencumbred Soul
> Mounts up, and leaves behind the Clouds and Starry Pole:
> From thence thy kindred legions mayst thou bring
> To aid the guardian Angel of thy King.
> . . . Now take thy steepy flight from heaven, and see
> If thou canst find on earth another *He* . . .

The search for 'another He' is successfully concluded in the appearance of the idealised David, whose speech leads us to the end of the poem (1026–9). God is remote and fleetingly observed, but like the trinity of Cigoli's painting this remote Godhead crowns and dominates the work. The Ossory elegy also serves to echo in positive terms the comic negativity of an earlier son-father relationship, that between Achitophel and his son:

> . . . that unfeather'd two-Legged thing, a Son;
> Got, while his Soul did huddled Notions try;
> And born a shapeless Lump, like Anarchy.

The comic image of Shaftesbury's live son, that suggests a plucked bird, the incongruity represented in the unsettled rhythms of the line, the emphasis on the gross physical nature of the conception, the dismissive brevity, the association with the forces of anarchy, are in complete and dramatic contrast with the dignified and extended praise of the dead Ossory, translated now to a world where realism has given way to reality.

The parallels with the methods of the painters is not apparent in the poem so much in actual passages of description as in the attitude towards the material. In baroque painting the objects depicted are not in the painting primarily to represent actuality but to tell us something about the ideal world which the actual world symbolises or foreshadows, if rightly understood. The mind is led by the senses from the actual to the spiritual. Frequently, therefore, the baroque painter resorts to allegory; but even if he stops short of systematic allegory his tendency is to use his images emblematically. This tendency is also found in Dryden's images. The architectural images, that have been the subject of adverse criticism, are chiefly to be understood in this way. The image of the falling fabric of the state (801–3) which French objects to, for instance, is to be seen not realistically as the picture of an actual building, but as a pictorial emblem, not only of man's political life, but of the insecurity of all earthly things.[20] It is possible that Dryden recalls Montaigne here: 'The great and glorious masterpiece of man is to know how to live to purpose; all other things, to reign, to lay up treasure, to build, are, at most, but little appendices and props'. Man must do no more than patch up the flaws and buttress the walls because to attempt more would be far worse than merely attempting the impossible; it would be going against God's will that temporal things should be impermanent. It would be placing the material above the spiritual: 'And mend the Parts by ruin of the Whole'. The ark that could be threatened is, again, not primarily to be thought of as a physical object, but a symbol of the divine will, which is beyond the 'ancient fabric', not merely spatially but symbolically superior to it – placed above and beyond it as it might be in a baroque painting. This emblematic use of properties is even more clearly seen in the passage in which Absalom is described by David as a 'young Samson' who will pull down the pillar of state and destroy himself along with the people (953–6):

> Kings are the public Pillars of the State,
> Born to sustain and prop the Nation's weight:
> If my Young Samson will pretend a Call
> To shake the Column, let him share the Fall . . .

Here the column is entirely emblematic, an emblem of responsibility; it has no more relation to the functional column of a building than those architraveless columns that are so frequently used as emblems in baroque paintings. A good example of this can be seen in Gimignani's *Adoration of the Kings* in Burghley

House, London, where on the extreme right hand of the picture a column continues upwards the framing given lower in the picture by the figure of Joseph, while towards the centre of the picture another column at a rather lower level from the first dissolves into clouds from which *putti* appear. Neither column has any realistic architectural function, but both help to frame the Virgin and child and suggest the divine framework of which the child's birth is the keystone (the Christ figure is actually shown against the keystone of the central column). The use of the column as an emblem of responsibility or uprightness became a stock property of the portrait painting of the period: a good late example can be seen in Hogarth's fine portrait of Thomas Coram. In the passage from *Absalom and Achitophel* Dryden links this pillar emblem with the story of Samson in a way that might at first seem incongruous, for Samson destroyed the arena of God's enemies the Philistines. But Dryden is continuing his use of the column as an emblem of the state. The call to *this* Samson is not a genuine call to defeat God's enemies and its result will be his own fall – a reference to the fall imagery in the earlier half of the poem in which Achitophel is depicted shaking the forbidden tree (203) in trying to bring about the fall of Absalom. Absalom here, then, continues his comic role, this time as a parody of the biblical Samson. But the comic role is seen even more clearly now to be self-defeating.

'The artist of the baroque age sought, not to attain the truth, but to demonstrate it'[21] writes Germain Bazin. Dryden's poem is a journey out of comic disorder towards a cosmic orderliness. It is, in a sense, the most devastating indictment of that world of comic scepticism from which so much Restoration comedy springs. It starts in the world of the sceptical, libertine assumptions of Charles II and his courtiers and takes the reader gradually from a mood of irresponsible cynicism into the solemn and real world of God's majesty. In doing so it transforms the King from the actual lecher he was into the symbol of the divine orderliness his sacred role as king demanded he should be. Whereas Marvell's *Last Instructions* presents the comic problem of the fisher king, Dryden's poem takes us through a process of an exorcism of comedy that effects the King's cure. It is typical of Dryden that his finest comic poem should be devoted to the solemn purpose of expelling the comic spirit.

he was also a man who could stand back from his experience, detach himself from it and laugh at both the world and himself. As a poet he learnt, in the satires, to control and harmonise these two sides of his nature that he could never reconcile in his life. As his poetry matures he increasingly learns to bring the two opposing impulses together. Three phases can be detected in his development as a poet. In the first he is largely writing light poetry, playing with conventional forms and ideas; for a short period (Vieth dates it 1672–3) he turns in *The Ramble*, *The Imperfect Enjoyment* and *Signior Dildo* to burlesque, abandoning the formal conventions, in order to express a deepening sense of the essentially chaotic nature of experience. In the last and great period of his work, though never abandoning his lighter poetry, he attempts to create an order with the aid of laughter that he can impose on the disorderliness of experience. It was this search for orderliness that produced the great satires. In his life, but not, it seems, in his poetry he took a further step and came, on his death bed, to accept the Christian view that man's ability to impose order on his experience is a reflection of the divine power.

At one extreme his poetry could almost be described as Romantic:

> Absent from thee I languish still;
> Then ask me not when I return?
> The straying fool 'twill plainly kill
> To wish all day, all night to mourn.
>
> Dear! from thine arms then let me fly,
> That my fantastic mind may prove
> The torments it deserves to try
> That tears my fixed heart from my love.
>
> When, wearied with a world of woe,
> To my safe bosom I retire
> Where love and peace and truth does flow,
> May I contented there expire,
>
> Lest, once more wandering from that heaven,
> I fall on some base heart unblest,
> Faithless to thee, false, unforgiven,
> And lose my everlasting rest.[2]

There is, even here, a certain amount of parody and sexual *double entendre*; Rochester was hardly ever wholly serious, except about the comic. But there is also unmistakably a note of personal sincerity, what John Oldmixon describes in his own verse as 'the real sentiment of my heart at the time I writ it'. Much of Rochester's verse is in some sense personal, and this alone marks him off from the majority of his predecessors and contemporaries. Usually, however, the personal element is distanced by the use of conventional devices. At his best he contrives both to present personal experience and at the same time remain, as poet, aloof from it. His greatest poetry is both passionate and analytical.

If there are moments when Rochester is expressing feeling directly, equally characteristic are those poems in which the poet appears completely detached from his creation and the feelings are presented through a veil of irony. Rochester's poetry certainly shows signs of a greater concern with things and less concern with the technicalities of expression than his predecessors. The Romantic cult of sincerity is already making an appearance in his poetry. Yet he is also very much of the tradition of the Renaissance gentleman, where the observance of convention was as much a guarantee of poetic good manners as conventional behaviour was of good breeding. Gentlemanly detachment, *sprezzatura*, was still as important to the Restoration aristocrat as it had been to his Elizabethan forebears, except that now aloofness had been reinforced philosophically by stoic and epicurean scepticism. Even Rochester's debauchery can be partly explained as a result of that epicurean curiosity described in Jean François Sarasin's account of Petronius as 'a nice and learned Artist in the Science of Voluptuousness'.[3]

As a gentleman poet, Rochester was not concerned with publication; his earlier poetry, at least, is casually conceived and often casually executed. Timon's account of his poetry at the beginning of the satire that bears his name, would certainly fit Rochester's at the time when the lines were written, in the spring of 1674:

> I vowed I was no more a wit than he:
> Unpractised and unblessed in poetry.
> A song to Phyllis I perhaps might make,
> But never rhymed but for my pintle's sake.

Rochester was never as detached from his 'pintle' as this remark might suggest; in fact he was as much attached to it as it was to him. But his ability to treat things of great concern with detachment reveals an aspect of him as a poet that goes far to explain his success as a comic poet. For one source of his comedy is in the sceptical detachment with which he could contemplate both himself and the world about him.

Rochester uses poetic convention, like most Renaissance poets, to place ideas and expressions of feeling in a critical framework. The conventions provide a standard of reference against which particular thoughts and feelings can be measured and assessed. Most of his poems can be seen as exercises in particular genres or sub-genres. His early pastoral poetry, for instance, such as the *Pastoral Dialogue between Alexis and Strephon* and the *Dialogue between Strephon and Daphne* are highly artificial exercises in the pastoral dialogue favoured by the French *précieux* poets. Because these poems could rely on a body of generally accepted convention they were susceptible to comic treatment; for instance, in the contrast of the artificial qualities of the genre with a realistic treatment of the subject matter. One of Rochester's most successful comic poems, *Fair Chloris in a Pigsty Lay*, exploits pastoral conventions in this way for comic effect. A few of Rochester's minor poems have been examined in some detail as examples of particular genres or sub-genres. *Upon Nothing*, for instance, has been shown by Rosalie Colie to be one of a long line of poems on the subject of 'nothing' that were used as an opportunity for Renaissance poets to show their ingenuity at handling paradox. At the end of the life of Rochester Dr Johnson quotes a long Latin poem by a sixteenth-century poet Jean Passerat on nothing, which Sir John Hawkins says Johnson had quoted from memory. Rosalie Colie mentions a collection of poems on the subject in Dornavius's *Amphitheatrum sapientiae Socraticae Joco-Seriae*.[4] The most famous variation on the theme of nothing is John Donne's sombre and magnificent *Nocturnall on St. Lucie's Day*. The praise of nothing was a sub-genre of the mock encomium. Another of Rochester's poems, *The Imperfect Enjoyment*, has been shown by R. E. Quaintance to be one of a series on the subject of sexual mismanagement, that originated in France and became popular during the Restoration.[5]

The highly conventional nature of much seventeenth-century poetry and the importance given to 'wit', that is, 'ingenuity', inevitably fostered a detachment favourable to the development of comic forms, and some of Rochester's poems can be seen as straightforward exercises in the kind of comic inversion represented by such forms as the mock encomium. One popular comic form was the mock song, to which at least one anthology of the period, *Mock Songs and Joking Poems* (1675), was largely devoted. Rochester wrote several of these comic songs. Frequently the mock song set out deliberately to parody a non-comic song. An example of this is Rochester's parody of Carr Scroope's song 'I cannot change as others do', which becomes in Rochester's version (perhaps predictably):

> I fuck no more than others do;
> I'm young, and not deformed.[6]

Rochester's uninhibited pornography manages to make funny a kind of poem that is almost invariably tedious elsewhere. Another kind of mock song involves the kind of contrast between form and meaning already mentioned in relation to the mock pastoral. The song was of course normally a polite form and it could be exploited for comic purposes by retaining the lyric grace to serve an incongruously ungracious subject matter. There are several examples in Rochester's poems, such as the lines 'On Mrs. Willis' which begins:

> Against the charms our ballocks have
> How weak all human skill is . . .

and another highly scatological song which begins with the conventionally poetic line: 'By all love's soft, yet mighty powers'. Related to these mock songs are the conventional 'anti-platonic' love lyrics that might retain the forms of the idealising or 'platonic' love songs, but present love in a harsh or comic light. Such 'realistic' accounts of love seem to have provided an antidote to the idealising tendencies of the Petrarchan love tradition for almost as long as there was a Petrarchan tradition. Indeed Petrarch himself, though normally solemn enough on the subject of love, provides one such poem among the sonnets in the poem beginning 'Io non fu d'amar voi lassato unquanco' (I was never tired of loving you). There are many examples of the anti-platonic love poem in English, Wyatt and Donne both exercise themselves in the form and the Drolleries abound in them. Rochester merely continues a long tradition, therefore, in such songs as 'Against Constancy',[7] the song 'How happy, Chloris, were they free'[8] and 'Love a woman? You're an ass!'[9]

These comic poems of Rochester are largely play poems, poems that are exercises in forms rather than explorations of experience. The poet seems to exist in them only as manipulator. They are machines for making the reader laugh, not for taking him on a voyage of discovery. Perhaps the best of these poems of complete detachment is the lyric called 'The Song of a Young Lady to her Ancient Lover'. This is an exercise in the 'contrast' poems that were so popular in the anthologies of the seventeenth century. The genre, or sub-genre, has not so far as I know been systematically explored but, like so many of the minor comic forms, it seems to have its basis in rhetorical exercises. Certainly the idea of contrasting such opposites as youth and age, black and white (especially black men and white girls), beauty and ugliness occurs early in rhetorical tropes; Sir Gawain and the Green Knight contains a formal contrast of youth (beauty) and age (ugliness) in the portraits of Bertilak's wife and Morgan. Particularly popular in the seventeenth century were poems about old men courting young girls or, less frequently, young men courting old women. Bishop Henry King has a poem called 'Paradox That it is best for a Young Maid to Marry an old Man',[10] emphasising in the word 'paradox' the element of witty ingenuity that the reader expected to find in such poems. Alexander Brome includes a similar poem in his collection Songs and Other Poems (1661).[11] A collection entitled Methinks the Poor Town (1673) has a poem called 'An Old Shepherd Courts a young Nymph'[12] and another collection, Merry Drollery (1661), has a poem on a similar subject called 'Lust Described' which may give a clue to an original moral intention behind such exercises.[13] Alciati in his famous book of emblems has an emblem under the heading 'Amor: senex puellam amans' (Love: an old man loving a girl)[14] which also is presented as a warning. A collection of 1675 has a song

beginning 'When a woman that's buxom a dotard does wed'
and Mennis's collection *Musarum Deliciae* (1655) has a poem
called 'A Young Man Courting an Old Widow'.[15] No doubt
there are a large number of similar poems in various collections
of the time which the reader will perhaps be pleased I have
not come across. It is important, however, to realise how
closely related to current convention much of Rochester's work
is, and to list a few parallels seems a good way of emphasising
this. Rochester's exercise in the 'contrast' poem is particularly
interesting, because he seems to have taken particular pains to
leave out any suggestion of moral judgement. The poem is
written as paradox. The young lady who addresses her ancient
lover in the poem adopts Bishop King's opinion that 'it is best
for a young maid to marry an old man'. But Rochester himself
is careful to keep so precise a balance between her advocacy
and the natural repulsion the situation evokes, that the poem
itself cannot be said to be suggesting any interpretation. It is
an excellent example of that rare, balanced, sceptical comedy
that neither apportions blame nor gives approval:

> On thy withered lips and dry,
> Which like barren furrows lie,
> Brooding kisses I will pour
> Shall thy youthful [heat] restore
> (Such kind showers in autumn fall,
> And a second spring recall);
>   Nor from thee will ever part,
>   Ancient person of my heart.
>
> The nobler part, which but to name
> In our sex would be counted shame,
> By age's frozen grasp possessed
> From [his] ice shall be released,
> And soothed by my reviving hand,
> In former warmth and vigor stand.
> All a lover's wish can reach
> For thy joy my love shall teach,
> And for thy pleasure shall improve
> All that art can add to love.
>   Yet still I love thee without art,
>   Ancient person of my heart.

The incongruity, here, arises in the contrast between the passionate sincerity of the young girl and the unattractiveness of the object of her attention. No judgement, however, is implied either of the young girl or the ancient. We are at liberty to interpret it as praise for the young girl's kindness or as blame for its misdirection. Both interpretations are equally plausible and the poem remains perfectly balanced between the two. Rochester is demonstrating the core of the comic dilemma: the inability of the mind to choose between two equally plausible interpretations of the same situation. So that the poet himself does not intrude any judgement into the poem Rochester adopts a favourite device of his, the device of impersonation, or 'prosopopeia', as the rhetoricians often described it. This was a common device of Renaissance literature by which the poet detaches himself from his subject matter in adopting a dramatic *persona*. Alexander Brome explains to his readers in the preface to his *Poems* (1661) that he cannot be held responsible for any views expressed in his poems as he is merely adopting views suitable for the particular *persona* he chooses in each case:

> But as to the men of a severer brow, who may be scandaliz'd at this free way of writing, I desire them to conceive those Odes which may seem wild and extravagant, not to be Ideas of my own mind, but characters of divers humours set out in their own persons. And what reflected on the Times, to be but expressions of what was thought and designed by the persons represented.[16]

The *Song of the Young Lady* is a comparatively simple, and entirely successful, example of comic scepticism. The sceptical implications are not stressed, though a comparison with other 'contrast' poems suggests that Rochester is not simply playing with ideas. Paradox here is more than just a game, it is a demonstration of the limitations of human thought processes. This is a favourite theme of Rochester; it is the underlying theme of the *Satyr against Mankind*, where logic is driven to absurdity. Much of Rochester's sceptical poetry dwells in the contradictions inherent in human nature. *The Disabled Debauchee*, for instance, develops the paradox that heroic self-sacrifice is a supreme form of egotism and conversely egotism a supreme form of self-sacrifice. Again the mood is of comic detachment because Rochester is not attempting to apportion praise or blame, but to present two opposed sets of values, the public and private, in juxtaposition. The balance between praise and blame is achieved by the characteristic Augustan devices of mock-heroic, the use of a dignified verse form for a low subject. The verse form used is the stanza used by William Davenant for his epic poem *Gondibert*, which Dryden also used for *Annus Mirabilis*. The subject matter too relates to Dryden's poem, for it is conceived as a parody of the celebration of naval battles of the kind Waller's much-parodied *Instructions to a Painter* (1665) had made popular. Rochester opens the poem with an epic simile, extended over three stanzas, likening his disabled debauchee to an ancient admiral watching a naval fight, which brings the gleams of battle to his eyes:

> From his fierce eyes flashes of fire he throws,
>   As from black clouds when lightning breaks away;
> Transported, thinks himself amidst the foes,
>   And absent, yet enjoys the bloody day.

This baroque image of power, however, serves only to make the ludicrous comparison of the heroic admiral with the old lecher who, no longer able to sustain his debauched pleasures, finds his enjoyment in spurring on younger men:

> Thus, statesmanlike, I'll saucily impose,
>   And safe from action, valiantly advise;
> Sheltered in impotence, urge you to blows
>   And being good for nothing else, be wise.

As often in the use of mock-heroic technique the effect is one of ambiguity. There is contrast, but also some of the heroic associations rub off on to the comic hero. At the end of the poem therefore, we are not sure, after all, whether we are meant to see the debauchee as a repellent old pervert or as a genuine hero, determined to maintain his heroic struggle against age and decrepitude to the last. The final stanza, which I have quoted, suggests by another ironic twist that the virtuous standards we have been assuming in the contrast between the heroic and the debased are perhaps the result of a bloodless, feeble attitude to life, that wisdom is after all another name for impotence.

Rochester achieves a fine irony by playing off two sets of standards: the social virtues of self sacrifice and restraint suggested by the normal assumptions we bring to the poem (by the restrained formality of the verse form and also by the battle imagery and the willingness of the old man to pass on his gifts to the next generation); and the individualistic virtues of honesty to our own feelings which his sexual heroism implies. Public and private virtues that were coming into conflict increasingly in the Restoration period here collide as two ludicrously irreconcilable and conflicting, but equally valid, sets of values. A comic balance of similar forces can be seen in Etherege's portrait of his hero, Dorimant, in *Man of Mode*. The comic contrast in Rochester's poem is heightened by the inevitable association of the debauchee's attitudes with what we know of Rochester himself, and in one manuscript version the poem is headed 'The Lord Rochester uppon himself'.[17] The conflict of values in the poem can therefore be seen as a comic juxtaposition of two aspects of Rochester's own character: the aristocratic pride, represented in the respect for epic form and convention, and the individualistic passion of the poem's subject matter.

Human love is frequently the subject of Rochester's comedy because in love these two opposing aspects of human experience, the pride and the passion, are most incongruously juxtaposed. And because this clash reflects impulses in Rochester's own character the comic hero of his poems is often closely related to the poet himself. In two of the lyrics the dilemma of man's sexuality is presented in general terms as a balanced comedy of irreconcilable values. The punning title of *The Fall* links loss of innocence with the loss of sexual potency. The theme is that universal dilemma so ably dealt with by the modern anthropologist Margaret Mead: 'the more [man] thinks, the less may he copulate'.[18] Before Adam's fall, Rochester declares, human kind lived a life of nature, in which the will was in complete accord with the senses:

> Naked beneath cool shades they lay;
>   Enjoyment waited on desire;
> Each member did their wills obey,
>   Nor could a wish set pleasure higher.

Now, however, our disastrous tendency to worry about everything denies us spontaneity and prevents our enjoyment. There is, as Rochester writes in a letter to his wife, 'so great a disproportion 'twixt our desires and what is ordained to content them'.[19] It is the disappointment of desires that provides the laughter, in accordance with Kant's formula of 'an affection arising from the sudden transformation of a strained expectation to nothing'.

The idea that modern man is a degenerate version of natural man is very ancient. It was made popular again in western Europe by Montaigne's *Essays*, especially the essay *Of Cannibals*, in which Montaigne argues:

> [The Indians] are savage at the same rate, that we say Fruits are wild, which Nature produces of her self, and by her own ordinary progress; whereas in truth, we ought rather to call those wild, whose Natures we have chang'd by our Artifice, and diverted from the common Order. In those, the Genuine, most useful and natural Vertues and Properties, are Vigorous and Spritely, which we have help'd to Degenerate in these by accomodating them to the pleasure of our own Corrupted Palate.[20]

And in another essay Montaigne writes:

> Nature always gives . . . better [laws], and more pure than those are we make our selves; witness the Picture of the Golden-Age, and the state wherein we see Nations live, who have no other.[11]

Montaigne does not usually link the idea of savage well-being to sexual enjoyment, having a somewhat jaundiced view of the pleasure of love, but in his essay on cannibals he envies the fortunate primitives for having only two principal concerns: fighting and women (1 30). Rochester could, however, have found such an association of natural virtue and sexual enjoyment in Donne's poetry. In *Elegy 17*, for instance, Donne writes:

> How happy were our Syres in ancient times,
> Who held plurality of loves no crime!

> Women were then no sooner asked than won,
> And what they did was honest and well done,
> But since this title honour hath been us'd,
> Our weake credulity hath been abus'd;
> The golden laws of nature are repeal'd,
> Which our first Fathers in such reverence held . . .

In 'The Relique' Donne refers to the sexual organs as 'the seals/ Which nature, injur'd by late law, sets free' – this could possibly be a reference to the new law of the Christian, especially because the poem described the lovers in Christian terms and compares their continence with the asexuality of the angels. It is likely, too, as Redpath points out, that Donne has in mind a passage of Ovid's *Metamorphoses* (x 329 ff). In Donne's *The Progresse of the Soule* the sexuality of earlier man is likened to animal sexuality and the suggestion is that the spontaneous life of both man and animal was superior to that of modern man (191 ff):

> In this world's youth wise nature did make haste,
> Things ripened sooner, and did longer last;
> Already this hot cocke, in bush and tree,
> In field and tent, ore flutters his next hen . . .
> . . . Men, till they took laws which made freedom less
> Their daughters, and their sisters did ingresse;
> Till now unlawful, therefore ill, 'twas not . . .

Neither Donne nor Montaigne suggests that this happiness of primitive man can be equated with the pre-lapsarian contentment of Adam and Eve, and Marvell in *The Garden* seems to think paradise would be better excluding women altogether. Adam and Eve's sexual enjoyment, however, is part of the bliss of paradise in *Paradise Lost*. In Donne and Montaigne the idea of a primitive golden age seems to be primarily classical in inspiration. It is a commonplace of seventeenth-century libertine poetry to link sexual intercourse with the recovery of paradise. Rochester does this himself in such lyrics as 'Absent from thee I languish still'. Carew in his libertine poem *The Rapture* describes the joys of Elizium:

All things are lawfull there, that may delight
Nature, or unrestrained Appetite;
Like and enjoy, to will, and act, is one,
We only sinne when Love's rites are not done.[22]

A poem called 'The Fall' in Edmund Waller's *Poems* (1645), a poem of equivocal lubricity, associates the pleasures of sexual intercourse with the Fall in the garden of Eden, though he does not exploit the paradox that the origin of our sin is the origin of our pleasure:

Thus the first lovers, on the clay
Of which they were composed lay;
So in their prime with equal grace
Met the first patterns of our race:
Then blush not (fair) or on him frown,
Or wonder how you both came down . . .

Waller's title is also a pun, associating the metaphorical fall of Adam and Eve with the literal fall of the lovers to the ground; but the implications of the pun are not developed. Rather closer to Rochester's poem in its association of the Fall with sexual limitations is the accusation levelled at Adam and Eve in the first of the *Sonetti Lussuriosi* of the sixteenth-century poet Pietro Aretino, which Rochester must surely have read:

And if we were allowed to fuck after death I should say to you; let us fuck until we die of it; after, we shall go and fuck Adam and Eve, who were the cause of this unlucky death. It is only too true, for if those wretches had not eaten the traitor apple I know well enough lovers would not cease enjoying one another.[23]

None of these examples, however, develop the paradox that is central to Rochester's poem, that guilt and pleasure are inextricably intertwined in sexuality. The libertine aims to defy the taboos that our sense of guilt places on sexual activity: Rochester's poem suggests that the taboos are inescapable. His purpose in associating our first parents with the golden world of primitive man is to exploit the paradoxical association of sexuality and innocence. Our fall (both spiritually and the

impotent fall of the sexual organ) shows our inability to dis-
associate sexuality from our sense of guilt. The result is comic,
because we long and strive for a state of innocence in which the
very act of striving is a sign of our sense of guilt. We are in the
absurd position of constantly striving for the unattainable. In
the last stanza of the poem therefore, Rochester's lover is left
with nothing to offer his girl friend but the abstract 'tribute of
his heart' when she is longing to share Eve's delights:

> Then Chloris, while I duly pay
> The nobler tribute of my heart,
> Be not you so severe to say
> You love me for the frailer part.

Here Petrarchism is stood on its head: instead of the courtly
code that leads the lover to a knowledge of beauty it becomes a
poor substitute for what before the Fall is a full-blooded sexuality. Platonic love is here the punishment for our fall from
Nature.

The complexity of man's attitude to sex, as both the ultimate
good and the primary source of our guilt, is exploited comically
again in a mock pastoral 'Fair Chloris in a Pigsty lay', which
Vieth regards as prentice work but which (though its unequivocally comic tone suggests that it was written before the
major satires) seems to me a work of considerable accomplishment. The poem tells how Chloris falls asleep among her pigs.
The sounds of their grunting make her dream that a young man
appears to warn her that one of the pigs is in danger 'hung on
the gate/That leads to Flora's cave'. The youth's real aim,
however, is to get her into the cave so that he can rape her:

> Now pierced is her virgin zone;
>   She feels the foe within it.
> She hears a broken amorous groan,
>   The parting lover's fainting moan,
>   Just in the happy minute.

> Frightened she wakes, and waking frigs.
>   Nature thus kindly eased
> In dreams raised by her murmuring pigs
>   And her own thumb between her legs,
>   She's innocent and pleased.

The rape has after all been self-induced, the result of her deepest, unconscious wishes. The ambiguity of sexuality here is well expressed. The 'piggishness' of human sexuality, which is suggested not only by the inspiration of the dream in the pigs' grunt and in the torpid, unromantic setting (the pigs complaining of the heat), but by the deceitfulness and brutality of the dream lover:

> This plot, it seems, the lustful slave
> Had laid against her honour,
> Which not one god took care to save
> For he pursues her to the cave
> And throws himself upon her.

The gods do not intervene, of course, because we are dealing in this poem with forces far more powerful than remote deities: we are dealing with the forces inside the girl's own body. Freud could hardly have stressed the potency of the libido more clearly. Here, however, Rochester takes the scene comically to illustrate the absurdity of the one event in human experience to which he usually attributes value. And just as the girl's natural fear of sexuality is well expressed in these images of dirt and violence, so the natural pleasures of submitting to these forces, the pleasure which animals and pre-lapsarian man enjoyed without fear, and without noticing the dirt, are expressed in romantic details that counterpoise the fear. The setting after all, is pastoral; Chloris and her dream lover are nymph and swain, she is 'fair Chloris', with 'snowy arms' filling her 'ivory pails', the love shoots from 'her brighter eyes' and the cave where the pig is hung up and she is raped is Flora's cave. It might be worth moving from the intentionally ridiculous to the sublime that Rochester is parodying by noticing that Flora is the goddess of the spring who, in Botticelli's *Primavera*, appears triumphantly bedecked in flowers which issue from the mouth of the earth nymph Chloris as she is 'inspired' by Zephyrus, the spirit of love in the world. A source of both painting and poem is the description of the rape of Chloris by Zephyrus on her transformation into Flora, in book five of Ovid's *Fasti* (II 195 f). We are dealing in this poem with something more than the simple comic inversion of a pastoral lyric. Behind the poem is the myth of the ambivalence of human sexuality. To Rochester the ambiguity of our attitudes is funny: he faces up to the impossibility of reconciling the two aspects of sexuality except in laughter. The ambiguity is finely presented in the last line: 'She's innocent and pleased'. Ironically, her unconscious has done what her conscious could not: reconciled her sense of guilt with her sense of enjoyment.

In the poems discussed so far Rochester as poet is standing outside the events of the poem even when, as in *The Disabled Debauchee*, the hero of the poem seems to have some resemblance to his creator. But human sexuality was not simply a dilemma for other people as far as Rochester was concerned, it was the central paradox of the human condition. As a sceptic of absolute values Rochester tended to look on sexual experience as one of the few meaningful experiences in life. Like some modern existentialists, he saw sexual fulfilment as one of the few ways man could create meaning in an essentially meaningless world. Sexual enjoyment, in enriching and transforming the moment, gave the illusion of permanence in an impermanent world. In a few of his non-comic lyrics he expresses this idea directly:

> All my past life is mine no more;
> The flying hours are gone,
> Like transitory dreams given o'er
> Whose images are kept in store
>   By memory alone.

> Whatever is to come is not:
> How can it then be mine?
> The present moment's all my lot,
> And that, as fast as it is got,
>   Phyllis, is wholly thine.

This poem is on the well-worn *carpe diem* theme so beloved by seventeenth-century poets; as usual Rochester is writing within a conventional framework. But his treatment of the theme is markedly different from other poets. When Anglicans like Donne, Herrick or Marvell implore their mistresses to gather rosebuds while they may, we sense that they are playing a game. In *To his Coy Mistress* the game may arouse considerable passion and, like Rochester's poem, may stress the meta-physical implication of the 'desert of vast Eternity' that awaits the lovers in death, as much as the lover's attempt at seduction. But Marvell's use of language is characterised by a verbal ingenuity, a cleverness, that allows him to employ such witty quibbles as the sexual puns on 'worms' (27) and 'honour'. Rochester's poem uses witty argument in the so-called 'meta-physical' (i.e. late Petrarchist) manner, but the language is, characteristically, more concerned with meaning than method. The poem is not only clever, we are persuaded it might be true; that it is not just a clever way of pretending to get the girl into bed or of surprising the reader, but a statement of a meta-physical reality. *To his Coy Mistress*, for all its profound sugges-tions of the ruthlessness of time, ends by convincing us that we are admiring a clever poet rather than confronting a solemn truth. Rochester's poem is not as skilfully written as Marvell's and the effect is to that extent weaker, but the opening two stanzas, especially, present us much more starkly with a view of metaphysical emptiness than any other *carpe diem* poem of the century. Perhaps the contrast with Marvell's fine poem is not clear-cut. The point becomes clearer if we contrast it with the work of a lesser poet, John Cleveland, whose poem *To Julia* is on the same theme:

> Now since you bear a Date so short
>   Live double for't
> How can thy Fortresse ever stand
>   If't be not man'd?
> The Seige so gaines upon the Place,
> Thou'lt find the Trenches in thy Face.
> Pitty thy self then, if not me,
> And hold not out, least (Like Ostend) thou be
> Nothing but Rubbish at Deliverie.

This is play poetry with a vengeance.

But just because sexuality was so important to Rochester its paradoxical nature was not something that could be left un-related to his own experience. In *The Ramble in St. James's Park* and *The Imperfect Enjoyment* he writes comic poems about the discrepancy between sexual desire and sexual reward, not from a detached point of view, but as it affects him directly. In these poems the source of the comic is different. It comes not so much from the exploration of the paradox that human sexuality is an irreconcilable conflict between the animal and the spiritual in our natures, but from the clash between the poet's involvement in the situations he describes and his need, as poet, to remain outside them. There is an incongruous view of the poet as both fool and guide. For *The Ramble* he adopts, not the formal stanzas of the lyric poems, but the disorderly form of Hudibrastic verse, and both poems contain burlesque elements. He is no longer detaching himself to analyse and state the paradox of human sexuality; he is part of the paradoxical world he describes. In both poems he is himself the clown hero, presenting his own humiliation as a sacrifice to the comic god. It is interesting that in these early attempts to reconcile his desire for self-expression with his comic vision of the absurdity of things he resorts to burlesque. For, as we have seen, burlesque shows a confusion of attitudes in which the poet mixes praise and blame indiscriminately. This is most noticeable in *The Imperfect Enjoyment* where, although the subject is the poet's own sexual humiliation, the result is not the self-satire we should expect. Nor on the other hand can it be described simply as a celebratory poem. There are two reasons for this lack of clear direction: firstly Rochester adopts a mock-heroic style which gives the poet-hero the ambiguous status usual to the mode; secondly a good deal of the blame for the poet's humiliation is transferred from the poet to the part of his anatomy that has caused all the trouble. The humiliation, therefore, is taken rather light-heartedly. The poet turns on his offending instrument at the end of the poem to give it a curse as elaborate as that given by Polyaenus on a similar occasion in the *Satyricon*:

> Thou treacherous, base deserter of my flame,
> False to my passion, fatal to my fame,
> Through what mistaken magic dost thou prove
> So true to lewdness, so untrue to love?
> What oyster-cinder-beggar-common whore
> Didst thou e'er fail in all thy life before?
> When vice, disease and scandal lead the way,
> With what officious haste dost thou obey!

> Like a rude, roaring hector in the streets,
> Who scuffles, cuffs and justles all he meets,
> But if his King or country claim his aid,
> The rakehell villain shrinks and hides his head;
> Ev'n so thy brutal valour is displayed,
> Breaks every stew, does each small whore invade,
> But when great Love the onset does command,
> Base recreant to thy prince, thou dar'st not stand.

In *The Ramble* Rochester also acts the part of the poet clown. But whereas the 'Rochester' of *The Imperfect Enjoyment* survives his humiliation and rounds on his tormentor like a Chaplinesque hero, *The Ramble* is more self-humiliating, in spite of a vehement curse addressed to the offending lady. The difference between the two poems is largely dictated by the verse form. In *The Imperfect Enjoyment* a well-groomed heroic couplet creates the ambiguities of mock-heroic and by its use the poet asserts a strict control; *The Ramble* makes what, for Rochester, is a rare use of the Hudibrastic line – though Rochester used the octosyllabic for the less personal burlesque, *Signior Dildo*. John Dennis suggests Butler was the model for some of Rochester's verse.[24] Like Butler's hero, Hudibras, the 'Rochester' of *The Ramble* is subjected to the humiliation of acting as hero in a shapeless world, the mere association with which is degrading. This is burlesque poetry, where satirical attack is not accompanied by any implied assertion of standards. Our response to the hero is a confused one: he is both humiliated and the centre of the poem's vitality. Rochester's scepticism here has become not simply a mode of contemplation but has undermined belief in the contemplation itself. Both poems have the same subject, the sexual humiliation of the hero and, when we consider the over-riding importance of sexual virility in Rochester's poetry, this humiliation becomes more than a temporary deflation. But in *The Imperfect Enjoyment* the hero overcomes his defeat. In *The Ramble* he is rejected by his Corinna who turns her attention instead on three fops whom the hero despises. Etherege subjects Dorimant to a similar humiliation in *Man of Mode* when Loveit lavishes her attentions on Sir Fopling Flutter: Dorimant, according to John Dennis, was modelled on Rochester. In both these poems the poet plays the role of clown, symbolising the absurdity of the society he serves. We have already seen the importance of this role for the poet in the Commonwealth anthologies, especially in those containing the work of Sir John Mennis and James Smith. Sir William Temple is still complaining in his dignified way, as late as the 1690s, that it is fashionable for gentlemen poets, who should know better, to adopt the role of the traditional fool:

> Another vein which has entered and helped to corrupt our modern poetry is that of ridicule; as if nothing pleased but what made one laugh . . . This was encouraged by finding conversation run so much in to the same vein and the wits in vogue to take up with that part of it which was formerly left to those that were called fools and were used in great families only to make the company laugh.[25]

The tendency to self-mockery is very strong in Rochester, especially in the earlier work. Occasionally the mockery turns into fierce self-satire, suggesting, as Burnet remarks, that he did not always regard behavioural standards as purely relative: 'So that in detestation of these courses [his debaucheries] he would often break forth into such hard expressions concerning himself as would be indecent for another to repeat'.[26] The most extraordinary example of such an outburst of self-satire are the lines *To the Postboy*:

Rochester: Son of a whore, God damn you! can you tell
               A peerless peer the readiest way to Hell?
               I've outswilled Bacchus, sworn of my own make
               Oaths would fright Furies, and make Pluto
                                               quake;
               I've swived more whores more ways than
                                               Sodom's walls
               E'er knew, or the College of Rome's Cardinals,
               Witness heroic scars – Look here, n'er go! –
               Cerecloths and ulcers from the top to toe! –
               Frighted at my own mischiefs, I have fled
               And bravely left my life's defender dead;
               Broke houses to break chastity and dyed
               That floor with murder which my lust denied.

> Pox on't, why do I speak of these poor things?
> I have blasphemed my God, and libeled Kings?
> The readiest way to Hell – Come, quick!

Boy: Ne'er stir.
        The readiest way, my Lord's by Rochester.

Even this poem, however, with its apparent autobiographical reference to the notorious Downs affair, in which Rochester and Etherege fled from an affray leaving their companion, Downs, to be murdered by the night watch, has a certain amount of comic distancing. The dramatic mode argues at least as much histrionic vaunting of his satanic talents as penitence. The suggestion is that Rochester here might be playing yet another part. There is also an element of literary parody, for the opening lines seem deliberately to echo the opening of a witty love poem by Suckling (with whose poetry Rochester was very familiar) called *Upon two Sisters*:

> Believe't young man, I can as easily tell
> How many yards and inches 'tis to hell.

Restoration literature remains bookish even when it appears impromptu.

Increasingly after the two burlesque poems Rochester's relation to his comic heroes becomes a good deal more oblique. In most of his satire proper he uses a *persona* which enables him to present feeling directly, but also to contemplate and analyse it. The 'Mulgrave' poems, *The Very Heroical Epistle to Answer to Ephelia*, *My Lord All-Pride* and *The Epistle of M.G. to O.B.*, are conceived, like *The Disabled Debauchee*, as mock-heroic. Here, however, the *persona*, 'Mulgrave', is more obviously denigrated and the result is less ambiguous, more satirical comedy. The mock heroic language and the mock serious tone set up expectations which the hero clearly cannot fulfil and the effect is closer to that obtained by Dryden in *Mac Flecknoe*. Rochester's irony, however, is subtler because, unlike Dryden, he does not associate the comic with the negative, with what has to be repudiated, but as always sees it as an inevitable condition of life. 'Mulgrave' is allowed to dominate his poems much more than Shadwell or Flecknoe dominate theirs. Both *The Heroical Epistle* and *M.G. to O.B.* are dramatic monologues, in which everything is seen from 'Mulgrave's' point of view. The exception to this is *My Lord All-Pride*, a lampoon, where the intense satirical tone precludes comic ambiguity. The ambiguity of the other two poems, however, is shown in the general assumption until very recently that they were autobiographical. Pinto, for instance, quotes *The Very Heroical Epistle* (1–36) to demonstrate Rochester's 'complete egotism'.[27] It was David Vieth who in his *Attribution in Restoration Poetry* first showed conclusively that these poems were dramatic monologues spoken by the *persona* 'Mulgrave'. Pinto's mistake, however, is understandable. The aggressively male selfishness with which 'Mulgrave' approaches love in *The Very Heroical Epistle* is not so different from attitudes found in such lyrics as *Against Constancy*,[28] though this, of course, is a conventional exercise and need not be taken to represent Rochester's own viewpoint. *The Very Heroical Epistle* is funny just because we are not entirely sure whether we are to accept or reject 'Mulgrave's' egotism. There is something genuinely grandiose, almost splendid, in the sheer outrageousness of his utterance:

> You may as justly at the sun repine
> Because alike it does not always shine.
> No glorious thing was ever made to stay:
> My blazing star but visits and away:
> As fatal, too, it shines as those i' th' skies:
> 'Tis never seen but some great lady dies.
> The boasted favor you so precious hold
> To me's no more than changing of my gold.

The imagery here is the baroque imagery of kingship and, although it gets added absurdity in referring to a subject not a king, we cannot help feeling it is either similarly absurd or similarly acceptable as the inflated imagery of baroque panegyric. Here again then, we have two opposed but equally valid viewpoints: the aggressive virtues of male sexual arrogance and the rational awareness of the strict social limitations within which male sexuality must be confined. Underlying the comedy are the incompatibilities of sexual fertility and of sexual taboo and limitations. 'Mulgrave', in the second half of the poem, soars into fantasy as he dreams of the happy Sultan he would like to be:

> Methinks I see thee underneath the shade
> Of golden canopies supinely laid,
> Thy crouching slaves all silent as the night,
> But, at thy nod all active as the light . . .
> Each female courts thee with a wishing eye
> Whilst thou with awful pride walk'st careless by.

This sexual fantasy highlights the actual inadequacies of the comic hero, but it is also heroic aspiration to which few male readers in their prime will fail altogether to respond. It is only because the fantasy gets completely out of hand that we come eventually to accept the deflation rather than the heroism. And how well Rochester handles his medium to create this satirical effect! The first half of the poem has the rough energy that seems to reinforce the masculine aggressiveness; it is only with the more sensuous language of the harem passage that we feel things have definitely gone too far to be entirely serious, even for our fantasies.

In *The Epistle of M.G. to O.B.* once again the incongruity arises from the clash between formal decorum and the indecorousness of the comic hero. The poem suffers, however, from a certain inconsistency in the presentation of 'Mulgrave' which results in unjustified changes in the level of the comedy. At times he is presented as a wit not easily distinguishable from the author:

> In wit alone 't [Providence] has been munificent
> Of which so just a share to each is sent
> That the most avaricious is content:
> Who ever thought – the due divisions such –
> His own too little or his friend's too much?

Vieth compares this passage to a passage from Descartes's *Discourse on Method* and the comparison suggests the extent the knowledgeable author is intruding into the personality of his satirical butt. At other times 'Mulgrave' is presented, as in *The Very Heroical Epistle*, as the boaster. Here, however the effect is less pleasing, more crudely satirical:

> But I who am of sprightly vigour full,
> Look on mankind as envious and dull.
> Born to myself, myself I like alone
> And must conclude my judgement good or none.

Another equally distasteful side of Mulgrave's personality is his predilection for expressing himself in scatological imagery. The total effect is to make 'Mulgrave' in this poem both inconsistent and repellent and the comic duality achieved in *The Heroical Epistle* is largely lost.

The satire of *The Heroical Epistle* and the balanced, sceptical comedy of *The Disabled Debauchee*, *The Fall* and *Fair Chloris in a Pigsty Lay* turn particular examples into statements of a general dilemma. In the great satire of 1674–5 Rochester broadens his themes to consider the human comedy on a larger scale.

7 Rochester:
The Major Satires

In the major satires Rochester solves the problem of reconciling formal decorum and passionate individualism by adopting a dramatic form that allows him to present feelings directly, but to place them in a critical medium. The satires are both a passionate expression of anger against man's ineptitude and ultimately a triumph of Augustan order over individualism. Like Hobbes, who was a major influence on Rochester's thought, and like Swift after him, Rochester comes to assume in the satires that there is a possibility, through the exercise of reason and common sense, of mitigating the consequences of the fall. The comedy therefore changes from the burlesque that Rochester favours in his earlier comic poetry, to a satirical comedy in which the foolish creature man as he is in actuality is measured against the less foolish creature he might be and occasionally is. The distance between the two views in the various satires is a measure of the comedy. In *Timon* and *Tunbridge Wells* the satirical targets are social; these are satires of manners in which the victims are judged by the standards of the libertine 'honnête homme', the man of sense, who judges from a naturalistic standpoint. In the *Satyr against Mankind* and the *Epistle from Artemisia in the Town to Chloe in the Country* the satirical target is mankind in general and in spite of the *Satyr's* satiric intensity, the viewpoint in both poems is more sceptical, more ironic. In *Artemisia* in particular we feel, to use Vieth's image, we are in a hall of mirrors, in which it is difficult to distinguish the real from its reflections. Rochester seems to be adopting an attitude described by St Evremond in his treatise *On the Morality of Epicurus* (1685):

Every object has different faces, and the mind, which is in continual movement sees them differently according to how it revolves; so, to speak truly, when we think we are gaining new knowledge we are merely seeing things from a different angle.[1]

Such scepticism was very much in the air in Restoration England. Another French visitor to England, François Bernier, a friend of Boileau, writes in a letter of 1682:

I have been philosophising, firmly convinced of certain things and lo! now I begin to doubt them! It is too bad: there is only one of them of which I have no doubt at all and that is despair of ever being able to understand anything.[2]

Similar sentiments are expressed in a letter sent to Rochester in the year of his death by his friend Charles Blount: 'all philosophy excepting scepticism is little more than doting'. Although there is no assertion of absolute standards in *Artemisia* there are preferences, and Rochester depicts a hierarchy of values, none of which have any ultimate sanction. In each of the great satires Rochester widens and deepens the personal themes of man's depravity of the Mulgrave poems, the *Imperfect Enjoyment* and *The Ramble*. Mankind itself becomes the subject.

Rochester's four major satires *Timon*, *Tunbridge Wells*, *The Satyr Against Mankind* and *Artemisia to Chloe* were written probably in that order between the spring of 1674 and the summer of 1675. Like most of the poems we have been looking at in the last chapter they are comic poems, but now Rochester finds a relationship between comic detachment and assertion which gives the comedy a consistent satirical direction. The standards that are asserted are tentative, relative; better than what is repudiated but having no ultimate sanction in a coherent world order. The world of the satires is still that described in *Upon Nothing*:

Matter, the wicked'st off-spring of thy [Nothing's] race,
By Form assisted, flew from they embrace,
And rebel Light obscured thy reverend dusky face.

With Form and Matter, Time and Place did join;
Body, thy foe, with these did leagues combine
To spoil thy peaceful realm, and ruin all thy line:

But turn-coat Time assists the foe in vain,
And, bribed by thee, destroys their short-lived reign,
And to thy hungry womb drives back thy slaves again.

The process we watch in the satire is of man's slide back towards
meaninglessness from a precarious state of coherence that is
never fully in his grasp. Each poem is a triumph over the
threatening chaos by means of laughter, a transient defeat of
nothingness which momentarily stems the reduction of everything to futility. *Artemisia* is the finest expression of this process.

Timon and *Tunbridge Wells* are rather more limited in scope.
They are both the kind of social comedy recommended by
Rochester's friend St Evremond in his address to the Marshall de
Crequi (1671):

Poetry requires a peculiar genius that agrees not over-much
with good sense. It is sometimes the language of gods,
sometimes of Buffoons rarely that of a civil man . . . Comic
poets are of all most proper for the converse of the world;
For they oblige themselves to paint naturally what passes
in it, and to express after a lively manner the thoughts and
passions of men.[3]

Timon is not merely a record of events, however, for like much
of Rochester's poetry, it borrows freely from literary models.
The poem is a close imitation of Boileau's third satire, which
itself takes its inspiration from the eighth satire of Horace's
second book of satires and the tenth satire of the earlier seventeenth-century poet Mathurin Regnier (1573–1613). Each of
these poems tells how the protagonist is invited out to dinner
and makes fun of his ridiculous host; but whereas Horace's
Fundanius mocks his host's absurd preoccupation with gastro-
nomic niceties, Boileau to some extent and Rochester completely
reverse this and satirise the grossness of the food and the conversation. The literary origin of *Timon* is important because the
model provides the conventions that enable Rochester partly to
objectify and distance the anger of his spokesman, Timon.
Rochester never entirely excludes a personal commitment in his
satire. It is one reason for the great intensity of his poetry: 'A
man could not write with life unless he were heated by Revenge'.[4]

Certainly Rochester's poem is angrier than Boileau's and there is a greater emphasis on the unpleasantness of Timon's host and his guests and less on their sheer absurdity. But this emphatic tone can again be explained as well in terms of literary tradition.

Contemporary manuscripts and the earliest printed text, the 1680 *Poems on Several Occasions*, head both *Timon* and the *Satire against Mankind* with the title 'Satyr'. This is the normal spelling in the period for our word 'satire', and suggests, and was intended to suggest, the supposed connection of the word with the Greek satyrs, the rough wood daemons, who were reputedly the fathers of the satiric genres. The Elizabethans believed in this uncouth origin of satire, as can be seen from Thomas Drant's introduction to his translation of Horace in 1566:

> A satyre is a tarte and carpyng kynd of verse,
> An instrument to pynch the pranks of men,
> And for as much as pynchyng instruments do perse,
> Yclept it was full well a Satyre then.
> A name of Arabique to it they gave:
> For Satyre there, doothe signifie a glave.
>
> Or Satyra, of Satyrus, the mossye rude,
> Uncivile god: for those that wyll them write
> With taunting gyrds and glikes and gibes must vexe the lewde,
> Strayne curtesy: ne reck of mortall spyte.
> Shrouded in Mosse, not shrynkying for a shower
> Deemyng of mosse as of a regall bower.
>
> Satyre of writhled waspyshe Saturne may be namde
> The Satyrist must be a waspe in moode,
> Testie and wrothe with vice and errs to see both blamde
> But courteous and frendly to the good.[5]

Donne observed this convention that satire must be harsh and uncouth, as did all the Elizabethan formal satirists:

> I sing not, siren like, to tempt, for I
> Am harsh,[6]

Dryden was the first to popularise the notion,[7] which he had obtained from the French scholar Isaac Casaubon, that the derivation of 'satire' from 'Satyr' was false. He puts forward this view in his *Original and Progress of Satire* (1693), though earlier writers like Thomas Langley in his translation of Polydore Virgil in 1546,[8] and clearly Ben Jonson, had been aware of an alternative tradition of a lighter, more comic satire. That the older tradition of the lacerating satirist was still very much current during the Restoration is clear from Dryden's lines *To the Memory of Mr. Oldham* in which Oldham's rugged verse is excused because 'Satyr needs not' smooth versification. As late as 1700 Samuel Cobb praises Oldham for adopting a style: 'Like satyrs, rough, but not deform'd as they'[9] while an anonymous author, a year later, regards it as manifestly absurd to have:

> Epic, Burlesque and Satyr seen
> Dancing i' the same Heroic mein[10]

and says polished verse is inappropriate for satire. That Rochester is consciously identifying himself with the scourging satirist tradition seems certain from his calling his satiric persona 'Timon', which recalls one of Shakespeare's most outspoken characters. Vieth suggests that Rochester might have either the original Timon of Athens in mind or Timon of Phlius, a Greek satirical poet, but it seems more likely to suppose that Rochester was thinking of Shakespeare's Timon, especially in view of his reference to Shakespeare in the *Allusion to Horace* as a master of comic satire (28–31). The mid-1670s saw a notable revival in interest in Shakespeare, evidenced clearly in Dryden's tribute to Shakespeare's 'sacred name' in the prologue of *Aureng-Zebe* (1676). Boileau's satirical spokesman is simply given the initial 'P'. The French were obviously familiar with the harsh satirist tradition, which was first formulated by continental humanists like Polydore Virgil, for Boileau's spokesman does not pull his punches and is noticeably tougher than his counterpart in Horace. Molière uses the satirical railer, too, in the character of Alceste in *Le Misanthrope*, just as Elizabethan dramatists had adopted the railing satirist for the stage. Wycherley had adapted Molière's play

for the Restoration stage in *The Plain Dealer*, again increasing
the savagery of the satire by recourse to the long-standing
English tradition.

In both *Timon* and *Tunbridge Wells*, as with Wycherley's
character Manly, we are to understand the satiric persona not
as a simple representative of the poet's viewpoint, but as a
dramatic character deliberately chosen as an appropriate
device for the satirical job in hand. The dramatic nature of
Timon is further emphasised by adopting from Horace and
Boileau a listener, interlocutor or 'adversarius' to open the
poem, which is thus given dialogue form.[11] Rochester's adversarius however is soon forgotten and the poem is largely
dramatic monologue. By tradition the satirical railler was
coarse and outspoken, not necessarily correct in his assessment
of a situation that none the less clearly justified complaint. In
both poems Rochester adopts the pose described very vividly
by the Elizabethan satirist Everard Guilpin in the conclusion
to his Epigrams:

> Viewing this sin-drown'd world, I purposely,
> Phisick'd my Muse, that thus unmannerly
> She might beray our folly-soyled age,
> And keep Decorum on a comick stage,
> Bringing a foule-mouth Jester who might sing
> To rogues . . .[12]

The use of this dramatic device implies that the poet himself
adopts not only a satiric attitude towards the people and events
described but also adopts an ironic attitude towards the satiric
agent. This implication is never fully realised in Elizabethan
formal satire. The sequence of Rochester's major satires shows
Rochester increasingly aware of the full ironic possibilities of
the arrangement. In *Timon* he is closest to his satiric mouth-
piece. Timon, for instance, shares his creator's fondness for
debauchery (2) and the attitudes expressed are seemingly
shared by poet and persona. It is not until *Artemisia* that he
develops the irony to the full. *Artemisia* is thus a more detachedly
comic poem, because no attitude is presented as unequivocally
correct and the alternative viewpoints are more nicely balanced.
Timon is the most satirical in tone because Rochester is closely

identified with the angry tone of Timon and this allows less
room for the juxtaposition of the alternative viewpoints that
pure comedy requires. Timon's scorn, like that of the Elizabethan satirist, sometimes comes near to obliterating what is
scorned. Whereas Boileau plays up the comedy by making his
satirical spokesman, like Horace's Fundanius, a genuine
gourmet, and the comedy comes from his thwarted expectation,
Rochester is more concerned with the contrast in attitudes
between Timon on the one hand, and the host and his other
guests on the other. Timon's superiority is more unequivocal.
He represents not simply a frustrated *bon viveur* like Boileau's
'P', but the libertine 'Honest' man, the man of 'natural' tastes
and standards, deploring the absurd artifices and the vulgar
affectations of the others. Characteristically his comments on the
absurdity make use of the 'anti-platonic' sex imagery which is
the inevitable reflection of his naturalistic viewpoint. Un-
prompted by Boileau, whose sense of decorum does not allow
such usages, the carrots at the feasts are as long as a countess's
'dildo', the table is so large the diners have as much room to
move as her lovers had in Lady Cullen's cunt. Timon's attitudes
are comic, but he is not like Boileau's spokesman part of the
absurd world he ridicules. Boileau's 'P' is himself ridiculous.
For instance, he makes an absurd fuss about not being able to
get ice in the height of summer:

> All the time I was hoping to sweeten the effect of the poison-
> ous wine by mixing large quantities of water with it. But
> who would have expected it? To crown the misfortune of its
> being so hot, there was not a scrap of ice. Good God, no ice!
> At the height Of summer! In the month of June! As for me,
> I was so beside myself that vehemently wishing the whole
> meal to the Devil, I was twenty times on the point of leaving
> the table![13]

Rochester reduces the affair of the ice to a passing reference of
half a line:

> And now the bottle briskly flies about,
> Instead of ice, wrapped up in a wet clout.

Timon is concerned with the coarseness of the proceedings, the
absurdity of the host's wife, who has no equivalent in Boileau's

satire, the absurdity of manners and conversation. In this way
the comedy is thrown less equivocally from the satirical agent
to the people satirised.

There is in fact plenty of comedy in *Timon* stemming from
the inherent absurdity of the world Timon describes. The
'anti-platonic' assumptions of Timon mean that the railing
satirist's view of the world in general is a comic one, and because
he is not merely a figure of fun we take this comic view seriously.
In this way Rochester manages to broaden the comic implications of his poem beyond the local comedy, of Horace and
Boileau, to the suggestion that after all these absurd creatures,
the host and his friends, are merely extreme examples of that
absurd creature man – a theme to be developed further in
Tunbridge Wells and most comprehensively of all, in the *Satyr
Against Mankind*. The host's wife, therefore, is not simply a
particular case of a contrast between outward protestation and
inward desire (58–63):

> My Lady wondered much how heaven could bless
> A man that loved two women at one time,
> But more how he to them excused his crime,
> She asked Huff if love's flame he never felt;
> He answered bluntly, 'Do you think I'm gelt?'
> She at his plainness smiled, then turned to me . . .

The lady's hypocrisy is apparent and the contrast between her
affected delicacy and Huff's coarseness provides a nice juxtaposition of pretentiousness with actual vulgarity. But the
'naturalistic' attitude of Timon towards woman's sexuality
provides a gloss on the hostess; like the Countess of Northumber-
land hiding her dildo under her pillow she is merely revealing
the equivocation of women in general towards sex and the satire
on the hostess becomes, therefore, a metaphor for the absurd
duplicity of women in sexual matters. In this instance Rochester
enriches and widens the scope of the satire into a sardonic
review of the way of the world in general. Where he is least
dependent on Boileau, in the hostess passages for instance,
it is noticeable that his satire bites deeper, whereas the literary
discussion and the custard pie ending to the feast are, though
equally well handled in both poets, of less serious import.

Boileau's feeling for the comic compared to Rochester's is circumscribed by his respect for order and the belief in an orderly world.

In *Tunbridge Wells* Rochester uses similar techniques for a similar purpose and the two poems, as Vieth suggests, are very much of a pair. However, there are some interesting changes, which both increase the irony and broaden the comic implications to embrace mankind in general more obviously and more completely. Again Rochester uses the dramatic persona of the railing satirist, but now makes his role rather more obviously comic. The opening for instance is couched in mock heroic terms, which contrast with the plain-spoken directness of the opening of *Timon*:

> At five this morn, when Phoebus raised his head
> From Thetis' lap, I raised myself from bed
> And mounting steed, I trotted to the waters,
> The rendezvous of fools, buffoons, and praters,
> Cuckolds, whores, citizens, their wives and daughters.

This is a burlesque opening which might be compared with the excerpt of Cotton's burlesque *Journey to Ireland* quoted in an earlier chapter. It at once suggests we are dealing with the poet in his role of clown, and this impression is strengthened in the next lines where we find the satirical persona going to take his medicine for a 'squeamish stomach'. Clearly we are not to be entertained with a balanced view of the proceedings at the wells. The satirist is 'physicking' himself not like Guilpin, to prepare himself to describe a corrupt world, but to calm a disturbed indigestion. Before he can drink the waters some of the other invalids appear and he begins to 'purge and spew' at the sight of them without needing any emetic. The shift in the satirist's position compared to Guilpin is important, for Guilpin suggests a deliberately controlled distortion, Rochester is creating a satiric character who is already partly out of control. There is a level of irony and comedy towards the satirical agent that is not apparent in the work of the Elizabethan satirist or in Rochester's earlier work. The irony is further reinforced when we remember that the waters of Tunbridge Wells are famous above all for curing the 'spleen', that is, bad temper. Thomas Fuller tells us in his *Worthies of England* (1661): 'Surely it runneth through some iron-mine, because so good for splenetic distempers'.[14]

Tunbridge Wells sets out to describe in satirical terms the stream of visitors that arrive to take the waters. It is much more loosely structured than the other major satires, being essentially a string of satirical portraits linked together by the comments of the satirical spokesman, who is seen rushing about in a frenzy of distaste with what he sees. The first visitor is a bawling fop whom the satirist avoids by slinking away, only to be confronted with a solemn fop, the Master of Ceremonies, who is equally absurd:

> I silently slunk down t'th' Lower Walk.
> But often when one would Charybdis shun
> Down upon Scylla 'tis one's fate to run,
> For here it was my cursed luck to find
> As great a fop.

Again the classical allusion suggests mock heroic and the Tom and Jerry game the satirist plays, slinking about, then rushing away – 'hence to the upper end I run' – only to be presented with yet another absurd group, makes us feel the satirist is almost as zany as the people he meets. He seems to combine the intelligence and idiocy of a Groucho Marx. Here it is not just the people seen but the person seeing who is infected with the general absurdity. We are in a world where absurdity is the norm and the standards being applied are being imposed by the poet from outside the world of the poem. The abandonment of an 'adversarius' in the poem, who might help to provide an element of sanity, contributes to the feeling of uncertainty. Here Rochester is beginning to develop the full ironic potential of the railing satirist technique, and the result is both a lighter comedy and yet a comedy that has a more wide-ranging seriousness.

Some of the vignettes are delightfully comic:

> Here waiting for gallant, young damsel stood,
> Leaning on cane, and muffled up in hood.
> The would-be wit, whose business was to woo,
> With hat removed and solemn scrape of shoe

Advanceth bowing, then genteely shrugs,
And ruffled foretop into order tugs,
And thus accosts her: 'Madam, methinks the weather
Is grown much more serene since you came hither.
You influence the heavens; but should the sun
Withdraw himself to see his rays outdone
By your bright eyes, they would supply the morn,
And make a day before the day be born.'
With mouth screwed up, conceited winking eyes,
And breasts thrust forward, 'Lord, sir!' she replies
'It is your goodness, and not my deserts,
Which makes you show this learning, wit, and parts.'
He, puzzled, bites his nail, both to display
The sparkling ring, and think what next to say,
And thus breaks forth afresh: 'Madam, egad!
Your luck at cards last night was very bad:
At cribbage fifty-nine, and the next show
To make the game, and yet to want those two.
God damn me, madam I'm the son of a whore
If in my life I saw the like before!'

The inanity of the conversation, the rushing about from group
to group, the representative nature of the groups, including as
they do, fop and clergy, the fashionable gallant, the mother who
has come to cure her daughter of headaches and her companion
who is hoping to cure her barrenness by taking the water, all
suggest a world of affectation where everything is in flux and
half-formed and nothing of any importance happens. It is
worth contrasting Rochester's dynamic, dramatic use of the
satiric portrait with Marvell's static emblematic portraiture,
the one emphasising instability and change, the other still
seeing the world in terms of immutable values. The looseness
of the structural device is an important contribution to the
feeling of formlessness, though the satirist's cynical comment on
the women at least provides a naturalistic standard of judgement. The best way of curing their complaints he suggests, is to
take advantage of the virility of some of the men who hang
about to serve the willing:

And ten to one but they themselves will try
The same means to increase their family.

is clearly some identification between poet and satiric persona, in *Tunbridge Wells* there is also a rather greater element of detachment. It is true that both the *Timon* and the *Tunbridge Wells* commentator detach themselves at the end from the absurdity; the latter riding off on the horse he finds superior to himself. Yet the poem itself, more than *Timon*, asks us to contemplate the absurdity, to rise above it in the contemplative act of laughter. We are less closely associated with the action of the poem here. The commentator himself is merely an observer of the events and not a participator in them like Timon, and the light humour with which some of the exhibits are treated suggests a detachment even further removed from them than the hysterical satirist's detachment. The more controlled verse form of *Tunbridge Wells* supports this feeling. We find here, then, the kind of layering of comic perspectives that is exploited most subtly in *Artemisia* and which suggest a hierarchy of comic values with the poet himself the least absurd participant in a crazy world. Most absurd of all is the comic world of everyday described in the poem. Above that is the 'honest' satirical commentator superior to the others, in that he sees this absurdity, but having nothing to offer but derision. Above that still, the poet himself, sharing qualities with the satiric persona, but also suggesting that man can, after all, be a creature capable of reason and capable of detachment, even if not a rational animal. The satire is based on the juxtaposition of relative values, in which the poet himself expresses the vanity of the world from a point of view of comparative sanity.

At first sight the technique of the *Satyr against Mankind* would suggest a closer involvement by the poet with his satirical persona than in the two poems already discussed, and the poem has generally been regarded as the fiercest and most personal, as well as the best, of Rochester's satires. There is no obvious use, here, of a satirical persona that can easily be distinguished from the poet. Yet the poem is not the savage personal denunciation of man it is often taken to be, but a comic poem in which comic detachment is obtained by a method that is used in *The Fall* and *Upon Nothing* and favoured by late 'metaphysical' writers like Marvell and Cleveland. The method is that of Swift and Shaw: to drive logic to absurd conclusions. But Rochester uses it not so much to show the inadequacy of logic as to show the absurdity of the situation revealed by this logic.

The theme of the poem is closely related to that of *The Fall*. It expresses the same paradox in a three-stage argument. In the first part of the poem Rochester argues that man above all the animals suffers from a fatal capacity for speculative reasoning. As in *The Fall*, man has lost the art of being natural and projects himself into an abstract world of ideas which he can only live by in defiance of his animal nature. This part of the poem then (1–122) depicts the consequences of the fall of man from the innocent state of nature, taking up the theme of the superiority of the animals that had been suggested in the conclusion of *Tunbridge Wells*. The cure for this fall from nature, argues Rochester at this stage of his thesis, is a right use of reason, or as he calls it, the use of 'right reason' (99) as opposed to speculative reason (96–109):

> Our sphere of action is life's happiness,
> And he who thinks beyond, thinks like an ass.
> Thus, whilst against false reasoning I inveigh,
> I own right reason, which I would obey:
> That reason which distinguishes by sense
> And gives us rules of good and ill from thence,
> That bounds desires with a reforming will
> To keep 'em more in vigor, not to kill.
> Your reason hinders, mine helps to enjoy,
> Renewing appetites yours would destroy.
> My reason is my friend, yours is a cheat
> Hunger calls out, my reason bids me eat;
> Perversely, yours your appetite does mock;
> This asks for food, that answers, 'What's o'clock?'

Rightly used, reason should be an aid to our natural desires not a means for projecting an abstract world and living a life, as Rousseau calls it, 'exterior to our natures'.[15] Less naively than Rousseau, however, and with the dialectical subtlety of William Blake in the oppositions between innocence and experience, Rochester follows this argument in the second part of the poem to a new stage, to show that the heaven that right reason can build in hell's despair is in fact 'a hell in heaven's despite', as Blake puts it in *The Clod and the Pebble*. In the first section of the poem, though he makes use of Hobbesian ideas, Rochester expresses the hedonist doctrines of such epicurean thinkers as Gassendi and Jean François Sarasin.[16]

The second major section of the *Satyr* (123–73) takes the logic of the first part to its ultimate conclusion by demonstrating what kind of creature man is in his natural state; showing him to be by nature the most unnatural of the animals. The consequence of allowing our reason to mediate for our feelings is to let fear triumph, because fear is our dominating passion. We find, paradoxically, that we enter the hell of the Hobbesian natural state where man is in perpetual war with his neighbour and is spurred on by fear. For man's nature, unlike that of the other animals, is cruel, because he projects his fears into every situation. His main distinction from the other animals is that he anticipates trouble, and by anticipating it, causes it. What we fear is of course an abstraction, so, paradoxically, when we allow our true natures to express themselves, we get just the condition we are intending to avoid, a situation as in *The Fall* and *The Imperfect Enjoyment* where our abstracting habit – our 'hope and fear' – destroys our spontaneous responses. Rochester contrasts the healthy 'naturalism' of the animal world with the nightmare world of natural man, described by Hobbes as a world of 'continual fear and danger of violent death, and the life of man solitary, poor, nasty, brutish, and short' (*Leviathan* I xiii) (127–58):

> Be judge yourself, I'll bring it to the test:
> Which is the basest creature, man or beast?
> Birds feed on birds, beasts on each other prey,
> But savage man alone does man betray.
> Pressed by necessity, they kill for food,
> Man undoes man to do himself no good.
> With teeth and claws by nature armed, they hunt
> Nature's allowance, to supply their want.
> But man, with smiles, embraces, friendship, praise,
> Inhumanly his fellow's life betrays;
> With voluntary pains works his distress,
> Not through necessity, but wantonness.
> For hunger or for love they fight and tear,
> Whilst wretched man is still in arms for fear.

For fear he arms, and is of arms afraid,
By fear to fear successively betrayed;
Base fear, the source whence his best passions came;
His boasted honor and his dear-bought fame;
That lust of power, to which he's such a slave,
And for the which alone he dares be brave;
To which his various projects are designed;
Which makes him generous, affable and kind;
For which he takes such pains to be thought wise,
And screws his actions in a forced disguise,
Leading a tedious life in misery
Under laborious, mean hypocrisy.
Look to the bottom of his vast design,
Wherein man's wisdom, power, and glory join;
The good he acts, the ill he does endure,
'Tis all from fear to make himself secure.
Merely for safety after fame we thirst,
For all men would be cowards if they durst.

The contrast between man's troubled state and the freedom from anxiety of the animal kingdom is a commonplace of seventeenth-century thought. Hobbes himself in chapter 17 of the first part of *Leviathan* contrasts man, who is 'most troublesome when he is most at ease', with the unreflecting contentment of animals. And Montaigne, in the *Apology for Raimond de Sebonde*, makes a similar contrast to Rochester's between man's capacity for abstraction and the immediacy of animal responses:

And if it be so, that he only of all the Animals hath this priviledge of the Imagination, and irregularity of Thoughts representing to him that which is, that which is not, and that he would have, the False, and the True; 'tis an Advantage dearly bought, and of which he has very little reason to be Proud: seeing that from thence springs the principal and original Fountain of all the Evils that befal him, Sin, Sickness, Irresolution, Affliction, Despair.[17]

We have already seen Rochester touch on the theme in *Tunbridge Wells* and Boileau makes use of it in the satire, the eighth, which was the immediate source of the *Satyr against Mankind*. The emphasis in this part of the *Satyr*, however, is not on the differences caused by man's intellectual powers in contrast to animal instinct, but a contrast between two instinctual natures, man's and the animals'. For this reason Rochester emphasises the ruling instinct which underlies all human behaviour as he conceives it: the instinct of fear. For having shown in the first part of the poem the disastrous consequences of trying to live by speculative reason, he is now concerned to show what are the natural impulses that inspire his conduct. To explain what man is like freed from the pursuit of the *ignis fatuus* of reason and to see whether 'nature makes amends' (124) to us for afflicting us with speculative reason Rochester has recourse to the explanation of man's motivation given in Hobbes's *De Cive* (1642). In this Hobbes argues that, in Peter's words: 'Everything we do springs either from the desire for power or fear'.[18] In particular Hobbes argued, the fear of death dominates everything we do: 'man shuns death by a certain impulsion of nature, no less than that whereby a stone moves downward'.[19] Rochester goes even further than Hobbes in explaining everything, even the lust after power, as a result of fear. As in *The Fall* and in *The Imperfect Enjoyment*, it is man's fear of what might happen that prevents him living the easy, untroubled life of the rest of the animal world. Even if we achieve a state of nature against our unnatural propensity for abstraction, as Adam once did and the libertines now sought to do, this would not help us, because we are by nature discontented.

Rochester has thus pursued his argument to a logical impasse. On the one hand by use of our speculative reason we cease to be our natural selves because we project ourselves into an unreal world of abstraction. On the other hand by being natural, by accepting our natures as they are, we accept a state of being dominated by fear, which is our ruling passion and our fears, ironically enough, are themselves abstractions (168–73):

> Thus, Sir, you see what human nature craves:
> Most men are cowards, all men should be knaves.
> The difference lies, as far as I can see,
> Not in the thing itself, but the degree,
> And all the subject matter of debate
> Is only: who's a knave of the first rate?

In the final section of the poem (174–221) Rochester tentatively, and perhaps ironically, suggests a solution for this impasse – again basing his argument on ideas obtained from Hobbes. This solution had already been suggested in *The Fall* (if this is indeed the earlier poem): that given our unnatural nature the best man could do was to construct an artificial nature from his abstractions. In the lyric this was the abstract 'noble tribute of my heart' in place of the more natural 'frailer part' of his body, which has become incapacitated by anxiety. In the *Satyr* he suggests the possibility of employing reason to construct an 'artificial' man who will live according to abstract concepts of virtue, though he implies sardonically that he has never actually found such a person:

> If upon earth there dwell such God-like men,
> I'll here recant my paradox to them,
> Adore those shrines of virtue, homage pay,
> And with the rabble world, their laws obey.
> If such there be, yet grant me this at least:
> Man differs more from man, than man from beast.

The last two lines emphasise quite rightly the totally different nature of the men Rochester is contrasting: the natural and the 'artificial'. The idea of constructing an 'artificial' man might well be by analogy with Hobbes's view of the state as an artifice created to modify man's nature. Hobbes himself seems to have believed that because reason was natural to man the rational behaviour involved in submitting our conduct to the will of the state was itself natural,[20] in spite of the fact that he contrasts man's behaviour in society with his behaviour in a 'natural' state. Rochester is being more logical than Hobbes in implying that if we live by a set of rules determined not by our nature but by their rational consistency then we inhibit our natures and become something other than we naturally are; though he leaves it as an open question whether in practice we are able to live according to abstract principles of virtue. The test would be how successful man is at actually living according to these abstract notions.

The *Satyr Against Mankind* has frequently been called a Hobbesian poem, but more correctly it should be regarded as a sceptical critique of Hobbes, which is why it takes the form of paradox. Rochester is not interested here in prescribing a solution to man's predicament as Hobbes is, but in describing the irresolvable tensions under which he must suffer. Like Swift's view of man in *Gulliver's Travels* the view of man presented in the *Satyr* is of a creature held between two extreme tendencies of his own nature, a Yahoo-nature which makes him even more bestial than the beasts and an Houyhnhnm – nature which is an ideal, rational state, artificially created by our intellect and bearing little relation to our biological nature. If there *is* a resolution of this tension it is in the possibility (which neither Swift nor Rochester endorse in actuality) of effecting a total change in our natures, becoming in effect 'artificial' men that in Swift's fable turn out to be more like horses than men. In reality we are forced to accept the unresolved paradox that the more natural we are the more unnatural we become and both Rochester and Swift in juxtaposing their two visions of man, find a resolution only in sardonic laughter. That we are intended to see the poem as paradox is not only clear from the poem itself (127) but also from contemporary comment like Parson's funeral sermon and the anonymous elegies which refer to the paradoxical nature of Rochester's poetry.[21]

Boileau's eighth satire is itself presented as a paradox, but Boileau's paradox is the traditional one that man, the only rational animal, is so frequently irrational. The satirist in Boileau's satire does not deny that man is a rational creature and that his rationality is in itself good:

Adversarius: That man has reason is beyond debate
                    Nor will yourself, I think deny me that;
                    And was not this fair pilot given to steer
                    His tottering bark through life's rough ocean
                                    here?

Satirist: All this I grant; but if in spite of this,
                    The wretch on every rock he sees will split,
                    To what great purpose does his reason serve...[22]

The worst that can be said at the end of the poem is the ass's comment 'man is a beast as much as we'.

The differences from Boileau are instructive. Rochester's theme is not only far more sceptical, but the methods he employs in presenting his theme differ considerably. Boileau's poem adopts the Horatian device of presenting a conversation between the satirist-persona and an adversarius representing orthodox opinion. The tone of the poem is accordingly more detached, both because the satirist is obviously a dramatic character rather than the poet himself, and because the normal view is presented by the adversarius. Boileau's satire is polite and carefully wrought in the Horatian manner. Rochester, as in *Tunbridge Wells*, drops the adversarius altogether and the poem is a dramatic monologue spoken by a satirical persona between whose views and those of the poet himself there is no immediate way of distinguishing. Rochester also adopts a rougher and more vigorous cadence than either Boileau or Boileau's English translator, Oldham. The effect is to give a dynamic immediacy to the speaker's words that suggest that the problem of man's double nature presented in the poem is not merely being rehearsed as an academic exercise but is a problem for the speaker and his readers. The opening lines, for instance, present a disgust with human nature that has all the conviction of a personal declaration:

> Were I (who to my cost already am
> One of those strange, prodigious creatures, man)
> A spirit free to choose, for my own share,
> What case of flesh and blood I pleased to wear,
> I'd be a dog, a monkey, or a bear,
> Or anything but that vain animal
> Who is so proud of being rational.

The rapid onrush of the syntax, defying the couplet divisions, the extraordinary suspension of the opening clause, the curious emphatic positioning of the 'am' in the first line, which seems to link it in some paradoxical way to the opening word of the line 'were' and led many early copyists of the poem (and at least one modern editor, Pinto) to place a nonsensical full stop at the end of the second line – all these and the egotism of the insistent first person, create a tension between syntax and formal metre that provides us with the emotional equivalent of the tensions presented in the paradoxical theme. Rochester is both 'placing' his satirist in a critical medium and participating with him in the role of satiric agent in the poem. As the logic drives remorselessly on, its implications became more and more confusing. The poet-satirist is himself caught in a situation in which the harder he drives the less progress he makes; the more he asserts, the less he can confidently say. The end is inevitably the weak, hypothetical compromise of the final lines. Weak endings are characteristic of Rochester. The ending of *Artemisia* is particularly, and deliberately, lame, while there seems to be a possibility that the magnificent four final lines of *Tunbridge Wells* were an afterthought and in any case both *Tunbridge Wells* and *Timon* end, not with any solution of the comic tensions, but with the satirist leaving the comic butts to their own devices. The preference for inconclusive endings is not surprising because true comic endings by their very nature, can resolve nothing. The rage at man's attempts at rationalisation and at man's natural depravity in the *Satyr* ends by cancelling itself out and the poet-clown is left rather disconsolately retreating from his own logic (174–82):

> All this with indignation have I hurled
> At the pretending part of the proud world,
> Who, swollen with selfish vanity, devise
> False freedoms, holy cheats, and formal lies
> Over their fellow slaves to tyrannize.
> But if in Court so just a man there be
> (In Court a just man, yet unknown to me)
> Who does his needful flattery direct,
> Not to oppress and ruin, but protect . . .

This is disingenuous: the satire has been a satire against mankind, not an attack on tyranny. But the poet has been forced to retreat into the putative world of a court where there is a just man who lives by the precepts of abstract virtue because of the unbearable implications of his own logic. Not inappropriately the sentence in which the just man is mooted breaks off without any syntactic resolution (190); we are moving into a world where coherence will not take us. He has found himself presenting a world where the alternative of either Houyhnhnm

or Yahoo are equally unpleasant and unacceptable but, as a
clown should, he refuses to accept the impasse. He is not such a
fool either, to believe completely in his phantom virtuous man,
retaining his sense of incongruity as he contemplates his own
hypothesis (212–15):

> But a meek, humble man of honest sense,
> Who, preaching peace, does practice continence;
> Whose pious life's a proof he does believe
> Mysterious truths, which no man can conceive.

Defiant to the end, the satirist pokes fun even at his own
artificial creation. If the creation of artificial man is the solution
to the human condition it is a highly comic solution. None the
less the poem is satire as well as comedy. Both mankind in
general, as victims of a cosmic joke by which we lose, whichever side of the coin of our nature comes uppermost, and the
satirist *persona* also, are shown in an absurd light. But the poet
himself in articulating the absurdity has scored some sort of
triumph over it, a standard has been presented, a system of
references by which the absurdity can be judged. For a moment
the poet has defied the limitations of logic and of his own nature.
The poem transcends the paradox out of which it is made.
Rochester has avoided the ambiguity of the earlier burlesque
poems in achieving the difficult feat of combining a passionate
identification with his fool hero with a cool appraisal of him
by use of a logical, almost syllogistic, structure for his poem and
by the use of an orderly verse medium.

Though *The Epistle of Artemisia to Chloe* is a more light-
hearted poem, and more obviously comic, its tendency is the
reverse of the *Satyr*: to progress from the comic to the non-
comic. As an Horatian Epistle we would expect it to have
a less uncompromising tone and greater irony. The ironic
detachment is certainly not complete, however, though the
standards implied are insinuated obliquely. The means by
which this tentative assertion of moral values is made is in the
structural framework of the poem. In this Rochester adopts
Marvell's method in *Last Instructions* of using a formal structure
to suggest values lacking or only partially presented in the
depicted world of the poem. Marvell chooses a structure that

asserts complete faith in the triumph of order, Rochester adopts a structure that suggests that order and civilisation (they are treated as two sides of the same coin) are a relative matter. He asserts, in the shape of the poem, that some attitudes and conventions are better than others, but that none can claim any absolute sanction.

To show this Rochester adopts an ingenious structure that might be compared to a nest of Chinese boxes, in which the value of the contents of each box diminishes as we get nearer the centre. As each layer is exposed we see not only what basic materials the surface sophistication is formed over and supported by, but also the raw material out of which civilisation is made. The poem progresses into the heart of sophistication's darkness. In this, like the *Satyr Against Mankind*, it borrows from Hobbes the suggestion that civilised man is an artifact made by the ingenuity of human reason out of the raw material of our animal passions.

The outer box in the poem itself is provided by the 'writer' of the epistle, Artemisia. Artemisia has much in common with her maker. She is witty, detached, treating herself with a good deal of self-irony, and like her creator she is a passionate person whose outburst in praise of love makes one of the finest moments of the poem. She is not, however, the poet. The difference of sex, for instance, is stressed:

> How would a woman's tottering bark be tossed
> Where stoutest ships, the men of wit, are lost?

She is a reluctant poetess, deprecating her friend Chloe's suggestion that she should write verse, though unable to resist the suggestion. And even at this stage we detect another level of irony, for the venture which Artemisia is beginning, the writing of a poem, is the venture which her creator, the 'man of wit' with whom she contrasts herself, has himself just embarked on, with a similar danger of shipwreck. Artemisia's assertions are already, therefore, boxed in by the poet himself, who provides an outer layer of reference by which all the events within the poem are to be judged.

When Artemisia addresses herself on the ironies of writing poetry, we are not only aware of Rochester's ironic comment on Artemisia but of irony at his own expense:

Dear Artemisia, poetry's a snare,
Bedlam has many mansions, have a care.
Your muse diverts you, makes the reader sad.
You fancy you're inspired; he thinks you mad.
Consider, too, 'twill be discreetly done
To make yourself the fiddle of the town,
To find th'ill-humored pleasure at their need,
Cursed if you fail, and scorned though you succeed!
Thus, like an arrant woman as I am,
No sooner well convinced writing's a shame,
That whore is scarce a more reproachful name
Than poetess –
Like men that marry, or like maids that woo,
'Cause 'tis the very worse thing they can do,
Pleased with the contradiction and the sin,
Methinks I stand on thorns till I begin.

This combination of standing outside life – the essential element of detachment required of the artist – and the need to be at the same time in the thick of life in order to be able to record the feel of it, is as much Rochester's dilemma as Artemisia's. That the impulse to write is also ambiguous – part self-gratification, part obligation – is itself a pattern of the central theme of the poem: how to accommodate the passionate and the rational in our own natures. Although Artemisia is eloquent in defence of genuine love, she distinguishes it clearly from mere unrestrained appetite, scorning women who 'hate restraint, though but from infamy' (58). Her attitude is that of the defender of 'right reason' in the *Satyr Against Mankind*.

Rochester's use of the heroic couplet throughout the poem indicates clearly his relation to Artemisia. It provides a formal framework within which his characters can operate. Accordingly, it is used with a considerable amount of discipline, the end-stopping for instance, is more obtrusive than in Marvell's poem and is much closer to the later Augustan ideals of correctness. On the other hand, it permits itself deviations, like the broken line in the passage just quoted. Here the passionate enthusiasm of Artemisia gets the better of decorum, so that the form is partly moulded to reflect Artemisia's feelings directly, partly as a standard by which to judge them.

Rochester's relationship to Artemisia is mirrored in Artemisia's relation to the 'fine lady' whose behaviour and conversation Artemisia reports at length in the middle section of the poem (73–188). This is the third 'box' of the series. Here the difference between the reporter Artemisia and the character she is reporting is rather greater. But the fine lady shares Artemisia's wit and urbanity as well as her interest in fashionable society. The difference between them lies in the fine lady's want of heart – want of that element of 'commitment' that Artemisia and, by implication, Rochester see as a necessary part of the cultivated stance. The fine lady is as concerned with her pet monkey as she is with her prospective lover – and rather more so than with her husband.

To deny one's passionate nature is to make oneself less not more rational. So Artemisia describes the fine lady as having the wit, the intelligence, the education befitting the civilised woman but not the essential qualities of feeling that give human meaning to these attributes. The fine lady suffers as much from her Houyhnhnm qualities as Corinna in the final section of the poem from her closeness to the Yahoos. So Artemisia meditates on the fine lady (147–68):

> I took this time to think what nature meant
> When this mixed thing into the world she sent,
> So very wise, yet so impertinent:
> One who knew everything; who, God thought fit,
> Should be an ass through choice, not want of wit;
> Whose foppery, without the help of sense,
> Could ne'er have rose to such an excellence.
> Nature's as lame in making a true fop
> As a philosopher; the very top
> And dignity of folly we attain
> By studious search, and labor of the brain,
> By observation, counsel, and deep thought.
> God never made a coxcomb worth a groat.
> We owe that name to industry and arts:
> An eminent fool must be a fool of parts.
> And such a one was she, who had turned o'er
> As many books as men; loved much, read more;

Had a discerning wit; to her was known
Everyone's fault and merit, but her own.
All the good qualities that ever blessed
A woman so distinguished from the rest,
Except discretion only, she possessed.

'Discretion' here would seem to mean something close to that
Hobbesian right reason which Rochester defines at some length
in the *Satyr against Mankind*: the use of reason to further our
desires and enrich our real experience. The lady fop, the
creature of fashion, is here associated with the philosophical
'formal band and beard' of the *Satyr*; both have denied the
passionate nature which defines our humanity and have chosen
to become the product of their own fantasies. They are empty
shells, having all the appearance of meaning and none of its
reality. So in this passage the fine lady and the philosopher are
associated together as equally remote from nature. God does
not make fools, they are a product of studious abstraction.
Artemisia's 'generous passion of the mind' may not be an
absolute value, may not have any sanction *sub specie aeternitatis*,
but it is greatly superior to not having any passion at all.

The attitude of Artemisia to the fine lady moves the tone of
the poem towards a harsher satire. The opening comic irony of
the poem defines civilised conduct as a delicate balance between
detachment and commitment. From this delicate balance the
poem moves increasingly to contrast these civilised standards
with the inhumanity of sense without feeling, and finally, with
feeling without sense. The portrait of the fine lady is still comic
because Artemisia is more interested in the absurdity of the
conduct – that is, in measuring it against the standards she
maintains – than in condemnation. In the final section of the
poem, however, where the 'fine lady' herself becomes the
reporter, the tone changes again towards more derogatory
satire as she scornfully tells the story of Corinna and her
'booby'. The implication is that comedy is a measure of
civilisation. The further we remove from civilisation the weaker
the element of comic detachment. This is the reverse of Dryden's
attitude to the comic and closer to Shaftesbury's in the next
generation.

The final section of the poem, the final 'box' of this nest of

Chinese boxes, is the most strongly satirical. Here the 'fine lady'
holds up to derision first Corinna and then the 'booby' she
cheats, for being slaves to their appetites. In this section we
have a picture of man as a Yahoo creature; a world, like the
Hobbesian world of natural man, in which life is largely a
continuous display of dog eating dog. As the fine lady puts it in
her cynical, heartless way, summing up the treatment the
booby gets from Corinna (252–5):

> Nature, who never made a thing in vain,
> But does each insect to some end ordain,
> Wisely contrived kind keeping fools, no doubt,
> To patch up vices men of wit wear out.

Artemisia and the poem itself does not endorse the cynicism,
but it supports the fine lady's repudiation of unrestrained
appetite. Corinna is presented as a prostitute who has been
'cozened at first by love' and has then learnt how to use men's
sexual appetite to advantage by cozening them in her turn. Her
ruin, however, is brought about by a man of wit, who turns out
to be too smart for her. She contracts a venereal disease from
him and is abandoned by him and all the other men of the
town. The restless pursuit of 'power after power, which ceaseth
only in death', as Hobbes puts it in *Leviathan* (1 x), requires
Corinna to take her revenge by deceiving some country
bumpkin into keeping her. She finds a suitable victim, takes all
his money and poisons him.

This descent into the 'nasty, brutish and short' life of the
natural man brings to a non-comic conclusion a poem whose
definition of culture is entirely in terms of the comic. The
structure of the poem implies a comic, sceptical attitude to
absolute values: the poet himself, it is implied, is simply one of a
series of commentators whose judgements have value only in
relation to the particular events recorded. Artemisia, who is
closest to the poet himself and as 'author' of the epistle stands as
a type of the poet, is relatively wiser, more civilised than the
fine lady who, in her turn, is superior to Corinna and the
booby. But Artemisia herself is treated ironically; the very
attempt to make these judgements is a fool's errand, there is
something ungainly, undignified about it, like a lady's riding
astride a horse. So by implication the poet himself leaves it

open to query whether he is not after all once again making a fool of himself in attempting any judgement at all. None the less, while there are no certain, absolute standards, within the work itself and (by symbolic extension) within our limited knowledge of the world as we find it, the poet does assert his preference for a scale of values where thought and feeling are kept in equilibrium, where like Artemisia we need to be both able to love and see the ironies in loving. It is a paradoxical attitude, fraught with contradiction and therefore, comic, but it is preferable to a world of heartless detachment or of mindless concupiscence. Artemisia therefore shows a shift in comic attitude from the complete detachment of a poem like *The Disabled Debauchee* to a more sympathetic comedy which combines feeling and attachment. In this poem Rochester, having rejected the detached language of the gods seems to be embracing that of the buffoon, as we have already found in *The Imperfect Enjoyment* and in *The Satyr against Mankind*.

The Satyr against Mankind and *Artemisia* are both deeply sceptical poems in that they cast doubt on our finding any ultimate sanctions for our behaviour. Yet they are also an attempt, and a successful attempt, to impose an order on a chaotic universe, an assertion of the power of the creative imagination to make order where there is none. Burnet records Rochester's views on morality towards the end of his life, and clearly in these satires he is moving towards this viewpoint:

> For morality, He confessed, he saw the necessity of it, both for the Government of the World, and for The preservation of Health, Life and Friendship: and was very much ashamed of his former Practices, rather because he had made himself a beast, and brought pain and sickness on his body, and had suffered much in his Reputation, than from any deep sense of a Supream being or another State . . . he confessed he had no remorse for his past Actions, as Offences against God, but only as Injuries to himself and to Mankind.[23]

If moral order does not exist then man must make it. Unfortunately there is always an immense gap between our ideas of order and our actual behaviour. It is the gap between the imagined order and the actual chaos which sparks off the comedy.

8 Conclusion

In the great variety of Restoration comic poetry some pattern of development and change seems to emerge from the complexity. It is a pattern whose changes are partly dependent on changing circumstances; partly on the idiosyncrasies of some of the major figures – this because the Restoration fostered for a brief period, at least in aristocratic circles, a cult of individualism which was another symptom of the breakdown of the older conventions of seeing and doing things. In the Commonwealth period comedy came to be a serious business for two reasons. Socially it came to have ideological connections with the Cavaliers, as a protest against the deliberate melancholy favoured by some of the Puritans, and at the deeper level it increasingly came to express the sense of uncertainty and incongruity that followed the questioning of the nature of authority.

We have seen in the Commonwealth drolleries the persistence of a joyful, amiable comedy that is a natural expression of an age confident in its own values. Such, looking back, Shakespeare's age appeared to the writer of 'An Old Song of an Old Courtier and a New' who contrasts the new courtiers of the king with the old courtiers of Queen Elizabeth; such was Aubrey's reaction to an age which had seen the fairies fly away for ever. Poems expressing regret at the passing of a simpler, more moral, age are common:

> Where is the decency become
> That your fore-mothers had?
> In Gowns of Cloth and caps of Thrum
> They went full meanly clad.
> But you must jet it in Silks and Gold,
> Your pride in winter is never a cold.[1]

Even this however gets mocking treatment in the poem that follows it in *Musarum Deliciae*. By now, not even nostalgia is sacred. In that earlier and happier age (earlier ages are always happier) even satirical comedy largely deals with conventional generalities or with local aberration. There is, of course, Jonsonian satiric comedy, the closest to Restoration and often its model. Jonson reminds us that even in Elizabethan times comedy was associated with evil, for his was a comedy that sought to purge itself of its comic element, to cure the individual of his individuality so that he could be restored as a healthy limb of a healthy, non-comic society. As in the middle ages the comic is thought of as the diseased. But equally the comic was treated lightly, as play, which no one was expected to take seriously.

Commonwealth comedy increasingly comes to mean something more disruptive even than Jonsonian comedy. It is often no longer play-acting – as it was for 'metaphysicals' like Donne, Carew and Henry King, even the young Marvell – nor is it a ballad humour of joyful assertion, though the drolleries still contain a great deal of both these kind of the comic. It is not only now in the 1650s that the poet can see crazy things in an essentially harmonious world; increasingly he seems to see a crazy world. This sense of deep uncertainty is rarely made explicit in Commonwealth verse, which goes on ostensibly asserting the values of the past. Indeed it only becomes explicit in the Restoration in the quite untypical scepticism of Rochester's poetry. We need not be surprised that lesser poets failed to understand the full implications of the breakdown in the old beliefs or to face up to the possibility that traditional teaching was in error. Rochester alone had the courage and genius to explore this possibility fully, even to the extent of challenging the Christian assumptions of his society. And subsequent generations hurriedly covered over what he had revealed by irrelevantly suggesting that his preoccupation with obscenity showed an unbalanced mind.

Instead, the general uncertainty comes to be expressed indirectly. One characteristic response of the period is to seek for certainty in reason and common sense in place of traditional authorities. This search in poetry frequently takes the negative form of trying to strip away illusion in the vain hope of arriving at the bedrock of truth. Play poetry such as the anti-platonic love poetry that had evolved from collections like Tottel's

Miscellany in the mid-sixteenth century as joking 'answers' to non-comic poems – now comes to be more important than the non-comic verse that once hosted it. In Suckling, especially, and in the verse his example inspired, this anti-platonic poetry comes to predominate and take on a life of its own, independent of the literature it started by mocking. The love poetry that seeks to destroy illusion has a conviction that the idealising love poetry totally lacks:

> Though we, like Fools,
> Fathome the Earth and Sky,
> And drayne the Schools
> For names t'express you by:
> Out-rant the lowd'st Hyperboles
> To dub you Saints and Deities,
>   By Cupid's Heraldry,
> We know you're Flesh and Blood as well as men,
> And when we will can mortalize, and make you so agen.[2]

The drolleries abound in this poetry of negative vision and it persists in the Restoration in the lyrics of courtier poets like Charles Sedley, Charles Sackville, Earl of Dorset and in Rochester. Swift's poetry continues the tradition.

Another way in which the uncertainty expresses itself is through a preoccupation with form rather than content. Form comes to be manipulated independently of meaning and gives rise to the beginnings of that mock heroic verse that the Augustan age exploited so successfully. We have seen, for instance, how Cleveland ceases to write about anything and becomes preoccupied with creating ingenious verbal forms. His verbal patternings, highly complex and sophisticated though these are, are made to cover a void. Most characteristic, however, is that half-form, burlesque, which both asserts and denigrates at the same time and leaves a confused impression because the comic writers themselves have become confused.

Burlesque becomes common in the drolleries of the 1650's and reaches a height of popularity with the publication of the first part of *Hudibras* in 1663, with its second part in 1664, and with the publication of Charles Cotton's imitation of Scarron's *Vergil Travestie* in 1664. Both these works had phenomenal success. *Hudibras* went into numerous editions in Butler's lifetime and he was the one Restoration poet, apart from Dryden, to be reprinted more or less continuously until our own time. Cotton's work did not survive in popularity quite so long, its last edition, the fifteenth, dating from 1807. It is interesting to speculate why *Hudibras* has lost favour just at a time when interest in other Restoration poets is reviving. It is Rochester's poetry – though bowdlerised – that is now available in paperback and *Hudibras* that can only be found in learned and expensive scholarly editions.

Burlesque, like anti-platonic love poetry, seems to start as parody. One of the earliest English burlesque poems, James Smith's *Meeting of Penelope and Ulysses*, written before 1640, guys the classical story, and soon Scarron is initiating in France the fashion for parodying classical texts that became the rage throughout western Europe for half a century. But like anti-platonic poetry burlesque increasingly becomes independent of its models, less an exercise in play poetry and more a serious expression of the doubt and insecurity that pervades life at mid-century. *Hudibras* is the most notable example. Butler, like Suckling before him and Swift after him, set out to destroy illusion, paradoxically trying to create a poetic world from which the poetic imagination was to be excluded. The purpose was to destroy whatever was fanciful and so leave the reader free to contemplate the natural world, which held the key to the discovery of truth, unencumbered by the distortions of the imaginative medium. The means of projecting this destructive creativity was a verse form that aimed to deny the formal conventions of verse: rhyme, rhythm, verbal decorum. For Butler the formal conventions merely concealed the plain truth that needed to be asserted. But again Butler runs into contradiction: you can only defy poetic convention by to some extent obeying it, a rhyme can only be successfully bad if it is a rhyme, rhythm can only be irregular if it creates a norm of regularity. So Butler finds himself creating a comic poetic world in *Hudibras* that is a comic world in its own right, in defiance of his destructive intentions. The result is a curious mixture of celebratory comedy in which Hudibras himself becomes the triumphant clown-hero and satirical, destructive comedy which aims to destroy what is being created. What sets out to be a poem to liberate the reader from the yoke of his imagination ends as an illustration of the impossibility of the task and witnesses to the very confusions it sought to disentangle.

It was left to the Restoration period proper to develop the most successful comic forms: stage comedy and comic satire. The major achievement in both these fields became possible as the destructive impulses that were expressed in burlesque were contained and placed in a perspective gained by a re-imposition of order. Restoration satire is a judgement on disorder from a new, if sometimes precarious, vantage point of orderliness. In Dryden's *Absalom and Achitophel* this perspective is won by resurrecting the old god-given order which had regained some credibility as Charles's regime gathered strength, especially after the discrediting of the Popish plot scare. Dryden's conservative mind expressed itself naturally by restating the heroic ideals of baroque: his heroic plays are the clearest statement of this reverence for the old idealistic order. But even in stage comedy his purpose is primarily to eradicate the disturbances indicated by the comic and restore a Romantic or heroic serenity. Comic characters like the comic lovers of *Marriage a la Mode* have to be cured of the moral aberrations that their comic roles indicate, and eventually they are reinstated in the romantic world of the main plot. Dryden's satire in *Absalom and Achitophel* is a mode of judging the comic forces of actual disorder against a background of baroque idealism, just as *Mac Flecknoe* is a consistent judgement on the physical from the vantage point of the spiritual. Both poems assert a coherent and consistent spiritual interpretation of the universe so that the comedy never wavers in its satirical intention.

Marvell, too, resurrects baroque ideals as a standard of judgement on the actual and again it is the difference between what is and what ought to be that is the source of comic incongruity. Marvell's sense of order in *Last Instructions* is, however, less secure than Dryden's; some ambiguity surrounds both his heroic figures like De Ruyter and the comic figures like Lady Castlemaine and the King, whose role seems particularly equivocal. This feeling of uncertainty is increased by Marvell's use of the couplet in the rough and ready manner generally thought appropriate for satire. Dryden's dignified, sonorous couplet reinforces his faith that order will inevitably triumph over chaos: Marvell, on the other hand, while he can use the couplet in this way, often uses it as an expression of disorder. Perhaps the analogy with mannerist painting is the correct one for assessing Marvell's achievement. Like the mannerist painters he works with the conventions common to the neo-classical tradition, but there is a constant distortion of perspective which has the effect, if not the intention, of emphasising the perplexities of human experience within the orderly universe, rather than of emphasising the order itself. Like Dryden, however, Marvell ultimately asserts the traditional order, even if it is more hardly won. And though the comic element is less obviously associated with evil, it is something ultimately to be repudiated.

Rochester is the most original and best comic poet of the period. His earlier poetry is not greatly superior to that of other lyricists and burlesque writers of the time. In *The Ramble* and *Signior Dildo* we find him following the fashion of Butler,[3] and in the earlier lyrics there is often little to distinguish his work from that of other court wits. Always a conventional poet, in the early work the conventions are put to no use for which they have not previously been tried. Some early poems, however – notably the mock pastoral 'Fair Chloris in a Pigsty lay' – show a complexity of treatment that is beyond the range of most of his contemporaries. It is in the great satires of 1674-5 that his full genius becomes apparent. *Artemisia* and the *Satyr against Mankind* in particular are extraordinary explorations of a world without God, in which man is forced to impose his own limited coherence on an incoherent world. The earlier poetry up to 1674 had simply reflected the confusions and uncertainties of the Hudibrastic world of the early Restoration. In the great satires Rochester not only reflects that world; he also judges it. In this case, however, not like Marvell and Dryden by the idealistic standards of the past but by the less dogmatic, more relativistic standards of a kind of sceptical rationality. Clearly much of his satirical technique was learnt from Marvell, but he uses these techniques less to reflect an inherent order, as Marvell had done, than to create an order out of the material of actuality. In Rochester's satires man is seen on his own. Unable to rely on a god-given order, he uses his rational faculties not to solve the problem of his being, for that is insoluble, but to come to terms with the fact of its insolubility.

All three of the major poets I have discussed, Marvell, Dryden and Rochester, attempt, in Dennis's resonant words, 'to restore the decays that happened to human Nature by the Fall, by restoring order'.[4] But whereas the two older poets look back to the past to obtain their coherent vision, when men could safely trust in the benevolence of an omniscient and omnipotent deity, Rochester has no such ideal to trust in. His universe is the Lucretian universe:

> Dead we became the lumber of the world.
> And to that mass of matter shall be swept
> Where things destroyed with things unborn are kept.
> Devouring time swallows us whole;
> Impartial death confounds body and soul.

Faced with an impersonal universe, the product of the chance collision of atoms, man must make his own temporary island of coherence in the universal flux. It is an absurd situation and man is essentially a comic creature, but by constructing his artificial island he momentarily triumphs over the meaninglessness. Laughter is the sound of the triumph.

After Rochester no one was to use laughter with such disturbing implications until our own century. There were imitators like John Oldham, who was willing to learn from Rochester's verse techniques, but not from his philosophy, and Ann Finch, Countess of Winchilsea whose pleasant society poem *Ardelia's answer to Ephelia* seems to owe a good deal to *Artemisia* without any of the latter's serious philosophical implications. Even the young Pope exercised himself in Rochester imitation, modelling his *On Silence* on Rochester's *Upon Nothing*. Comedy does not cease to be important in Pope's generation, though Pope and Swift seem somehow to be fighting a rearguard action against the rise of sentimental literature. Laughter itself becomes more amiable again and Addison distinguishes between satirical mirth, of which he disapproves, and Christian cheerfulness.[5] There are some interesting indications of this transition. Henry Carey is exasperated to find readers treating his pathetic tale of *Sally in Our Alley* as a satire on a notorious prostitute and issues a disclaimer with the edition of 1729:

For as innocence and virtue were ever the boundaries of his muse, so in this little poem he had no other views than to set forth the beauty of a chaste and disinterested passion, even in the lowest class of human life . . . but being then young and obscure, he was very much ridicul'd by some of his acquaintance for this performance, which, nevertheless, made its way into the polite world, and amply recompensed him by the applause of the divine Addison, who was pleased more than once to mention it with approbation.

Pope ran into similar difficulties over a sentimental little epitaph he had written about two country lovers killed by lightning. He sent the poem to Lady Mary Wortly Montagu asking her to shed a tear over them 'from the finest eyes in the world'. Lady Mary replied in the best tradition of courtly wit with the tart comment:

His endeavoring to shield her from the Storm was a natural action and what he would have done for his Horse if he had been in the same situation.[6]

She then offers her own version of the epitaph, which begins:

Here lyes John Hughs and Sarah Drew
Perhaps you'l say, what's that to you?

Pope of course was not slow to see the funny side of things and replied in his turn:

Here lye two poor Lovers, who had the mishap
Tho very chaste people, to die of a clap.

It took a long time for comedy to die away completely and then it would not lie down. In the *Essay on Gibing* of 1727 the author (possibly Swift), though he can still claim 'a spirit of Humour, and Raillery seems to have taken Possession of all orders and Degrees of Man', complains that the range of subjects permitted to comic treatment is narrowing.[7] Restricting the range of the comic to exclude delicate subjects is a sure sign the comic is being taken less seriously and it is not surprising that before long we hear the cry: 'The comic muse long sick is now a dying'.[8] Earlier than this Goldsmith complains of the increasing solemnity of manner in poetry and that critics have 'proscribed the comic or satyrical muse from every walk but high life"[9] This is not many years before Dr Johnson is having Imlac reprove two lady companions for finding a mad astronomer funny: 'Ladies, to mock the heaviest of human afflictions is neither Charitable nor wise'.[10] Dr Johnson, one feels, would have amused Queen Victoria. Laughter became less and less important in literature and we may be forgiven for imagining that some of the great Romantic writers, emulating Jesus, never laughed.[11] Laughter was less and less permitted in serious poetry, though we have it on Max Beerbohm's authority that even Matthew Arnold was never wholly serious.

Notes

CHAPTER 1: INTRODUCTION

1. Letter of Jean-Baptiste Rousseau to Brosette 24 July 1715: 'J'ai souvent oui dire à Despréaux que la philosophie de Descartes avait coupé la gorge à la poesie.'
2. Aubrey, *Brief Lives*, ed. Lawson Dick, p. xxxiii.
3. Preface to 'Rival Ladies', *Critical Essays*, ed. Watson, 1 4.
4. See my collection of verse elegies on Rochester in *Rochester, The Critical Heritage*.
5. *Satires*, ed. R. Lamar, p. 246.
6. Eleven poems on the subject were edited by E. F. Rimbault for the Percy Society, 1844, vol. IX.
7. *Critical Essays of The Seventeenth Century*, ed. J. E. Spingarn (Oxford, 1908) II 118.
8. *Poetics*, Penguin edition (1965) pp. 35–6.
9. *Satires*, p. 44.
10. Samuel Butler, *Characters*, ed. A. R. Waller, p. 409.
11. Ibid., p. 330.
12. G. R. Wasserman, 'Samuel Butler and the Problem of Unnatural Man'. *MLQ* 31 (1970) 192.
13. Burnet's 'Life of Rochester' from *Critical Heritage*, ed. Farley-Hills, p. 54.
14. See, for instance, *Proverbs* 14:6; *Eccles.* 2:2; *Ecclesiasticus* 21:23; *Ep. to Ephesians* 5:4; *Ep. of St. Peter* II 3:3–4. For Patristic views see E. Curtius, *European Literature in the Latin Middle Ages*, (London, 1953) p. 422.
15. George Stanhope, *The Duty of Rebuking* (London, 1703).
16. Alexander Brome, *Songs and Other Poems*, Sig. A7ʳ.
17. Richard Flecknoe, *Diarium* (1656) A3ᵛ–4ʳ.
18. Davenant, *Dramatic Works* (1873) IV 30.

CHAPTER 2: COMIC POETRY OF THE COMMONWEALTH

1. 'The Author's Epistle to this new Edition', *The Academy of Complements* (London, 1646) Sig. A6ʳ.
2. Hugh Crompton, *Pierides or the Muses Mount* (1658) Sig. A2ʳ.
3. *Athen. Ox.*, ed. Bliss (1817) III 623.
4. Ibid.
5. *Brief Lives*, ed. Lawson Dick, p. xxix.
6. *Wit's Recreations*, ed. Dubois p. 440.
7. Ibid., p. 460.
8. *Sportive Wit*, Sig. A2ᵛ–Aa3ʳ (The pagination of this volume is chaotic. There are two gatherings signed A, the second going from A1–Aa2–4; this poem comes in the second, after G8).

9. Francis Beaumont, *Poems* (1640) Sig. H4ᵛ.
10. *Sportive Wit*, p. 33.
11. *Poems of John Cleveland*, ed. Morris and Withington, p. 20.
12. J. L. Kinney, 'John Cleveland and the Satiric Couplet in the Restoration', *P.Q.* 37 (1958) 410–23.
13. See G. Williamson, *Seventeenth Century Contexts*, ch. 10 and Jonson, *Conversations with William of Hawthornden*, ed. R. F. Patterson (London 1923) pp. 1–2.
14. 'Le poète est créature, il bâtit un monde sur un point; ainsi peu import qu'on chante un héros ou un Pupitre; mais on a tort si ou n'a point réussi'. Charles Batteau, *Parallèls de la Henriade et du Lutrin.* Quotedby R. P. Bond, *English Burlesque Poetry, 1700–1750* (Cambridge, 1932) p. 51.
15. Thomas Fuller, *Church History*, ed. James Nichols (London, 1837) I 528.
16. Thomas Wilson, *Arte of Rhetorique*, ed. G. H. Mair (Oxford, 1909) p. 146.
17. See G. Kitchin, *A Survey of Burlesque and Parody in English*, p. 198.
18. Chiome d'argento fine, irte ed attorte / senz'arte intorno ad un bel viso d'oro . . . *Oxford Book of Italian Verse* (Oxford, 1952) p. 191.
19. *Westminster Drollery*, p. 77.
20. *Wit and Drollery*, p. 32. John Wardroper in his *Love and Drollery*, pp. 168–70, publishes a longer version from B.M. Add. MS. 24665 and in a note records several MSS where it occurs, including one in the Bodleian which ascribes it to Mr Lawson of St John's College; it seems to have been written at the beginning of the seventeenth century. It is also in *Westminster Drollery*, II 74.
21. Advertisement to *Pendragon or the Carpet Knight, his Kalendar* (London, 1698) Sig. A3ʳ⁻ᵛ.
22. *Poems of Charles Cotton*, ed. Beresford, p. 304.
23. Ibid., p. 312.
24. 'The Answer of Mr. Hobbes to Sir William Davenant's Preface before Gondibert', *Critical Essays of the Seventeenth Century*, II 59.
25. *Characters*, p. 47.
26. William Walsh, *Letters and Poems*, Sig. A3ᵛ.
27. John Dryden, *Original of Satire*, ed. Watson (Everyman ed.) II 76.
28. John Oldmixon, *Poems on several occasions*, Sig. A6ʳ.
29. *English Work of Giles Fletcher*, ed. Berry (Wisconsin, 1964) p. 76.
30. *Musarum Deliciae*, ed. Dubois, p. 29.
31. Ibid., p. 27.
32. C. H. Firth, 'The Reign of Charles I', *Transactions of the Royal Society*, 3rd ser. VI (1912) 30.
33. *Antidote Against Melancholy*, p. 20.
34. 'Wit's Recreation', in *Facetiae*, ed. E. Dubois, II 405.

CHAPTER 3: *Hudibras*

1. 'Address to the Reader', *Hudibras in three parts with notes and preface by Zachary Grey* (London 1744) p. vii.

2. Dennis, *Critical Works*, ed. Hooker 1 7–9.
3. *Coleridge on the Seventeenth Century*, ed. R. F. Brinkley (Durham, N. Carolina, 1955) pp. 164–5.
4. *Hudibras*, ed. John Wilders (Oxford, 1967).
5. Dryden, *Critical Essays*, ed. Watson, II 147.
6. Lines contributed to Soames's translation of Boileau's *Art of Poetry*, see Dennis, *Critical Works*, I 433.
7. 'Life of Butler', *Lives of the English Poets*, ed. G. Birkbeck Hill (Oxford, 1905) I 210.
8. *Lectures on the English Comic Writers* (London: Everyman ed.) p. 65.
9. *Hudibras* (Edinburgh, 1854) I vii.
10. Quotations are from the edition of John Wilders (Oxford, 1967).
11. *Characters*, p. 401.
12. Ibid., p. 461.
13. Ibid., p. 336.
14. Ibid., p. 328.
15. Ibid., p. 340.
16. Ibid., p. 56.
17. Ibid., p. 54.
18. Ibid., p. 452.
19. *Hudibras* 1 i 509–18.
20. *Characters* p. 408.
21. Ibid.
22. Ibid., p. 53.
23. Ibid., p. 406.
24. See Wasserman, 'Samuel Butler', p. 192.
25. *Characters*, p. 330.
26. *R.E.S.* IV (1928) 163.
27. *Characters*, p. 468.
28. Ibid., p. 470.
29. *Satires*, 34–5.
30. Aubrey, *Brief Life of Samuel Butler*.
31. *Journal*, ed. F. M. L. Poynter (1963) p. 157.
32. *Satires*, 56–9, 211–21.
33. Ibid., p. 211.
34. *Characters*, p. 271.
35. Ibid., p. 449.
36. Ibid., p. 36.
37. Ibid., p. 346.
38. D. Gibson, 'Samuel Butler', *Seventeenth Century Studies*, ed. R. Shafer (Princeton, 1933).
39. *Characters*, p. 466. 'He that seriously considers the Miraculous ways of our coming into this world, and how much wee are Surpriz'd with ourselves, will finde Reason to thinke that our Departure out of it, is not the last Change of Condition that wee are to expect'.
40. *Hudibras*, p. xxii.
41. *Characters*, p. 459.
42. Ibid., p. 462.

43. Ibid., pp. 112–23, 114–15.
44. *Satires*, p. 44.
45. *Characters*, p. 115.
46. Ibid., p. 438.
47. Ibid., p. 429.
48. Ibid., p. 456.
49. Ibid.
50. *Hudibras*, p. xxii.
51. *Characters*, p. 339.
52. Wasserman, 'Samuel Butler', p. 180.
53. *Characters*, pp. 337–8.
54. Ibid., p. 338.
55. Ibid., p. 381.
56. *Satires*. p. 38.
57. *Characters*, p. 434.
58. Ibid., p. 339.
59. Ibid., p. 339.
60. Ibid., p. 470.
61. See Gibson, 'Samuel Butler'.
62. *Characters*, p. 273.
63. Ibid., p. 339.
64. Ibid., p. 330.
65. A. H. West, *L'Influence française dans la Poesie Burlesque en Angleterre entre 1660 et 1700* (Paris 1930) p. 149.
66. See, for instance, Ian Jack, *Augustan Satire* (Oxford, 1952) p. 17.
67. Johnson, *Life of Butler*, ed. Hill, 1 218.

CHAPTER 4: *Last Instructions to a Painter*

1. There are an increasing number of honourable exceptions, e.g. Ruth Nevo in *The Dial of Virtue*, and J. H. Summers, 'Private Taste and Public Judgments' and a few lines of Brian Morris's essay 'Satire from Donne to Marvell' both in *Metaphysical Poetry, Stratford Studies*, vol. II 1970.
2. H. E. Toliver, *Marvell's Ironic Vision*, p. 84; Earl Miner, 'The Poetic Picture, Painted Poetry of Last Instructions', *MP* LXIII (1966) 288–94; M. Gearin-Tosh, 'The Structure of Marvell's "Last Instructions to a Painter"', *Essays in Criticism* XXII (Jan 1972); A. S. Fischer,' The Augustan Marvell', *ELH* 38 (1971).
3. All quotations are from the edition of George Lord in *Poems on Affairs of State*, vol. I (New Haven, 1963).
4. Ibid., pp. 55–66. For a discussion of the authorship question see *Evidence for Authorship*, ed. D. Erdman and E. G. Fogel.
5. The emendation indicated by the square brackets is my own.
6. J. R. Sutherland, 'Marvell's Satires', *PQ* XLV (1966) 46. In a recent article on *Last Instructions* (see note 2) Michael Gearin-Tosh has demonstrated the careful structure of the poem; this chapter was largely written before I had seen Mr Gearin-Tosh's article, but is, with reservations, in agreement with it.

7. A. S. Fischer, 'The Augustan Marvell'.
8. 'Ad Patrem', 17–19: Nectu vatis opus divinum despice carmen, / Quo nihil aethereos ortus, et semina caeli . . . commendat.
9. For a discussion of Restoration views on the appropriate style for satire see chapter 7 on Rochester's major satires.
10. For other references to Marvell's reputation as a comic poet see Defoe's *The Review*, 29 March 1711; 28 March 1713 and Dryden's disparaging reference to Marvell as an expert in satire and 'rayling', preface to 'Religio Laici', *Poems* ed. Kinsley I 308.
11. For a comprehensive list of poems that use the convention see M. T. Osborne, *Advice to a Painter Poems 1633–1856*.
12. See Hagstrum, *The Sister Arts* for an account of this tradition of imitating painting in poetry.
13. 'The Poetic Picture, Painted Poetry of *Last Instructions*' in *Andrew Marvell*, ed. George Lord (1968) p. 173.
14. For an account of seventeenth-century attitudes to satire see Ruth Nevo, *The Dial of Virtue*, from which these two quotations are taken.
15. *The Rehearsal Transpros'd*, ed. D. I. B. Smith (Oxford, 1971), pp. 160–5.
16. See G. Williamson, *Seventeenth Century Contexts* (London, 1960) p. 243.
17. K. E. Toliver, *Marvell's Ironic Vision*, p. 206.
18. Hagstrum, *The Sister Arts* pp. 195–6 et passim.
19. Sypher, *Four Stages of Renaissance Style*, pp. 185–201.
20. Compare Carew, 'Upon the King's Sicknesse', *Poems* (1640) p. 59. 'Entering his Royall limbs that is an head, / Through us, his mystique limbs, the paine is spread'.
21. John M. Wallace, *Destiny his Choice* p. 182.
22. Pepys, *Diary* 10 June 1667.
23. Ibid., 13 June 1667.
24. Both these examples are given in M. Pogue's unpublished dissertation, 'The Restoration Verse Satires of Andrew Marvell'.
25. Freud was not the first to see the significance of the association of money and sex. Money images for sexual activity are frequent in Rochester's poetry (e.g. *Imperfect Enjoyment* 69; *Ramble in St. James's Park* 102; *On Mrs. Willis* 16 and especially *A Very Heroicall Epistle in Answer to Ephelia* 24–31).
26. Defoe, *Review* 28 March 1713 (though there is some doubt now whether the *Dialogue of the Two Horses* referred to is by Marvell).

CHAPTER 5: JOHN DRYDEN

1. Shadwell, *Complete Works*, ed. Montague Summers (London, 1972) v. 253.
2. *Critical Essays*, edited Watson II 153.
3. Ibid., II 115.
4. Thomas Rymer, *Tragedies of the Last Age*, ed. Zimansky, p. 75.
5. Charles Gildon, *The Laws of Poetry* (London, 1721) p. 124.
6. *Critical Essays*, edited Watson II 15.
7. Preface to 'Rival Ladies', *Critical Essays*, edited Watson I 4.

8. For further examples see R. W. King *MLR* xxix (1934) 435–6.
9. Thomas Fuller, 'David's Heinous Sin' (1631) 1 st. 19, *Poems and Verse Translations*, ed. Grossart (Liverpool, 1868).
10. Ibid., iii st. 13.
11. *Parnassus Biceps*, ed. George Thorn-Drury, p. 20.
12. Schilling, *The Conservative Myth*, p. 148.
13. Arthur Hoffman, *John Dryden's Imagery* p. 75.
14. L. L. Brodwin, 'Miltonic Allusion in *Absalom and Achitophel*', *JEGP* 68, (Jan 1969).
15. A. L. French, 'Dryden, Marvell and Political Poetry', *Studies in English Literature*, viii 397.
16. *Life of Dryden*, ed. Hill i 436.
17. Hoffman, *John Dryden's Imagery*, p. 73.
18. Hoffman explores the parallels between Achitophel and Satan in some detail, ibid., pp. 78–84.
19. *Ben Jonson: The Complete Masques*, ed. Stephen Orgel (Yale, 1969) p. 3.
20. I use the word emblem in the sense defined by E. Panofsky, *Albrecht Dürer* (Princeton, 1955), p. 173, 'images which refuse to be accepted as representation of mere things but demand to be interpreted as vehicles of concepts'.
21. Germain Bazin, *The Baroque*, p. 40.

CHAPTER 6: JOHN WILMOT, EARL OF ROCHESTER

1. Gilbert Burnet, 'Some Passages in the Life and Death of John Wilmot, Earl of Rochester', *Rochester, The Critical Heritage*, ed. Farley-Hills, p. 51.
2. John Wilmot, *The Complete Poems*, ed. Vieth (New Haven and London, 1968) pp. 88–9. All quotations are from this edition.
3. 'Life of Petronius written by Mons. St. Evremont' (actually Sarasin), *The Satyrical Works of Petronius*, trans. Thomas Brown (London, 1708) p. iv.
4. Rosalie Colie, *Paradoxia Epidemica*, p. 5, et passim.
5. R. E. Quaintance, 'French Sources of the Restoration Imperfect Enjoyment Poem', *PQ* xlii (1963) 190–9.
6. I give the Gyldenstolpe MS version, which is rather more dramatic than Vieth's version; see *The Gyldenstolpe Manuscript*, ed. Danielsson and Vieth, p. 132.
7. *Complete Poems*, 82.
8. Ibid., 83.
9. Ibid., 51.
10. *Poems*, ed. Crum (Oxford, 1965) p. 180.
11. Alexander Brome, *Songs and Other Poems*, pp. 29–31.
12. *Methinks the Poor Town*, p. 30.
13. *Merry Drollery*, pp. 76–7.
14. Alciati, *Emblemator*.
15. *Musarum Deliciae*, p. 39.
16. Alexander Brome, *Songs and Other Poems*, Sig A4^v-A5^r.
17. Sackville (Knole) MS 79.

18. Margaret Mead, *Male and Female* (Pelican ed., 1962) p. 197.

19. Harl. MS 7003, 191.

20. *Essays of Montaigne*, translated by Charles Cotton, I 336.

21. Ibid., III 479.

22. Thomas Carew, *Poems*, p. 87.

23. I have not seen a version of Aretino's sonnets in the original Italian. This translation is done from a nineteenth-century (?) French version.

24. Dennis, 'Preface to Miscellanies', *Critical Works*, I 8.

25. Temple, 'Of Poetry', *Five Miscellaneous Essays*, ed. S. H. Monk, p. 196.

26. Burnet, 'Life of Rochester', *Critical Heritage*, p. 54.

27. V. Pinto, *Rochester* (London, 1963) pp. 170–1.

28. D. Vieth, *Attribution in Restoration Poetry* (New Haven, 1963) p. 82.

CHAPTER 7: ROCHESTER – THE MAJOR SATIRES

1. St Evremond, 'Sur la Morale d'Epicure', *Oeuvres Mêlées*, ed. Charles Giraud, I 177. Tous les objets ont des faces différentes, et l'esprit, qui est dans un mouvement continuel, les envisage différement, selon qu'il se tourne; en sorte que nous n'avons, pour ainsi parler, que de nouveaux aspects, pensant avoir de nouvelles connoissances.

2. Quoted by T. F. Mayo in *Epicurus in England*, p. 11.

3. *Works of St. Evremond*, trans. J. Duke (1711) II 9–10. La poésie demande un génie particulier, qui ne s'accommode pas trop avec le bon sens. Tantôt, c'est le langage des dieux; tantôt c'est le langage des fous, rarement celui d'un honnête homme . . . De tous les poètes, ceux qui font des comédies devroient être les plus propres pour le commerce du mond; car ils s'attachent à dépeindre naïvement tout ce qui s'y fait, et à bien exprimer les sentiments et les passions des hommes. Ed. Giraud i 95–6.

4. Burnet, 'Life of Rochester', *Critical Heritage*, p. 54.

5. Quoted by John Peter in *Complaint and Satire*, pp. 301–2.

6. Donne, 'To Mr. S.B.'

7. For an account of the importance of Dryden's Essay in this respect see William Frost's article 'Dryden and Satire', *Studies in English Literature 1500–1900*, XI 401–16.

8. See O. J. Campbell, *Comicall Satire* (San Marino, 1938) p. 27.

9. Samuel Cobb, *Poetae Britannici*, p. 17.

10. *The Dissertator in Burlesque*, p. 8.

11. Cf. M. C. Randolph, 'The Structural Design of Formal Verse Satire', *PQ* XXI (1942) p. 379. 'Whatever else they may not have known about the form, Renaissance and early seventeenth century satirists were certain of the principle that the genre was a semi-dramatic one held together by the figure of the Narrator-Satirist, and became extremely clever at devising and revising dramatic devices to give life and color to what might have been forthright, unadorned imprecation against vice'.

12. Everard Guilpin, *Skialetheia* (London, 1598) ed. in facsimile G. B. Harrison (1931) Sig. B7.

13. Nicolas Boileau-Despréaux, *Satires*, ed. Boudhors, p. 32.

> Toutefois avec l'eau que j'y mets à foison,
> J'esperois adoucir la force du poison.
> Mais qui l'auroit pensé? Pour comble de disgrace,
> Par le chaud qu'il faisoit nous n'avions point de glace.
> Point de glace, bon Dieu! dans le fort de l'Esté?
> Au mois de Juin? Pour moi, j'estois si transporté,
> Que donnant de fureur tout le festin au Diable,
> Je me suis veu vingt fois prest à quitter la table . . .

14. Thomas Fuller, *Worthies of England*, ed. Nutall II 120.
15. Rousseau, *Discours sur l'inégalité* (Pléiade ed.) III, 189.
16. For an account of Epicurean thought in the seventeenth century see T. F. Mayo, *Epicurus in England 1650–1725*. The nearest definition of 'right reason' in Hobbes to Rochester's is in *De Cive*, *Works* II, 16: 'By right reason in the natural state of man I understand not, as many do an infallible faculty, but the act of reasoning, that is the peculiar and true ratiocination of every man concerning those actions of his, which may either redound to the damage or benefit of his neighbours . . . the law of Nature, that I may define it, is the dictate of right reason conversant about those things which are either to be done or omitted for the constant preservation of life and members, as much as in us lies'.
17. *Essays of Montaigne*, II 214.
18. Richard Peters, *Hobbes*, p. 143.
19. *De Cive, English Works*, II 8.
20. See Peters, *Hobbes*, pp. 162 ff.
21. See my *Rochester, The Critical Heritage*, pp. 46, 111, 113.
22. Boileau, *Satires*, VIII 234–8:

> L'homme, venez au fait, n'a-t-il pas la raison?
> N'est-ce pas son flambeau, son pilote fidele?
> Oui. Mais dequoi lui sert, que sa voix le rappelle,
> Si sur la foi des vents tout prest à s'embarquer,
> Il ne voit point d'écueil qu'il ne l'aille choquer?

23. *Rochester, The Critical Heritage*, p. 56.

CHAPTER 8: CONCLUSION

1. 'Will. Bagnall's Ballad', *Musarum Deliciae*, p. 73.
2. Alexander Brome, 'Plain Dealing', *Songs and Other Poems*, p. 2.
3. John Dennis, 'Preface to Miscellanies', *Critical Works*, I 8.
4. Dennis, 'The Grounds of Criticism in Poetry', *Critical Works*, II 336.
5. *Spectator* 381.
6. Lady Mary Montagu, *Letters*, ed. Halsband (Oxford 1965) I 445.
7. *Miscellanea in Two Volumes* (London 1727) II 17.
8. Goldsmith, prologue to *She Stoops to Conquer*.
9. 'An Enquiry into the Present State of Polite Learning', Goldsmith, *Collected Works* ed. Friedman (Oxford, 1966) I 319–20.

10. Samuel Johnson, *Rasselas*. ch. XLIII.
11. See J. R. Caldwell, 'The Solemn Romantics', *Studies in the Comic* (California, 1941).

Bibliography

The bibliography is divided into three parts (1) Modern editions of seventeenth century texts in alphabetical order by author (these are the texts from which I have quoted throughout) (2) Seventeenth-century books listed in chronological order (3) Critical works. The lists are intended as a guide to the reader of the area covered and are not intended to be comprehensive.

(1) *Modern editions of Seventeenth-Century Texts:*

An Antidote against Melancholy, 1661, ed. J. P. Collier (London, 1870).
Facetiae: Musarum Deliciae, 1656, Wit Restor'd, 1658, Wits Recreations, 1640, new ed. E. Dubois, 2 vols (London, 1874). (A revision of Thomas Park's ed., 1814). *Merry Drollery Complete . . . reprinted from 1691 edition* J. W. Ebsworth (Boston, Lincs., 1875).
Supplement of Reserved Songs from Merry Drollery, 1661, ed. J. W. Ebsworth (Boston, Lincs., 1875).
Westminster Drolleries 1671, 1673, ed. J. W. Ebsworth (Boston, Lincs., 1875).
Parnassus Biceps or Several Choice Pieces of Poetry, 1656, ed. G. Thorn-Drury (London, 1927).
Covent Garden Drollery, 1672, ed. G. Thorn-Drury (London, 1928).
Love and Drollery, ed. J. Wardroper (London, 1969).
John Aubrey, *Brief Lives*, ed. A. Clark, 2 vols (Oxford, 1898).
John Aubrey, *Brief Lives*, ed. O. Lawson Dick (London, 1949).
Nicolas Boileau-Despréaux, *Satires*, ed. C. H. Boudhors (Paris, 1966).
Samuel Butler, *Characters and Passages from Note-Books*, ed. A. R. Waller (Cambridge, 1908).
Samuel Butler, *Satires and Miscellaneous Poetry and Prose*, ed. R. Lamar (Cambridge, 1928).
Samuel Butler, *Hudibras*, ed. J. Wilders (Oxford, 1967).
John Cleveland, *The Poems*, ed. B. Morris and E. Withington (Oxford, 1967).
Charles Cotton, *Poems*, ed. J. Beresford (London, 1923).
John Dennis, *Critical Works*, ed. N. Hooker, 2 vols (Baltimore, 1943).
John Dryden, *Poems*, ed. J. Kinsley, 4 vols (Oxford 1958).
John Dryden, *Of Dramatic Poesy and Other Critical Essays*, ed. G. Watson, 2 vols (London, 1962).
(Andrew Marvell), *Poems on Affairs of State*, 1, ed. G. de F. Lord (New Haven and London, 1963).
Andrew Marvell, *Poems and Letters*, ed. H. M. Margoliouth, 2 vols (Oxford, 1952).

Andrew Marvell, *The Rehearsall Transpros'd*, ed. D. I. B. Smith (Oxford, 1971).
John Milton, *The Student's Milton*, ed. F. A. Patterson (New York, 1930).
Samyel Pepys, *The Diary*, ed. H. B. Wheatley, 9 vols (London, 1893–6).
Thomas Rymer, *Critical Works*, ed. C. A. Zimansky (New Haven and London, 1956).
St. Evremond, *Oeuvres Mêlées*, ed. Charles Giraud, 3 vols (Paris, 1865).
Thomas Shadwell, *Complete Works*, ed. Montague Summers (London, 1927).
Sir John Suckling, *The Works*, ed. H. Williams, 3 vols, 2nd ed. (Oxford, 1958).
Sir William Temple, *Five Miscellaneous Essays*, ed. S. H. Monk (Michigan, 1963).
John Wilmot, 2nd Earl of Rochester, *The Complete Poems*, ed. D. Vieth (New Haven and London, 1968).
John Wilmot and Other Restoration Poets, *The Gyldenstolpe Manuscript* ed. in facsimile B. Danielsson and D. Vieth (Stockholm, 1967).
(John Wilmot), *Rochester the Critical Heritage*, ed. D. L. Farley-Hills (London, 1972).

(2) *Seventeenth-Century Books:*

Thomas Carew, *Poems* (London, 1640).
The Academy of Complements (London, 1640, 1646 (7th ed.), 1650, 1663, 1671 (as *Windsor Drollery*), 1684, 1705).
Wit's Recreations (London, 1640, 1641, 1645, 1650, 1654) and as *Recreations for Ingenious Headpieces* (1663, 1667, 1687).
Edmund Waller, *Poems* (London, 1645).
A Preparative to Study or the Virtue of Sack (London, 1653).
Nathanial Hookes, *Amanda, a Sacrifice to an unknown Goddess and Miscellanea Poetica* (London, 1653).
The Loves of Hero and Leander, a Mock Poem with . . . other Choice Pieces of Drollery (London, 1653).
Thomas Weaver, *Songs and Poems of Love and Drollery* (1654).
John Mennis and James Smith, *Musarum Deliciae or the Muses Recreation* (1655, 1656).
'I.C.', *Wits Interpreter*, (London, 1655, 1662, 1671).
Sportive Wit, the Muses Merriment, a new Spring of Lusty Drollery (London, 1656).
Cupid's Masterpiece or the Free School of Witty and Delightful Complements (London, [1656?], 1685).
The Academy of Pleasure (London, 1656).
Choyce Drollery (London, 1656).
Hugh Crompton, *Pierides or the Muses Mount* (London, 1658).
Naps upon Parnassus, A Sleepy Muse nipt and pincht, though not awakened (London, 1658).
Wit Restor'd (London, 1658).
Le Prince d'Amour or the Prince of Love (London, 1660).
Alexander Brome, *Songs and Other Poems* (London, 1661).
Wit and Drollery, Joviall Poems, by Sir J(ohn) M(ennis), Ja(mes) S(mith),

Sir W(illiam) D(avenant), J(ohn) D(onne) and the most refined wits of the age (London, 1661).

Merry Drollery or a Collection of Jovial Poems, Merry Songs, Witty Drolleries (London, 1661).

An Antidote against Melancholy (London, 1661).

Henry Bold, *Poems, Lyrique, Macaronique, Heroique etc.* (London, 1664).

Matthew Stevenson, *Poems* (London, 1665).

Joseph Glanvill, *A Whip for the Droll, Fiddler to the Atheist*, 4th ed. (London, 1668).

W(illiam) H(ickes), *Oxford Drollery* (Oxford, 1671).

(Richard Head?), *Cupid's Courtship or the Celebration of a Marriage between the God of Love and Psiche in a Droll, poem by the author of the English Rogue* (London, 1671).

The New Academy of Complements (London, 1671).

New Court Songs and Poems by R(obert) V(eal), (London, 1672).

A Collection of Poems written on Several Occasions by several Persons, collected by Hobart Kemp, London, 1672, revised edition, (London, 1673).

Holborn Drollery, or the Beautiful Chloret Surpris'd in the Sheets, (London, 1673).

W(illiam) H(ickes), *London Drollery or the Wits Academy*, (London, 1673).

Methinks the Poor Town has been troubled too long, or a Collection of all the New Songs (1673).

Wit at a Venture or Clio's Privy Garden (London, 1674).

A New Collection of Poems and Songs written by several persons, collected by John Bulteel (London, 1674).

Mock Songs and Joking Poems (London, 1675).

Joseph Glanvill, *Seasonable Reflections and Discourses to the Conviction and Cure of the Scoffing and Infidelity of a Degenerate Age* (London, 1676).

Thomas Duffett, *New Poems and Songs* (London, 1676).

Essays of Montaigne made English by Charles Cotton (London, 1685).

John Dennis, *Poems in Burlesque* (London, 1692).

(William Walsh), *Letters and Poems, Amorous and Gallant* (London, 1692).

(John Oldmixon), *Poems on Several Occasions* (London, 1696).

Poems on Affairs of State (London, 1697).

Samuel Cobb, *Poetae Britannici, a Poem Satyrical and Panegyrical* (London and Cambridge, 1700).

The Dissertator in Burlesque (London, 1701).

(3) *Critical Books and Articles:*

Bazin, G., *The Baroque*, trans. Wardroper (London, 1968).

Bond, R. P., *English Burlesque Poetry 1700–1750* (Cambridge, Mass., 1932).

Brodwin, L. L., 'Miltonic Allusion in Absalom and Achitophel', JEGP 68 (1969).

Bruser, F., 'Disproportion: A Study in the work of John Wilmot, Earl of Rochester', *Univ. of Toronto Quarterly* xv (1946) 384–96.

Caldwell, J. R., 'The Solemn Romantics', *Studies in the Comic* (California, 1941).

Campbell, O. J., *Comicall Satyre and Shakespeare's Troilus and Cressida* (San Marino, 1938).

Case, A. E., *A Bibliography of English Poetical Miscellanies 1521–1750* (Oxford, 1935).

Colie, R., *Paradoxia Epidemica; the Renaissance tradition of Paradox* (Princeton, 1966).

Davies, P. C., 'Rochester and Boileau: A Reconsideration', *Comparative Literature* XXI (1969) 348–55.

Evidence for Authorship: essays on problems of Attribution ed. D. Erdman and E. G. Vogel (Ithaca, 1966).

Fischer, A. S., 'The Augustan Marvell', *ELH* 38 (1971).

French, A. L., 'Dryden, Marvell and Political Poetry', *Studies in English Literature*, VIII.

Frost, W., 'Dryden and Satire', *Studies in English Literature 1500–1900*, XI (1971) 401–16.

Frost, W., *Dryden and the Art of Translation* (New Haven, 1955).

Fujimura, T., 'Rochester's Satyr Against Mankind: an Analysis', *SP* LV (1958) 576–90.

Gearin-Tosh, M. 'The Structure of Marvell's Last Instructions to a Painter', *Essays in Criticism* XXII (1972).

Gibson D., 'Samuel Butler', *Seventeenth Century Studies*, ed. R. Shafer (Princeton, 1933).

Hagstrum, J. H., *The Sister Arts* (Chicago, 1958).

Hoffman, A. W., *John Dryden's Imagery* (Gainesville, 1962).

Jack, I., *Augustan Satire 1660–1750* (Oxford, 1952).

Kinney J. 'John Cleveland and the Satiric Couplet in the Restoration', *PQ* 37 (1958) 410–23.

Kitchen, G., *A Survey of Burlesque and Parody in English* (Edinburgh, 1931).

Mayo, T. F., *Epicurus in England 1650–1725* (Texas, 1933).

Milburn, D. J., *The Age of Wit 1650–1750* (New York, 1966).

Miller, H. K., 'The Paradoxical Encomium', *MP* 53 (1956) 145–78.

Miner, E., 'The Poetic Picture, Painted Poetry of Last Instructions', *Andrew Marvell*, ed. G. de F. Lord (Englewood Cliffs, 1968).

Morris, B., 'Satire from Donne to Marvell', *Metaphysical Poetry, Stratford upon Avon Studies*, 11 (London, 1970).

Nevo, R., *The Dial of Virtue a study of poems on affairs of State in the Seventeenth Century* (Princeton, 1963).

Osborne, M. T., *Advice to a Painter Poems 1633–1856* (Texas, 1949).

Peter, J., *Complaint and Satire in Early English Literature* (Oxford, 1956).

Peters, R., *Hobbes* (London, 1956).

Pogue, S. M., *The Restoration Verse Satires of Andrew Marvell*, unpublished dissertation, Univ. of Missouri, 1967.

Quaintance, R. E., 'French Sources of the Restoration Imperfect Enjoyment Poem', *PQ* XLII (1963) 190–9.

Quintana, R., 'Samuel Butler, A Restoration Figure in a Modern Light', *ELH* 18 (1951) 7–31.

Randolph, M. C., 'The Structural Design of Formal Verse Satire', *PQ* XXI (1942).

Richards, E. A., *Hudibras in the Burlesque Tradition* (New York, 1937).

Richmond, H. M., *The School of Love, the Evolution of the Stuart Love Lyric* (Princeton, 1964).

Righter, A., 'John Wilmot, Earl of Rochester', *Proceedings of the British Academy* 53' (1968).

Schilling, B., *Dryden and the Conservative Myth: a reading of Absalom and Achitophel* (New Haven, 1961).

Summers, J. H. 'Andrew Marvell: Private Taste and Public Judgment', *Metaphysical Poetry*, Stratford upon Avon Studies, 11 (London, 1970).

Sutherland, J. R., 'Marvell's Satires', *PQ* xlv (1966).

Sypher, W., *Four Stages in Renaissance Style* (New York, 1955).

Tave, S. M. *The Amiable Humorist, Comic Theory and Criticism of the eighteenth and early nineteenth century* (Chicago, 1960).

Toliver, H. E., *Marvell's Ironic Vision* (New Haven, 1965).

Wallace, J. M., *Destiny His Choice* (Cambridge, 1968).

Wasserman, G. R., 'Samuel Butler and the Problem of Unnatural Man', *MLQ* 31 (1970).

West, A. H., *L'Influence française dans la Poésie Burlesque en Angleterre entre 1660 et 1700* (Paris, 1930).

Williamson, G., *Seventeenth Century Contexts* (London, 1960).

Index